For DAD
Love, John + Patty

Christmas 1976

Horse Tradin'

HORSE TRADIN'

by Ben K. Green

Illustrations by LORENCE BJORKLUND

ALFRED · A · KNOPF

New York · *1975*

The chapter "Gray Mules" appeared in the July 1965
issue of *Southwest Review*.

The following chapters appeared in
Horse Conformation by Ben K. Green:

> "Gypsy Hoss Trade," "Homer's Last Mule,"
> "Nubbin'," "Angel," "Maniac Mule," "Matched Mares,"
> "The Rockcrusher and the Mule," "A Road Horse
> for a Broodmare,"
> "Cowboy Trades for a Wagon 'n' Team,"
> "Poor Heifers—the Judge
> —Wild Mules," "The Parson's Mare, Bessie,"
> "Horse from Round Rock," "Mule Colts,"
> "Mine Mules," "Traveling Mare,"
> "The Schoolmarm and Ol' Nothin'."

Preface

Books have been written about horses in all the known languages; and if all the books written in English alone about horses could be loaded on a Conestoga wagon, it would take a six-horse hitch of Ohio-bred Percherons to untrack the wagon. Tribute has been paid to the breeders of rare individual horses in all breeds by the number of generous awards and distinctions for their accomplishments.

Yet historians and writers of other categories have completely neglected the greatest brotherhood of mankind ever associated with the horse. Three generations of people have passed on since the beginning of the machine age, and today the thought of power automatically implies automobiles, tractors, etc., with origins in Detroit and the other manufacturing centers of America. But when horses and mules were the sole source of power for farming and all methods of transportation, it was necessary that big business be involved in the buying, selling, and distribution of horses and mules from the areas of the United States where they were raised to the different parts of the country where they were needed. In 1900 the value of horses and mules in the United States totaled more than that of all the cattle, sheep, goats, and hogs on the farms and ranches in the United States.

The Mississippi Valley and all the territory east of the Mississippi Valley did not produce more than a small number of the horses and mules that were needed in their own territory. The middle west and northwest raised on the range vast numbers of draft horses that had to be marketed and distributed to other parts of the United States. The western and southwestern states produced most of the light-boned horses that were needed and practically all of the mules used in the southern states. Mules are by nature adapted to hotter climates and were much easier raised in the southwest; and by their nature again were more readily adaptable to the summer temperatures in the fields of the southern states.

The marketing of vast numbers of horses and mules required men of good judgment with a general knowledge of the horse power needs of the various parts of the United States. The purchase, shipment, and sale of horses and mules demanded the use of millions of dollars in capital investments. The managers of the central markets, who were also the financers of the horse and mule industry, had to know the types of soil and the amount of rainfall in the various parts of their trade territory which would, in any case, cover several states. These men also had to have a thorough knowledge of the crops to be grown and of the seasons of the year when the demand for horses and mules was best in each locality.

For a big dealer in a central market to be successful he also had to acquire a keen understanding of human nature, since he was in a sense the wholesale dealer relying on country shippers to furnish him with stock and then ship them out on account to local dealers to be sold to farmers. None of the knowledge needed by a high-class horse and mule dealer could be learned from books or schools, and it would be well understood that these men were usually middle age or over.

Last but not least, he had to be a man with a lot of nerve, who was willing to back his own judgment and that of his buyers and to face the risks involved in shipping, loading, and unloading (together with the possibility of various ship-

ping diseases) that were a hazard of the business. There
were necessarily other risks in collecting for the mules that
were shipped out to be sold in the country by local dealers.
It is easy to see that with money going out in both directions
it took larger amounts of capital, accompanied by a good
nerve and judgment, to be a successful central market dealer.

A number of central markets (Chicago, Kansas City, St.
Louis, Memphis, Tenn., Ft. Worth, Denver, etc.) sprang up
after the Civil War; before the 1900's they were financed
by horse and mule dealers and conducted on the highest
ethical basis of good business. These were men of keen judgment and good finance, who in turn picked men who knew
horses and mules and were well distributed over the states
that had the most stock. Most any good, responsible horse
and mule man could go to one of the central markets and get
a big dealer furnish him a checkbook. There were never
any written contracts. Generally, a short visit and a hand-
shake could seal a partnership that might endure for a lifetime. The horse and mule buyer from the country carried
the big dealer's checkbook and bought horses and mules in
whatever number they were available in his territory at
prices that would yield a profit. The profit was usually split
fifty-fifty between the buyer who rode the country and
bought the stock and his partner in the central market who
furnished the money for purchase and all expenses such as
transportation, feed bills, shipping, etc., as well as the con-
tacts for the sale of the livestock.

A good country horse and mule buyer needed to have a
thorough knowledge of the many classes that he would be
offered while buying in the country. There are no more
models and types of vehicles today than there were horses
and mules for specific purposes when they were the means
of power and transportation. A country buyer who rode up
on a mixed lot of horses and mules would need to know
what number of them would go for farm "chunks," and

which would be good enough for heavy draft to go to city streets for dray wagons; and if there was a team of nice wagon horses that were generally thought of as being light draft that would move a load at a trot he needed to recognize them for what they were worth. There might also be a horse good enough to go for a hunter or jumper or maybe a light harness team for fancy driving, and many other classes that could all be mixed up in some farmer's lot or rancher's pasture; and in most cases a good country buyer would strike an average price and take the bunch. Knowing where to place them was part of his central market partner's operation —but they had to be brought to where each horse would stand on his own average price and make a profit. A good country buyer was often referred to as a man that would bid on anything that walked.

This same dealer many times had customer accounts in the farming regions of the agricultural part of the United States that were short on work stock. These customers would come to the auctions at the central markets or might even place an order for so many carloads of horses and mules of given weights, ages, heights, and sometimes even designate the colors they wanted. These customer accounts were usually sold on credit and financed until they had sold the horses and mules in teams to their customer, the farmer, who might have been from one to two hundred or two to three thousand miles from where the teams he purchased were raised.

History heretofore has ignored these men of finance, foresight, and brains who actually furnished the distribution and finance for the horse power of early America.

The next class of dealer was the good, responsible, solid citizen who lived in the county seat or other better town of the farming areas of the United States. He had his regular customers, whether plantation owners who used several hundred mules or his neighbor farmer who only had a team or two. He shipped his mules and horses from the central markets and in most cases guaranteed them satisfactory for whatever purpose he sold them for. He usually took in trade the older or worn-out or horses or mules that were unsatisfactory for any reason in trade and drew the difference in cash or notes or maybe even other classes of livestock such as cattle. He was the sort of citizen who helped establish the first banks, general mercantiles, and who served on the local school board.

His counterpart in the buying and shipping of horses and mules was the good live buyer, operating maybe on his own money or maybe with the central market money of some partner. By furnishing a market to the growers in the range country at a reasonable price, he handled thousands of head at a marginal profit in order to provide a market for the growers who had furnished him stock for many years and with whom he hoped to do business for as long as he was active in the horse and mule trade. The same individual might be attending an auction at some central market with orders from customers to ship them stock for resale; in the course of a day's business at a central market generally from one to two thousand or more would be sold at auction in singles and teams. A good live buyer and seller would ofttimes have contracts for several different classes of stock. He could by buying small cotton mules weighing about 800 to 900 pounds that he would probably be shipping to Georgia, maybe with no limit to the number he needed to fill his orders; and at the same time be buying fancy sugar mules that were a high-class trade weighing from 1,000 to 1,250 pounds that went to the sugar cane plantations. And while he was watching for these two types of mules coming through the auction, he might be looking for farm "chunk"-type mares to be shipped to some Dutch settlement hundreds of miles from where the mules were going. All these operations required large sums of money, keen judgment, and the highest order of human integrity.

There were other members of this great brotherhood of horse and mule men who had very special kinds of customers and business. One example was the importer who bought breeding stock in foreign countries and imported them into the United States to be sold for the improvement of the quality of our domestic livestock.

Another class of dealer catered to the "carriage trade," a term that is still in use in modern times to denote quality. He handled only the finest of light harness and heavy harness horses (coach horses) for the carriage trade needed in the cities for transporting people in business to and from trains or other central points, as well as the horses that were used purely for driving pleasure. This same dealer would probably buy and sell a great many of the very choicest saddle horses to be used for pleasure and practical purposes by the city dwellers.

In times of war, the veteran country horse buyers and horse dealers were relied on by the government to assemble thousands of horses for cavalry or artillery purposes, and thousands of mules for wagon and pack animals; and I say with due respect that neither America, England, France, nor any other nation that ever depended upon the American producer and the American buyer to furnish horses and mules has ever lost a battle for the want of horsepower.

The local horse and mule business usually referred to as trading was carried on at the Country Trade's Day—usually First Monday, or some other designated Monday in the separate towns where they had their local trade squares—and farmers gathered and brought in something they didn't want to trade to somebody else for something he didn't want, both of them with the full intention of cheating the other.

Many humorous stories, most of which were true, originated from the instances that occurred at the local trade's days, and the champion characters of such occasions were the road traders who were gypsys—though many were Irish-

Gypsy crossbreeds or any other nondescript who cared to drift across the country and live in a camp wagon with his family, leading his stock to trade in the form of various kinds of "snide" stock hooked to the back of his wagon or many times having the children drive or lead the extra trading stock as they moved along the road from some trade ground or campsite down the creek bank all over the farming regions of the United States. This form of horse trader was opposed to work and unacquainted with the principles of honesty, but had an ever-abiding sense of humor and light-heartedness as long as he managed to cheat a few farmers and other traders sufficiently to keep in a good supply of groceries and tobacco and a reasonable amount of hard whisky.

I claim to be one of the few men left this side of walking-cane age who took advantage of early educational opportunities around the wagonyards, livery stables, and mule barns that afforded me a genuine wagonyard background. No modern-day horseman will ever have the opportunity to gain such inside knowledge of the horse business since the passing of these old institutions.

These Hoss Trades of Yesteryear are retold just as they occurred during my early years of experience as a horse trader. Nothing has been added or left out in order to varnish them for modern reading. It is my hope that they will add to your pleasure, and possibly cause many of you to reminisce over some humorous incidents that may have occurred to you in your experiences with horses and horse traders.

BEN K. GREEN

Contents

Horse Tradin'

Gypsy Hoss Trade

My family had a high standard to raise children by, and as soon as they could tell that one wasn't going to be a credit to the family name, they shipped him West—which explains why I left home at such a tender age. After I was full grown and was an experienced cowboy and horse trader of about sixteen years old, I'd drift back to the farming country to visit my kinfolks, rattle my spurs, and loll around the farm boys.

I rode one good horse on this particular trip which was going to last about thirty days, and led another one that I hated—and only rode occasionally to rest my good horse. This horse was one of the few paints I had ever owned or rode. He was a nice-made horse and had a very stylish way of traveling. He walked and trotted just like he couldn't hardly stand to hit the ground. This beautiful paint horse had more bad habits than any horse I think I ever had. With all his style—and at that time his color was popular, too—he had about as much sense as a weak-minded West Texas jackrabbit. He was hard to saddle, hard to mount, and because he was so snorty, snaky, and boogery, he was hard to ride—although he was not bad to buck.

One of the worst of his many bad characteristics was the way he pulled back when you tied him. He broke his bridle reins and the headstall of his bridle several times, and I had made a habit of tying him with a rope halter. He had his head pretty well skinned up around his ears and across his nose from settin' back when he was tied hard and fast to a gentle telephone pole or a nice big tree that would hold him.

While I was visiting, I had let him out in a little pasture, and in a few days the skinned places around on his head had healed up and peeled off; he had a little bit of grass bloom on him and was in nice shape to trade off. On Trades Day in Greenville, Texas, I got up early in the morning, rode him pretty hard about fifteen miles into town, and came in on the trade square with some sweat and lather showing around on him.

It was middle morning, and the trade square was covered with work horses, work mules, the general run of

4

milk cows, wagonloads of pigs, and so forth that might be seen at any trades day. Very few saddle horses were in sight.

I moseyed around awhile on my horse and found a trader's wagon with a number of saddle horses eating fresh hay out of the wagon. There was a good dappled gray gelding about fifteen hands high, in hard, sound flesh, and he was properly shod. The hair was rubbed short over his loins, there was a light mark on each side where the cinch ring of the saddle had rubbed, and you could tell by his general appearance that he was very much a usin' horse.

Pretty soon the trader spotted me looking at his horses and came over. He walked around my paint and asked: "You want to trade stock?"—which was the usual way of opening up conversation.

I told him that I wasn't hurtin' to trade, that I was pretty well mounted, but that I did like the looks of the gray horse. He made an awfully big speech about the gray horse but wound up by saying that he couldn't trade him for a few days yet because he had made a man a proposition and had promised to wait until he heard from him. That was pretty rare and a little hard to believe, but still I didn't know any different, so I looked around the wagon. On the other side tied to the front wheel was a real nice bay mare. She was about fourteen-two, which was about the size of my paint, and she was well kept and very gentle.

This little short, fat, squatty trader had every appearance of being an Irishman or some other breed of white man. He suggested to me that this was a mighty nice mare; he had known her a long time and knew her to be nice and gentle. He untied the little bay mare, jumped on her bareback, rode her off across the trade ground and back toward me. She traveled nice and smooth, had clean legs, and was a very nice kind of a little mare. When I was a boy, there were hundreds of horses that had never been ridden bareback, and when a horse would ride bareback it was proof of its gentleness—and it was generally assumed that it would ride even better with a saddle.

I got down, looked in her mouth, and she was about an honest eight-year-old. Her feet and legs were exceptionally clean, and she didn't give any appearance of ever having been used hard or mistreated. The trader asked to ride my horse, so I handed him the reins and he rode off. The paint horse wasn't shod and was a little tenderfooted. The trader rode back, got off, and said he thought this would be a pretty nice horse if I had some shoes on him—that he was too sore to travel. The trader didn't know it, but that horse came nearer to traveling when you could stand to ride him tenderfooted than he would have shod.

We had quite a visit, and I finally gave him $20 boot. He took the halter off the little mare and I took my bridle off the paint, unsaddled him, and pitched my blanket and saddle on the bay mare. I reached under her and started drawing the cinch up. All of a sudden she swelled up like a toy balloon, walled her eyes, bawled, ran backward for about twenty feet, fell over on her side, and started groaning. I looked over at the trader and he showed every expression of shock and surprise and appeared to be terribly embarrassed. He said he didn't know that a nice mare could act so bad.

My first fast young impulse was to stomp her head in

the ground or kick her in the belly and make her get up. About the time I was about to hit her, the trader yelled: "Wait a minute!"

He walked over to her head, reached in his pocket, got her a lump of sugar, patted her, and talked sweet to her. He reached down, loosened the cinch, and the mare got up.

By this time we had a bunch of other horse traders and farmers gathered around watching the show. I tried to draw that cinch up about three more times, and every time she fell he would give her a lump of sugar and say: "Don't hit her. Hittin' her won't do no good."

I left my saddle up on her without the cinch being tightened and walked away rattling my spurs and leading my mare. I always felt like a cowboy ought to set up and let his feet hang down when he moved, and that walking didn't agree with my disposition and caused my little feet—that were carrying those big spurs—to complain about the way they were being treated. You could hear a little giggle and noise among the traders and farmers as I walked away, which didn't add none to my ego.

I went down to Ingram's wagonyard, and as I started in the gate I met Uncle Barney. He had worked for about everybody breaking horses, and he said: "Mister Ben, what you gone and done now? That there is a gypsy mare."

I asked: "Do you know this mare?"

"No, but I knows that gypsy man. He don't look like no gypsy, but he am, an' iffen you ever breaks even swappin' with a gypsy, you's done made a hoss trader. She sho looks nice, but that's just the top side."

7

I went back to the back side of the wagonyard and put my mare in the lot. By now it was dinnertime, so I went off and ate a little. Then I moseyed back down to where I had left my mare in the lot and my saddle hanging on the fence. I decided that without that bunch of onlookers and helpers, I might saddle her up by myself—but when I pulled that cinch she reared up, fell backward, rolled over, and groaned.

Al Eiland, who was a very fine horseman and a Southern gentleman, came strolling to the fence. As usual, he was wearing a starched white shirt and a black bow tie and looked every part the distinguished individual that he was. I looked up and said: "Howdy, Mr. Eiland." He had been my neighbor when I was a small boy, and we had always been great cronies.

He looked over the fence at my mare lying on the ground with my saddle on her. He turned, looked all around behind him and saw that no one was listening, then said: "Ben, you have traded for the Sleeping Beauty." He told me the gypsies had raised that mare from a baby colt on a bottle, and had started having her lie down for sugar when she was small enough that they could pick her up and lay her down to give her sugar. He said this Irish-looking gypsy was married to a very black gypsy, and that there were several of them camped down on Long Branch. He went on to explain that before the day was over, they would offer to give me my horse back and keep whatever money I had paid difference. He said the Sleeping Beauty had kept that particular band of gypsies in grub money for several years.

As he started to walk away, as an afterthought it seemed he stopped and said: "Did they have a good gray horse about seven years old and about fifteen hands high tied to their wagon?"

I had already thanked him for wising me up, but I wanted to repay him, so I described the gray horse. He said they had traded Mr. Marshall at Terrell, Texas, some other kind of a snide for him, and that Mr. Marshall had too much pride to buy the horse back. Mr. Marshall was his good friend and had asked Mr. Eiland to try and buy the gray horse back from the gypsies.

Mr. Eiland was going on toward the wagonyard gate when I had a bright idea and called him to wait. Times have changed now, but at that time a young boy didn't holler at a grown man and tell him to *com'ere;* so he waited while I trotted up to him. I told him that if the Sleeping Beauty was as valuable as he said, I'd get the gray horse by night and he didn't have to worry. He didn't quite understand, but a twinkle came in his eye and a smile came on his big, fat face, and he said: "I'll give you a chance, Ben, and I won't bother with the gypsies until you're through with them."

I didn't leave my little mare, and about four o'clock here came about three or four copper-colored gypsy kids who stuck their heads through a crack in the fence. I knew then that the scouting party had arrived and the news would get back to the trading wagon fast. The little kids made quite a few strange noises to themselves, then one of them said: "What you doin' to our mare?"

I kind of grumbled at him: "That ain't your mare no more."

The biggest one of the kids said: "What you got all dem ropes on her foots for?"

I said in a normal, unconcerned tone of voice that

9

when I untied her, she would have been lying there long enough that she would want to stand up—when I turned her loose.

It wasn't twenty minutes until that Irish-looking gypsy man, followed by a couple of darker, skinnier, more typical-looking gypsies, came stepping down through the wagonyard like dry steers that had just smelled water. They looked over the fence and saw the Sleeping Beauty lying on the ground with all four feet tied together and my saddle cinched hard and fast. They jabbered a while in their unknown tongue, then said if I was sick of the Sleeping Beauty, they would give me my horse back and keep the $20.

I told them that I wasn't sick of her, but that she was going to get sick of me, and that I was going to leave her tied on the ground until she went to having nightmares instead of dreams of lumps of sugar. Then they decided they would give me half my money back and my horse. I told them that if I'd wanted that skunk-colored horse, I wouldn't have traded him off to start with.

Up to now I hadn't hit or whipped the Sleeping Beauty, but I reached over and kind of kicked her in the belly for their benefit. All three of them walked off a piece, then the one I had traded with came back and said he would give me all my money and my paint horse, too, if I would untie the Sleeping Beauty and trade her back to him. I told him no, I wanted to break her of that habit she had, and I believed I should keep her. As they left the wagonyard they were waving six or seven or eight hands and talking to themselves and to each other.

In no more than about half of a little bit, here came a wrinkled old gypsy woman moving swiftly as a ballet

dancer. These modern gals think they invented petticoats
—they ought to have seen that old woman. She was wearing lots of them, and all were of a different color. She
had gold earrings dangling to both shoulders, and the gold
bracelets on her arm sounded like chain harness when she
waved her hand. As soon as she got within smelling distance and rattling distance, the Sleeping Beauty raised her
head off the ground and nickered in a moan that was
nothing short of a pitiful, whipped cry, and began strain-
ing her legs against the ropes she was tied down with.

That old gypsy woman went down on her knees in
that manure lot with all those petticoats and kissed the
mare on her face, rubbed her, talked to her, and fed her
some sugar. The mare had shown no sign of emotion
when the men and kids came around, but she sure did
take on when that old gypsy woman got there. The
woman turned to me with soulful eyes and in a very ex-
pressive, deep voice said that I had a heart of stone to have
tied the little mare to where she couldn't get up. You
never heard such begging and beseeching from a human
being. She reached over to put her hand on the ropes
I had tied all the mare's four feet together with, and with
those nimble old fingers she was about to undo my tying
knots. I had a buggy whip in my hand, and I just tapped
her a little stinging lick across her wrist and said: "Gypsy,
get away from my mare."

She made a bunch of crosses on the ground and a lot
of loud noises and gave me the most awful lecture that
anybody ever got about being brutal to the Sleeping
Beauty. She told me that she had put in many years training that mare since she was a wee bambino, and now I was
ruining her. I told her no, I wasn't ruining her, I was just

untraining her to where she could stand a saddle on her while she stood up.

This old gypsy then stood up and hollered right loud, and here came the whole tribe through the gate. By this time it was getting rather late in the afternoon, and it didn't look to them like they had a chance to get their Sleeping Beauty back before night, so finally they asked me what did they have that I wanted. All the time they kept insisting they would give me the paint horse back and more money than I had given them.

We had a whole wagonyard full of cotton farmers looking and listening, and I was leaning against the back side of the fence with my buggy whip facing that tribe of gypsies. There wasn't any giggling going on in that bunch of cotton farmers standing behind them. I had remarked that my paint horse was too tenderfooted to ride, and that I didn't want him back at all. The spokesman for the gypsies said: "We'll go to camp and shoe the paint horse, then give you him and all your money back."

I kind of flipped my whip over against some corn cobs in the corner of the lot, like I was doing some deep thinking, then looked up and asked the spokesman of the tribe how long it took a gypsy to shoe a horse. He said in a very hopeful voice that he would be shod in an hour. I thought a minute and told him to bring that paint horse, well shod, and all my money in an hour—or to bring the dappled gray gelding that I had wanted in the first place.

They scattered to their camp like a covey of quail, but I knew there wasn't enough gypsies west of the Mississippi River to shoe that paint horse. The only time he had been shod, it took six good cowboys and he crippled some of them—which was just another one of the bad faults which I had failed to mention. So I crawled up on the fence and sat down.

The farmers all went to asking me questions. I wasn't in too good a mood with them because they had snickered at me when I left the trade ground leading my saddle; so I didn't have too friendly a conversation to offer the waiting onlookers.

Just at dark the old gypsy woman came rushing back to the wagonyard, down to the pen, and said: "They bringin' your horse. I untie my little baby."

I kicked a little dry manure on that pile of petticoats and said: "Gypsy, get away from my mare."

She wheeled and ran out of the wagonyard, and again the Sleeping Beauty nickered and cried at the sound of that old woman's voice.

In a few minutes, here came the Irish-looking gypsy who had traded with me to start with, leading the dappled gray horse. I untied the Sleeping Beauty, took my saddle off her, and let her up.

I rode by Mr. Eiland's and put the gray horse in his lot, left my saddle, and walked on the short distance to where I was staying. The next morning Uncle Barney admitted that I *had* made a horse trader. Mr. Eiland paid me a good price for the gray horse on behalf of his friend who wanted him back, and I saddled my good horse and started back to West Texas.

Rebel Commander

Along about August of one year in the middle thirties it seemed to me that we were about to have an early fall in the farming country. I had a nice set of three- and four-year-old mules that I had kept over from the spring mule business, had summered them on good pasture, and they were fat, ready to be hooked up and worked. Of course a trader looks to see if mules are ready to be hooked up and start to work because that's when they bring the most money. I thought these mules ought to bring a bigger profit for me than they would ordinarily make at the Fort Worth horse and mule market, or even at the Memphis, Tennessee, mule market, which at that time was the biggest mule market in the world.

I began to inquire around among horse and mule men about where the earliest cotton crop would be picked. I felt that if I got into a territory early, when the fall harvest began, I would probably sell some mules before the rest of the mule men got their barns and pens stocked and were ready to do business.

The more I inquired around the less I found out. Then one day I picked up a copy of the *Farmer-Stockman* while I was sitting in a barbershop waiting to get a haircut. This was a brand new issue, and I saw where they had a big cotton crop along the Mississippi River. The harvest had begun, and some farmers had been getting prizes for bringing the first bales of cotton into the various little towns. I sat there with my mind way off while the barber cut my hair, and I made up my mind then that I'd just as well see about that cotton crop in Mississippi. After all, money would be flowing there as soon as they started ginning and baling cotton—and I hoped I'd be the first on the ground with a set of fresh, fat young mules.

I got out of the barbershop and went around the corner of the square and down the side street where I had a saddle horse tied. I got on my saddle horse and started out to the edge of town to an old friend of mine to tell him what I had on my mind. I wanted him to wait until I got down in Mississippi somewhere, and then when I wired or called I wanted him to load my mules on the train and ship them to me. I felt I'd better get there first and make some arrangements for some kind of a pasture or barn or trading ground—some place to hold these mules while I traded on them. I would need a few days to do this before I got the mules in, since I was shipping to a strange country and didn't know anybody I could call to have me something ready when I got there.

My old friend was agreeable to this arrangement and said that he would look after whatever livestock I had around until I got back from selling my mules. I didn't know much about Mississippi. I picked out a spot on the map that showed to have a great big, wide, fertile valley and a good railroad running through it. It looked to me like that was all I needed for a future mule market. That evening I went home, turned out my best saddle horses—I never wanted anybody else to ride my own saddle horses when I was out of the country—and packed my rigging in my car.

I was driving a little six-cylinder, two-toned Buick coupé with a jump seat in the back—which in that time was a sure enough fancy rig for a young man to have for transportation. Of course this fancy automobile was just for special occasions. I didn't run around town and squeal the wheels on it like I see these flat-top, hot-rod kids doing this day and time. Instead of that, my rig stayed in the barn with a wagon sheet pulled over it until I had some reason to need it. The rest of the time I rode horseback and looked after my cattle, horses, and mules—and did on horseback whatever other business I had to do that didn't call for a long, fast trip.

Next morning way before daylight I was up and mounted on this little two-toned, fancy Buick automobile with its spare tires mounted on the sides of the front fenders. It sure was a fancy rig, and I felt like a big operator. I could drive just about as far as the road was cut out in a day, or in a day and night, or from the time I started until the time I stopped. I was young and tough, and sleeping and eating were just something I did on the side when it was convenient and I didn't have anything else to tend to.

The next morning about nine o'clock I drove into Dixon, Mississippi, which was a real nice little town. The stores were opening up and the gins were humming and there was a whole lot of activity up and down the streets. There were lots of teams and wagons and Negroes going to and from the gins. There were cotton pickers with sacks on their backs—I'd been meeting them since daylight. It sure looked like everybody was fixing to have a big fall.

This was a heavy-land country, and it would take good big heavy stout mules to work in this sure-enough black delta land—and that was just the kind of mules I had. The more I looked at the country, the more I thought it was the place to bring my mules. I pulled up in Dixon and parked this fancy rig of mine and got out and walked up and down the street like I was a big operator from way out West—just as though I was looking the country over to see if I wanted to buy all of it or part of it. I stomped around a while and found the town drugstore. It was sure a nice old-timey country drugstore—great long black mahogany shelves with glass doors on them, nice marble-covered soda fountain, pretty little square-topped fountain tables with the chairs hung on each corner leg, and when you got up these little chairs slipped back under the glass-case tabletop that had merchandise in it. This drugstore was the sociable spot of the town. It was where the people gathered and drank cokes and drank coffee and talked about what had happened the night before and what was going to go on from here out.

I didn't strike up acquaintance with anybody much that morning. I saw a lot of natives in and out, and you could tell the ladies that clerked in the stores and the men that came in from the bank. The village druggist was one of those good-natured, smiling, kind of half bald-headed fellows about fifty years old that knew everybody and knew what was going on. If you want to find a man that knows about the community, when you go to a new place, a country druggist knows a heap more about affairs of state than the banker or the lawyer or the sheriff or anybody else in town.

In those days the druggist was the one that opened his store first in the morning, and the drugstore was the last place that closed at night. If you were going to the farm or to the field or leaving town, the first place you would come by was the drugstore. When you went to the picture show or had a date with your girl or for any reason—shipping stock or something—were up late, the drugstore was the place in town you would go by before you went home at night. These modern drive-ins with their jukeboxes and their automatic coke machines will never see the day that they have the hospitality and the congenial atmosphere of friendliness that the old country drugstore didn't have to boast about—everybody knew it.

Well, this was a typical drugstore in the Old South. Everybody spoke with a long, slow drawl and was in no particular hurry. They were in no hurry to wait on you and in no hurry to see you leave. They would like for you to loaf around so they could find out about your business and maybe they could brag a little about their own. Strangers weren't too plentiful in this little town, and you could tell right off that people were looking at me, but of course I didn't scare. I had on high heeled boots that were shop-made, a 3x beaver Stetson hat, and I wasn't wearing any common britches, either. They could tell at a glance that I was from way out West, and whether they noticed it or not I was proud of it.

I started to walk out the door and the druggist said: "Needn't hurry."

I said: "No hurry, I'll be back to see you later in the day." I smiled and said it in a light tone of voice and waved as I went out the door.

I drove up and down the streets of the nice little town. The houses were well kept, the lawns were pretty, and there was moss hanging from the trees that grew around. Some of those nice, old-timey white panel fences had gates swinging in and out over concrete sidewalks up and down the residential part of town.

I circled around, went up and down the back streets and the four or five little roads that led out of town in different directions. I would drive out them a piece and come back. I met cotton wagons bringing in cotton and empty wagons going back out, some of them hauling the seed and some of them not. Little kids, black ones and white ones both, would be playing in the cottonseed on the wagons that were started toward home. Wagons you'd meet coming to town—the man driving the team would be buried down in the front in that beautiful white handpicked cotton, and there might be somebody up higher on the load just going along for the trip to the gin. The roads were dry but not too dusty. My car didn't kick up a lot of dust, and the wagons weren't throwing up too much. The air was clear. It was late summer or early fall —anyhow, the weather wasn't too hot, and everybody had an air of being busy and being happy about it.

About noon I pulled up in town and stopped my car and got out and walked a while. There was just one great big beautiful old hotel in town. It was a colonial frame hotel with big white pillars and a long gallery running across the front. When you went inside, you entered a nice big hall. This might at one time have been built for a mansion, but now it was a hotel. There were three big dining rooms on the ground floor, and the sleeping rooms were all upstairs.

You could tell right off that the hotel was the place town people ate at. They were kinda making headway for it. Well, I had known for a long time that I could eat anything that anybody else could (and maybe like it better) so I sort of joined the parade to eat some dinner with the folks. It was a nice big old comfortable hotel for a small town, and everybody was visiting and friendly and asking about one another's business—and about their children and where they went last Sunday and what they expected to do the rest of the week, and when the ladies aid society was going to meet. Everybody in the whole dining room was friendly. They were native citizens except for just three or four drummers that were sitting over to the side, sort of at a table to themselves. Well, I didn't want to be accused of being a drummer, and it was easy to tell at a glance that I wasn't a native, but I sat down at one of the long tables where some more of these nice people were eating.

This hotel was one of those sure-enough eating places where you sit down at a long table covered with all kinds of homegrown vegetables, fresh meat, country fried chicken, fried pies, and cakes. You just sit down there and "pitch till you win." By the time I asked two or three people to pass me some stuff—and by the time two or three voluntarily passed me something they wanted me to try some of—I wasn't a stranger at that table. We had begun to exchange remarks about how good the food was, how nice the weather was, and all that kind of business. These people sure were polite. They didn't want to pry into my business any, and I had by that time let my name come out and they were putting the "Mister" on it pretty heavy. For a right young man, that "Mister" sure did make an impression that would make you throw your head up and pay some mind when somebody said something to you.

Of course, right off I didn't hesitate to let them in on the fact that I was from Texas. They all had some kind of story to tell about Texans: some of them had been to Texas and the others all wanted to go. I told them what a great country it was—the wide open spaces and the big herds and the good horses and the mules. I confessed right quick that I didn't know too much about the farming business, that I'd made my living on a horse about all of my life. But I told them I had a high regard for the people that tilled the soil and fed the world and provided fiber that made the clothes, and I knew that this type of citizen was the salt of the earth. I also put in my little speech something about what a fertile land the Mississippi Valley was and how much of the rest of the world Mississippi could feed and clothe. I also dropped in that I knew the Mississippi Valley was stocked with some of the finest old Southern people in the nation because that wasn't going to hurt my cause any either.

There was a beautiful lady sitting across the table from

me. You could tell she was one of the town's business women. She had a nice tone of voice and a nice way of carrying on conversation, and directly she said: "Mistah Green, what brings you to Mississippi?"

I thought it was time for me to let the folks in on what I was doing there—before they thought I was a sheriff or something—so I said: "Well, I'm a horse and mule dealer. I have some good mules that came out of the west, and I was looking around for a likely spot to ship them for selling to people that wanted to till the land." I told her that these were exceptionally fine mules, good, deep bodied, and well cared for, the kind it would take to till the soil of the Mississippi Valley. I said I was thinking of shipping them to the town of Dixon.

This beautiful lady wasn't real young, but she wasn't middle-aged either, and she just radiated charm as she burst forth: "How delightful! My fathah has been the mule dealah heah at Dixon for many years, until he aged beyond tending to his affaihs, and I know he could be of some help to you if you decide to send youah mules heah. He would be so delighted to help a young mule man that might be following in his footsteps."

I said: "That would be wonderful. I'm looking for a barn or a pasture or someplace I could keep my mules after I get them unloaded off the train. I'd be glad to meet your father. Perhaps he could suggest someplace."

She literally beamed and gushed out that her father's old mule barn was vacant, and she just knew he would be delighted for me to use it. When I finished my "dinnah" she would be glad to go with me down to her home where her father would probably be taking a nap after his noonday meal.

We drove up in my two-toned, six-cylinder automobile—which she had already admired considerably and told me her daughter would like a car like that, too—and sure enough, the old man was sitting on the porch. He was a typical fine old Southern gentleman—white headed and wearing a small, well-trimmed mustache, a nice blue serge suit, and a white shirt with a black bow tie. His name was Colonel Bob Dixon.

He was so glad that I had come to Dixon, he said, and he would just be delighted to be of service to me in any manner he could. He could introduce me to all the people who needed good mules to work their plantations. He and I drove his daughter—widowed but still called Miss Belle Dixon—back up to town to her ladies ready-to-wear store; then we drove off down behind the business part of town just three or four blocks and, sure enough, he had one of those rare old-timey, livery-stable-looking mule barns.

This barn had a big square storefront across the top of it above the hallway. It was a big hallway that ran down through the barn, which was floored with heavy oak. On one side of the hallway were some harness and feed rooms, on the other side were some great big stalls, and toward the back were four great big pens, two on each side of the hall. The barn was way over two hundred feet long and about fifty feet wide, and you could tell it had been the scene of many big horse and mule deals.

Colonel Bob pulled his hat down over his eyes a little, leaned back on his walking cane, and began to reminisce. He told me about having bought carloads of horses and mules from people in Texas; he mentioned the names of several reputable horse and mule men that I knew well—

Ross Brothers and Burnett and Yount, C. B. Teams and
Charley Neal. I could see that he was well steeped in this
horse and mule business and could, if he desired, be a tremendous help to a young man in a strange country.

The barn hadn't been used to speak of in three or four
years. It was pretty dirty and had dry hay lying around in
all the stalls. There were lots of cobwebs and stuff up
around the corners and at the top of the hallway where it
joined the loft. The place needed cleaning up and shoveling out and fixing up. A few hinges needed to be fixed on
the gates. I told Colonel Bob that it would be my pleasure
to get some men and straighten up the place and put it
back in order in just a few days, if he saw fit to rent it to
me.

"Rent it to you! Why, my boy, I want you to use it
just like it was youahs, and I have nigras—that you can
take and pay what you want to—that have worked for
me for yeahs. They know how to clean this barn and how
to take care of youah hosses and mules. And you just pay
me whatevah it might be worth to you when you are
ready to go, and I hope you don't go soon. I'll be glad
for you to stay all fall and wintah."

I said: "Colonel Bob, that sounds like a Texas trick,
and I appreciate it very much. I'll just make arrangements
to have my mules shipped to me and unloaded here at
Dixon. I'll take over the barn, but I'll expect you to come
down and make yourself at home—loaf with me and
advise me and entertain your old friends here—just as if
you had never been out of business."

"Young man," he said, "it does my heart good to
know there are still men in the hoss and mule business
endowed with the principles of the old school. I want

you to know that you are welcome heah in my barn, and you are welcome in my home as my guest. I want you to feel free to do anything in Dixon that you would do in youah own home town."

I said: "Colonel, that's spoken like a Southern gentleman, and I'm going to take you at your word."

We both had a little chuckle, and he said: "Now, suh, if you will take me back home. I don't take long trips away from the house anymore, and I didn't —you know —quite get my nap out. But I'm going to be looking forward to some interesting visits with you."

We drove back to his old home on the south side of town. It was a beautiful old colonial house, well kept on the outside, but up to now I hadn't seen the inside. We bid each other good-bye, and I spent the rest of the afternoon driving around getting the lay of the land. I went down to the depot and wired my friend in Texas to ship my mules to Dixon, and then I moved into the hotel.

About four o'clock I drifted into the village drugstore. The druggist shook hands with me and said: "Mr. Green, I'm glad you are going to stay in Dixon a few days. Hope it will be longer. Make yourself at home and use my drugstore as your headquarters. We'll take your calls, and we'll do anything we can to make your stay in Dixon pleasant."

About that time a young man walked up and the druggist introduced him to me. He knew about my mules, he said, and added: "You've no idea how much good your visit here will do Colonel Bob. I do hope your mules will be of a quality that he can have pride in representin' to his old friends and customers."

I assured this young man—and also the druggist and

some other people within earshot—that the mules would be as fine as Texas ever grew, which was a fact.

It was surprising to me, as I thought about the situation, how suddenly everybody in town seemed to know about my business. The grapevine worked fast, and these people were willing and delighted to take in a fresh young stranger who might be a new experience to them. Things are sometimes dull in a little town, and I just thought to myself that they might be intending to make some diversion out of my visit—either at my expense or for my pleasure; I couldn't tell yet which it would be.

That night at supper everyone took on and said how glad they were I was coming to Dixon, and maybe I'd see fit to make it my future home. They needed me, since Colonel Bob wasn't able to take care of the horse and mule business of the town like he used to, and they thought the mule business vital to the agricultural pursuits of the people. I appreciated all this and tried to put on my best manners and eat with one hand at a time and not take too many second helpings.

Next morning I got to the barn pretty early, and there were three Negroes there—two middle-aged and one old white-headed man. The two middle-aged fellows were sweeping and shoveling and cleaning out the barn. You could tell they had been there a good while and sure had been stirring around. The old white-headed man was a kind of dignified old Southern Negro. He took off his hat and introduced himself and said that he was William, the other was Jake, and the third was Munroe. I said howdy to all of them and talked to William a little while.

Finally I asked: "William, do you want a job?"

He said: "Oh no, suh. Ah takes care of the Rebel Commandah for Colonel Bob."

"The Rebel Commander?"

"Yassah, that's Colonel Bob's private drivin' hoss. Colonel Bob, he's gettin' him ready for the fall fair. He'll drive him in the fall fair. We worries about Colonel Bob a-drivin' the Rebel Commandah, but maybe he ain't in no dangah much. Well, since you's heah, I'd bettah go on back over to Colonel Bob's. These boys heah knows what to do. Ah hopes youah mules gets heah in a few days."

I thanked William and told him I would see him some more. The other men were busy working and not asking me any questions about what to do, so I said: "Well, boys, I believe I'll go on off uptown."

They both tipped their hats and said: "Yessah, yessah. We'll be heah when you gets back."

I stepped into my fancy automobile and drove on up town and pulled up in front of the drugstore. It was about that time in the morning when everybody gathered, so I walked in and Miss Belle said: "Mistah Green, come ovah to the table. I want you to meet some of my friends."

She introduced me to two or three nice ladies, and when a young man walked in—a little younger than she was, maybe—she said, "Tom, Tom come heah."

Tom walked over to the table, I got up, and she said: "I want you to meet my brother Tom, Tom Dixon. He runs the bank."

Well, I shook hands with Tom and told him I was glad to meet him, and he immediately said: "Oh, you are the man that's usin' Papa's barn and goin' to bring us some mules. We're so glad to have you. If we can do anything for you at the bank, just let me know."

I just thought to myself: I got in business faster and with less effort in Dixon, Mississippi, than any place I'd ever been. I sure did have to make good for these people with my stock. I would bring in the best mules that Texas had, and you just couldn't tell—this might be the spot for me to spend the winter.

I socialized around and drank a coke and visited and listened to some of the nice things people had to say. I was polite, but I had kind of begun to tell about a few of the wonders of Texas. They found this all very interesting and were very attentive when I started to tell something and, of course, a man from Texas in Mississippi would appreciate a good listener. I kind of got my visit out and paid for all the drinks in the house, which I thought was awful cheap for dues, and stepped out of the front door. Coming down the street I saw Colonel Bob driving a beautiful black horse with shiny black leather harness on him. This horse had his head reined up high and was hooked to a beautiful red-wheeled gig. He was stepping at a smooth, nice rate of speed that showed he was a real harness horse with a lot of breeding and a lot of speed.

Colonel Bob looked neither to the right nor to the left. He drove right on through town and toward his house.

The druggist saw me watching. He stepped out of the door and said: "Colonel Bob has a farm on the other side of town. He drives out occasionally and looks things over, but he tries to get back to the house pretty early in the morning."

I said: "He's driving a beautiful horse."

"Yes, but we worry about Colonel Bob driving the Rebel Commander. You know he has been raced and is so spirited. We just hope the horse doesn't hurt him. The whole town is fond of Colonel Bob."

I told him I could readily understand that; I was fond of Colonel Bob and I'd known him just two days.

The druggist laughed a nice little chuckle and said: "Mister Green, the town's getting fond of you, too. We hope you make your visit a long stay."

I thanked him and went on off to the depot to check up on when my mules would get in. The depot agent said that if they were shipped when I thought they were, they ought to get to Dixon the next afternoon about four o'clock. Well, it seemed to me that would be a nice time of day to get in a load of mules. You could unload them and get them to the barn, feed and water and look them over before dark.

I spent the rest of the day socializing around the town. After supper that night I sat around in the hotel lobby and listened to the radio and listened to the people tell me about the country. They talked about the cotton crop and how long the staple was—what a good fall it was going to be for everybody.

Next morning I visited around town again and made coke-time at the drugstore, dropped by the bank and visited with Tom for a minute, went over by the post office and started back down to the mule barn; then I decided all of a sudden it would be nice to go by and get Colonel Bob and take him to see how the barn looked after his men had gotten through with it. I turned and drove up in front of Colonel Bob's house, but he wasn't in sight. I stepped out of the car and went up to the front door and knocked. One of the house servants came to the door and told me the Colonel was out at the barn, she thought, seeing about Rebel Commander.

Well, I had been wanting to get a firsthand look at this Rebel Commander; so I went around the side of the house, through the garden, and out to the barn. Sure enough, Colonel Bob was standing in the hallway. Old William was currying and brushing Rebel Commander. I cleared up my throat and whistled a little bit so he would know I was coming, and he turned around and propped himself on his walking cane and said: "Why, Ben, my boy, it's a pleasah to see you this mawnin'. I want you to look at the Rebel Commandah."

I walked around this good black horse. He was about fifteen-one hands high and would weigh eleven hundred. His legs were clean and sound, his feet were good, and he had the top line and shape of a horse that could trot. The muscle development on his forelegs and the stifles of his hind legs plainly indicated he was a horse of terrific speed.

As I observed all this I said to Colonel Bob: "He's truly a fine animal and a fine specimen of the Standard blood horse."

"I'm glad you appreciate good hossflesh, Ben. The Rebel Commandah is a direct descendant of the great horse Pilot Medium on his sire's side. On his dam's side he runs into Peter the Great."

I knew both bloodlines and commented on what good breeding he carried. He had a beautiful patent leather bridle on him with black patent leather blinds on it. They were drawn up tight, and the reflected light made his eyes just sparkle. He was truly a beautiful horse.

Colonel Bob and I started walking back up toward the house, and I told him why I had come by. He said: "Ben, that is very thoughtful of you, but I have had my morning's outing. I hear youah mules will be in heah this afternoon. Let me come by and see them in the mawnin'."

I said: "That's fine, Colonel Bob. I'll come after you."

"That's a lot of trouble to you, my boy."

"It's no trouble. It's a pleasure, and I'll be after you in the morning."

I was leaving the front steps and started toward the yard gate. As I glanced up, one of the most beautiful young ladies you ever saw was coming through that yard gate. She was blonde, as small and petite and cute as they come, and she traveled with more style than the Rebel Commander would ever have. She had long, wavy, naturally honey-colored hair, beautiful big blue eyes, and a smile that was very contagious. She glanced up at me and said: "Good morning, sir."

Colonel Bob turned around on the porch. "Mistah Green, that's my granddaughtah, Baby Belle."

I grabbed my hat and told Baby Belle what a pleasure it was to meet her—that I had met her mother, I was very much impressed with her grandfather, I had met her Uncle Tom—and we had quite a little talk. The old man watched us a minute—you could see the half-smile that came over the corners of his mouth—and he turned and walked on back toward the back of the porch. Then Baby Belle said she was delighted to have met me and for me to come back to see them again.

I thanked her and left, but for the next couple of

hours I thought more about the way Baby Belle looked than I thought about how my mules were going to look when they got here.

That afternoon when the train came in, I unloaded two carloads of good Texas mules: twenty-four to the car, forty-eight head in all. My men led them and drove them on foot down to the barn where we divided them into pens, put some of them in stalls, and got them separated where they wouldn't be fighting and bothering each other. I got plenty of feed and water for them, and had them pretty well located by late afternoon when a number of townspeople dropped by to see them. Nobody said anything that wasn't complimentary, and justly so because they were good, straight, sound young mules with plenty of size and plenty of flesh. They were the right kind to do a good job in that heavy land along the Mississippi Delta.

By suppertime I was satisfied my mules were in good shape and they weren't bothering me much—but Baby Belle was. I couldn't get that doll off my mind—which wasn't exactly normal for me. I had always attended to horses and mules and business a heap better than I had tended to social affairs. The general run of fillies didn't upset me too much when they trotted by, but there weren't very many of them moved like this one—and didn't any of them that I'd seen lately have the style that she had. She moved about as nice as anything I'd seen since I sold my last race horse. She had a sweet, Southern-drawl kind of voice, a bright flashing blue eye, and smooth peaches-and-cream complexion. She was a Southern belle, if there were any left on this earth. Just from what I could

32

see, she was away outgrown that term "Baby." A belle— but she wasn't a baby belle.

I ate supper at the hotel like I had been doing, but as soon as I finished eating I didn't loaf around the lobby to see what kind of smart talk the old people were going to carry on. I stepped out on the gallery, looked around a few minutes, and walked on down to the drugstore. I didn't get in my car. I just thought I would amble around afoot a little bit and take in some fresh air. The air had begun to have that fallish feeling after dark—a cotton-picking time of year smell to it—and it was a very pleasant time of day.

I walked in the drugstore. Nobody was there but the druggist and some man sitting at the back reading a magazine. The druggist and I got to talking a little bit, and he said that he'd heard I had some nice mules and folks felt like I was going to do well with them. I thanked him and told him I believed I would too, but I wouldn't be ready to show them for a day or two—until I got some of the rough knocked off them and until they filled up and got over looking chowsed and drawn from shipping.

I moved over to the fountain and asked him to draw me a big coke. I was just sitting there, wondering how to pass off the time of night, when I glanced up in the mirror and saw Baby Belle bounce in through the door with another beautiful young girl. These kids were three or four years younger than I was, but they hadn't noticed it and I wasn't going to bring it up. After all, they were grown girls and I was a grown boy, and they were far the most interesting people I had seen around. Mule business could get kind of dull if that's all you had to do. So

I stepped up real quick off my stool, turned and took my hat off, and spoke to the ladies. Baby Belle introduced me to her friend Charlotte. Charlotte was a real nice young girl. She didn't have near the style that Baby Belle did, but she was good company. Of course I asked them to join me in a drink, and we moved over to one of those little tables where the seats swung out from under the glass-case tabletop.

We carried on a lot of light conversation. Baby Belle told Charlotte I was the mule man from Texas that was using her granddaddy Bob's barn, and so on. I asked them what they were doing out in the night air, and they said they had started to the picture show. I didn't waste any time telling them I hadn't known there was one in town and that I liked to see a picture show. I wondered if I could come along. You could tell they were kind of sparring for that, and we didn't have much argument. I got up and paid for the drinks and we all went to the picture show.

After it was over and I was going to walk the girls back home I said: "Why don't we go by the hotel and get my automobile?"

Baby Belle answered: "I'm just dying to ride in that car, but I dasn't to tonight."

"Dasn't to—where did you get that?"

"That is good Southern English, I'll have you to know!"

"Well," I said, "then why dasn't you to?"

"I haven't asked Mamma Belle."

I said: "I know how we can fix that. It's kind of early yet—let's go get the car and we'll go down and get Mamma Belle and we'll all go riding."

That turned on a good note. She said: "That just might work."

We drove up to the house, and she called her mother to come out to the car. I said: "Don't be hollering at your mother. Let's go up to the gallery." So I got out and opened the door for her like a gentleman.

Sure enough, when we got up to the porch Mamma Belle was standing in the front door listening to the commotion. I pled guilty and told her it wasn't Baby Belle's fault that she had ridden in the car without asking. I told Mamma Belle we had just come by to get her, and that seemed to please her. So Mamma Belle and Baby Belle and Charlotte and I, we all drove around a while and made light conversation and told some cute little things. Mamma Belle entered into everything, but finally she suggested maybe it was about time we had better go home.

We took Charlotte home, and then we drove up to Daddy Bob's house where I said my good-byes. I thought I'd had a pretty good day. I'd got my mules unloaded, put in the barn, and fed and watered. I'd got to take Baby Belle to the picture show, and Mamma Belle when I left them that night had said: "Mistah Green, you feel free to come callin' any time."

It looked to me like I was getting off to an awful good start in the town of Dixon, Mississippi.

I was down at the barn by daylight the next morning. My helpers were already there, and we started brushing and currying and cleaning off mules. Later I got in my car and went after Colonel Bob. The old gentleman had just finished his breakfast. As I stepped on the porch he was coming to the door, and he said: "Ben, my boy, I heah you have some good mules."

I said: "Colonel Bob, I don't think anybody could tell quite as much about that as you could. I would value your opinion. Will you go down with me to the barn and look at my mules? Of course, I'll bring you back."

"Oh, that will be fine, Ben." And he reached over on the hatrack at the side of the door, got his old black Southern hat, and pulled it down over his eyes. He reached over again and got his walking cane and started out to the car with me.

Just as I opened the car door for Colonel Bob to step in, Baby Belle bounced up from somewhere. She came dashing out of the yard, ran between Colonel Bob and me, and sat down in the car seat. She flopped those long golden curls and rolled her blue eyes at her grandfather and said: "Daddy Bob"—the way she said it, it fairly jingled—"Daddy Bob, I want to go, too."

You could see that it delighted the old man, but he said: "Baby Belle, honey, you are a nuisance I seem to enjoy. Come on, we'll try to . . ." and he looked at me. "Young man, I'll try to not let my granddaughtah get in the way of the mules or cause you too much trouble."

"Colonel Bob," I said, "we won't bother about her." Of course I caught his eye off and gave her a short wink after I said it.

We got to the barn and Colonel Bob got out and Baby Belle bounced out over the steering wheel on my side, and we started down the hall of the barn. I showed the Colonel several matched pairs that I had stalled off to themselves. He found another pair, and still another, that he wanted to see. He called Jake, and he called Munroe, and had them bring out the mules so he could walk around them. You could tell the old man just reveled in having that barn full of mules and hollering at Jake and hollering at Munroe. He was living a lot of his horse and mule business over again at my expense. But it wasn't an expense, really, it was my pleasure.

The old man said: "You won't have any trouble selling these mules, young man. Are you going to take in trade, or are you going to have to sell for cash?"

I said: "Why, Colonel Bob, I didn't know you could sell mules straight out for cash. I'll trade for whatever they have to offer. Of course I'll want to draw enough boot in between to assure that I can sell what I take in at a profit."

"Oh," he said, "I understand that, Ben. These are the kind of mules my customers will appreciate, and I feel suah you will get them sold to an advantage."

I thought it would be a nice time to put the old gentleman on notice, so I said: "Colonel Bob, I would like to trade for some nice kind of saddle mares to take back West—some nice fox trotting, gaited mares, and even a driving horse or two. Of course, I'll trade for the old mules and fat mules and things that farmers want to trade off. And," I said, "I just wonder what the policy of the bank would be—I haven't discussed it with Tom—if I want to take some notes and mortgages on these mules. Would the bank consider discounting and buying the paper?"

"That's what ouah bank enjoys, Ben. We would be pleased to buy the paper you take on any of our customers around heah. There might be a few that are not too good, but you can discuss it with Tom. I think you can reach an agreement with him."

By this time Baby Belle had been all up and down the barn and was back in the car waiting for Colonel Bob and me. We started out and Colonel Bob said: "Now if you care to, we'll go by the bank and discuss this with my son Tom."

I said: "Colonel Bob, needn't to bother. I haven't got any paper yet. I may not even take in any."

"Well, if you do, I think it can be arranged so we can take care of it at Tom's bank." The old man never laid any claim to the bank's being his. He always mentioned it as "Tom's bank."

The old man was wise, and when we got back to his house and he had thanked me for coming after him and bragged on my mules he said: "Ben, don't let Baby Belle go back to the bahn with you. I think her mother wants her in heah aftah while for something." He winked and walked off.

Baby Belle sat long enough for me to ask her for a date that night. She seemed delighted and said there was a party out at somebody's house—that I didn't know and, of course, didn't care—and she would like for me to escort her to that party. I thought nothing could be nicer than going to a Southern party with a Southern belle, and I told her so.

Anyhow, that set things off good for the day, and I started back to the barn to see about my mules. By dinner I had sold two spans of mules—one for cash, and I took a pair of big fat old mules in on trade for the other. I just charged the man what my mules cost for boot and cleared his team, which was sort of the custom with horse and mule dealers in those days. Anyhow, I had gotten off to a good start. I had sold four mules the first half-day I had them ready to show.

That night there was a man came to the hotel to see

me about buying four more. I was trying to get away from him because I had a date with Baby Belle, but he didn't seem to be interested in leaving. He wanted me to tell him about the wonders of Texas, build up my mules, and so forth. I told him it seemed to me it would be to his advantage for me to describe the mules and tell him about them in the daylight when he could be looking at them— and long about now I had some other things to tend to.

He kind of got the hint, and I got up and got loose from him and went on out to Colonel Bob's home. I went in and waited around for Baby Belle to get dressed— visited with Mamma Belle and Colonel Bob and told them about my mule trades for the day. He mentioned several people that ought to be interested in some mules—told me which direction from town they lived, and that kind of stuff. I thanked him and told him I would be by in the morning and take him to see the mules I had traded for.

"Nevah mind, Ben. Wait a few days until you have moah in."

But I repeated that I would like to trade for some saddle mares to take back to Texas.

About this time Baby Belle showed up and we went off to the party. She was getting to be a delightful habit with me, and I enjoyed her a lot. She was fun and never complained or grumbled about anything. If we went somewhere to eat, it was always better than she had expected. And if we met somebody, they were always nice. And she just didn't complain about anything or make fun of anybody or criticize anybody's clothes or say anything unkind. That was different from a lot of the snooty little fillies I had known, and I really began to appreciate Baby Belle.

By the time I had been in town ten days, I had sold more than half of my mules and traded for a few. I had traded for two nice saddle horses, a chestnut and a bay. In the meantime I had discovered that Baby Belle had a saddle horse, and we had been riding horseback in the late afternoons. Charlotte and some of the other young people in the town had saddle horses, and we had all been out on some moonlight picnics ahorseback. We'd had parties and romped and played and had fun just about ever since I got there. Besides that, I was doing a thriving business selling my mules.

Nobody complained too much about the prices on them. Some farmers did want to trade in old, fat mules and get rid of them at too high a price—but I had bought my mules the year before and summered them and I owned them worth the money. They were sure doing me a lot of good. About this time I had gathered a little paper on some of them—took in some mules on trade and sold some on a credit with me holding the mortgage. I mentioned this one day to Tom in the drugstore.

"Why come on in the bank, Mistah Green. We'll see what we can do." So we walked on over and he said: "Now, we'll discount this paper about ten dollars a mule and buy it from you."

He looked for me to fight him a little over that, and I didn't want to disappoint him. I said: "About five dollars a mule?"

"Well," he said, "make it seven and a half."

"Make it six." I didn't want him to think I was too easy.

He said: "Well, that will be fine. Discount it six dollars a head a mule, and since you are writing these mortgages for eight per cent interest, it will be all right. The bank will get the interest and the six dollars a head. Now," he said, "I suppose you want to send this money to some bank in Texas and apply it on the mules?"

"Apply it nothing," I said. "That money's mine. If I sell a mule, I deposit it if I want to—and I can deposit it in your bank."

He brightened up considerably. He thought I had borrowed money to buy those mules. Well, I have borrowed money to buy thousands of mules, but it so happened that I owned these two carloads. And when I went for a coke the next day, Mamma Belle was a lot nicer.

That weekend there was fall fair and Old Settlers reunion coming up. They were going to have it down on the creek, close to town in a big grove of pecan trees, and the town was busy getting ready. They were going to have a big program—speakin's, dinner on the grounds, games, something for everybody—come one, come all. They were going to have some horseback riding, horse showing, and some harness racing. I had been hearing about this for several days.

About two days before the reunion, Baby Belle asked me if I would enter a horse in the horse show. I had traded for some nice saddle mares and had been riding one of them around with the rest of the young set, so I told her I would enter the five-gaited class. That morning I went by horseback to get Baby Belle. She rode a beautiful chesnut mare—stocking-legged, flax mane and tail—that was a real jewel and a real saddle mare. Baby Belle looked good on her, and they moved off together like they should. We spent all day at the Old Settlers reunion.

Visitors had come from far and near, but I was kinda

different. I had on boots and a big hat, and of course I was by that time telling them a lot about the Lone Star state. It seemed like everybody was getting a big kick out of my conversation. They had a big feed on the grounds, and I bragged on their cooking. I bragged on their cake and their pies and their chicken. Everything they shoved at me, I would try a batch of it—and directly here would come another nice old Southern lady and say: "Mistah Green, I would just like for you to taste a bite of this . . ." And I just kept a-tasting, and I bragged on all of it. I guess I ate more cooking from strictly secret Southern recipes at that Old Settlers reunion than you ever heard of at any other gathering in the world.

The political speakings were held in the morning and didn't anybody pay much mind to them. They had a band that played all day, and people sat around on the ground and listened to the music. They had different kinds of contests and games, but the big feature of the day was the afternoon harness racing. There was a half-mile track, and they had some fast trotting horses and some fast pacing horses. Most of them were local horses with local people driving them, so everybody was interested in every race.

We sat on our horses beside the track—a bunch of us young people—and watched the drivers score their horses, turn them around to their little two-wheeled driving sulkies, and bring them up to the starting line. When all of them were in place, the judge would fire his little gun and the race would be on. Of course if the horses weren't lined up just right, the judge would call them back to rescore; then the horses would get hot and lathering and excited, and the drivers' tempers would flare.

The fifth race was for drivers over seventy years old. Colonel Bob was close to eighty, but when the six horses came up to score this race, there was Colonel Bob driving the Rebel Commander. The horse never fretted nor frothed nor got mad; he scored and came back with the most perfect manners.

"Mamma and I are scared stiff," said Baby Belle. "We ah so afraid the Rebel Commandah is going to hurt Daddy Bob yet."

I said: "Well, I don't see how. That horse seems perfectly mannered."

"He has been a race hoss," she said. "Daddy Bob bought him off the track, mainly to have him for this Old Settlers reunion and to win this race."

They had to rescore several times, but directly the judge shot the pistol and the race was on. When they passed the grandstand, Colonel Bob was neck and neck with another horse. The Rebel Commander was moving out smooth and easy and had plenty left—he hadn't felt any strain and he wasn't hurting himself in the least. On the back stretch, Rebel Commander moved out about two lengths in front of the rest of the field. Colonel Bob was sitting very erect and holding his reins high. He was making a beautiful drive as they made the turn to come in by the grandstand. As I said, this was a half-mile track, so they had to make two circles. Colonel Bob pushed Rebel Commander out a little bit more—then he just took a tight hold on him and held him there. He made this first half-mile just in front of the other horses in the field. They came by the grandstand and started around again; then as he came into the home stretch the last time, Colonel Bob shook the bits a little and leaned forward and spoke to the Rebel Commander. You couldn't hear what he said, but that black horse must have believed it. He moved out and won the race by ten lengths—and the crowd went wild.

Colonel Bob scored Rebel Commander and brought him back by the judges' stand—he was in perfect manner —stopped, and stood still. The judges came out and presented Colonel Bob with a big trophy, then old William dashed up to lead Rebel Commander off the track by the side gate. They headed back home.

Baby Belle was excited beyond expression. It seemed everybody was delighted that Colonel Bob had won the race—except, I guess, the drivers of the other five horses. All in all, it was a good day. We went back to Colonel Bob's home and had a light supper and talked about the events of the day, and I left and put my horse in the barn at a reasonable hour.

The next week I had more horse and mule business than you could shake a stick at. Every trade I made was a good one, and I made money. By the end of the third week, I had sold out of all the fresh mules I brought from Texas. I didn't have quite a carload of saddle mares and trade mules to take back to Texas with me.

As things developed, it was time for Baby Belle to go to Gulfport to the girls' finishing school—whatever that was. So far as I was concerned, she was already finished; but it seemed that Mamma Belle thought she needed to go to this girls' school. I told Mamma Belle that so far as I could see, the only reason Baby Belle needed to go to that school was so that unfinished girls would know what they ought to look like and how they ought to act. Of course that made a big hit, and I told it in the drugstore where everybody laughed.

Baby Belle said: "Ben, you embarrass me!"

On Sunday night before I was going to ship out, Colonel Bob and Mamma Belle and Baby Belle had me down to the house for a family dinner. There was a beautiful table set and a lot of food. It was a little cool, and afterwards we sat around the fireplace in the spacious, high-ceilinged living room instead of out on the gallery. Hanging over the mantel was a portrait of Baby Belle's grandmother that quickly told you this was a family of gracious and beautiful women. It explained, too, why Colonel Bob was so fond of his granddaughter—she was the very likeness of her grandmother for whom Colonel Bob had built this house. Anything fine that had been hard to obtain but could be brought from afar—it was in this old Southern home.

We reminisced and talked and visited, and I told them how much I had enjoyed my stay in Mississippi. Before this time I had settled with Colonel Bob for his barn. I had asked Tom what he thought the Colonel expected. He said $25 would be enough; so I had given the old man $100—which was cheap aplenty for all the help he had been to me. He was delighted. Tom's bank was going to make some money, too, off the paper that I had sold them. All in all, it seemed that my visit there had been pleasing to everybody concerned. I had made more money in that month than I had made in other ways all year.

Colonel Bob excused himself and retired early that evening. I was sitting on a long sofa with Baby Belle curled up to my side in front of that fireplace. Mamma

Belle was sitting over in a great big chair next to the corner of the fireplace. "Ben," she said, "I have a problem I would like to discuss with you."

I couldn't imagine her having any problems, but I said: "I'd just be glad to help you if it is something that I would know about."

"You would certainly know about it. I live in constant feah that the Rebel Commandah is going to hurt Daddy Bob. I was wondering, as a favor to me, would you try to buy the Rebel Commandah and load him with your hosses and take him back to Texas?"

I said: "Why, that would be doing me a favor—not you."

"Daddy Bob is not going to want to sell the Rebel Commandah. It may take more money to buy him than he will ever bring you in Texas. I was wondering if you would go ahead and try to buy him, and let me give you the difference in money."

I said: "Oh, I doubt if that will be necessary. Let me ask Colonel Bob tomorrow what he will take for the Rebel Commander."

"Please don't let him know," she said, "that I've asked you to buy him, because then he wouldn't sell him at all. And we do want to get rid of that hoss before he hurts Daddy Bob."

I said: "He is beautifully mannered and well behaved. I don't see how he would hurt Colonel Bob—and he seems to get a great pleasure out of driving him."

"I know, but at Daddy Bob's age there is danger in his driving such a spirited hoss."

Baby Belle hadn't entered into this conversation, and she didn't say anything after Mamma Belle quit talking.

But Mamma Belle said: "Well, find out in the morning if you can buy the horse from Daddy Bob, then tell me what he says."

She excused herself and went on off to bed. Baby Belle and I sat by the fire and talked and told each other about our plans. She was going to that girls' finishing school, and I was going back to Texas, but she would write me. And I told her I never did answer anybody's letters—but I might hers.

She said: "You mean you might?"

I said: "Well, you can try me and see." And after while it was late, and I went back to the hotel.

Early next morning I went by to see Colonel Bob. He was out at the barn, and the Rebel Commander was in a dark stall in the corner. Of course I knew that you kept a black horse in a dark stall to keep his hair good. I knew that was all right, and I didn't ask him to get the horse out. I just stepped in the stall and walked around the horse a little bit. He was very nice and quiet and gentle—and I spoke to him and put my hand on his neck and rubbed him a little and walked out. Then I said: "Colonel Bob, I have traded for some saddle mares to take back to Texas, but I don't have that driving horse I wanted. I just wondered if you could be persuaded to part with the Rebel Commander?"

"Oh," he said, "Ben, I'd hesitate to part with him. After all, he's just an eight-year-old hoss, a nice drivin' hoss, and probably the last great hoss I'll ever own. It grieves me to think that I should sell him. Howevah, I would rather sell him to you and let him go out West where I won't see him again than sell him heah in town."

I said: "Colonel, I can appreciate that. I don't know

what he might cost, but if he is not beyond my means I'll try to buy the horse."

"Well, Ben, with all the quality and breeding and speed of the Rebel Commandah, I wouldn't think of taking less than five hundred for him."

I said: "Colonel, I am sure he is worth that, but I don't know whether or not I have a customer who would give that for him. Before I ship out tomorrow, I'd like to talk to you about it again."

"Well, it doesn't mattah much whether I sell him or not."

"I'm sure of that," I said, "but I'll see you after while."

I drove down to the drugstore and got out and went in —and here came Mamma Belle. "Have you talked to Colonel Bob?"

"Yes," I said, "and he wants five hundred for the Rebel Commander. That's a tremendous amount of money this day and time for a horse—and I doubt that I can sell him and break even on him."

She said: "Ben, I wish you would buy him, and let me give you a hundred on the five. Then he won't have to bring so much in Texas."

I ran that through my mind. I knew that the horse was not going to bring more than $250 in Texas—but I'd had a big time and made lots of money on this trip and the Dixons had been such a delightful part of it all—I told her that I would go ahead and buy the Rebel Commander. She could do as she pleased about giving me the $100.

About that time Tom came in the drugstore and she said: "Tom, go in the bank and get a hundred to give Ben." I'd got way past that Mistah Green stuff—hadn't anybody called me Mistah Green for a week.

Tom turned around and pushed the pencil tight up against his ear and went off to the bank. Directly he came back with two fifty-dollar bills and handed them to Mamma Belle. She turned and handed them to me and thanked me so much.

I went back to the house and told Colonel Bob that I would buy the horse. I gave him a check on his own bank where I had been keeping my money. He thanked me very much and said he would have William bring the horse to the stock car when I got ready to load out. I told him I would wall off a place in the stock car—where the Rebel Commander wouldn't be riding with the common horses and mules. He said he appreciated that.

I loaded my stock out in the middle of the next afternoon. Then that night I had Colonel Bob and Mamma Belle and Baby Belle and all the folks that had been so nice to me for dinner at the hotel. The good lady at the hotel fixed us a private table off over in a private dining room, and I put on a pretty nice farewell dinner for a fellow that had made his money in the horse and mule business. We told each other good-bye, and the next morning I left before daylight and started back to Texas.

I sat up straight and drove hard and got back home before my load of horses and mules got in on the train. I had drawn my money out of the Mississippi bank, and I got home thinking about how well I had done on this trip.

The next morning the train came in with my stock. The first thing I did was unload the Rebel Commander. I got him on the ground and brushed and curried him a little bit and led him out by the bridle. When we had started to load the horse in Dixon, old William told me that Colonel Bob had included the patent leather bridle with the patent leather blinds. He left it on the Rebel Commander because, he said, it belonged to him. Old William said I would understand later on.

There was a doctor in my home town that I thought might buy the Rebel Commander. The way it was in our country in the wintertime, a doctor sometimes needed a buggy, and he was still keeping a buggy horse, even though he had some automobiles. I knew the Rebel Commander would appeal to him.

I let the horse rest that day, but the next day I had him cleaned up and brushed off and groomed nicely. I hooked him to an open-top runabout buggy—a nice kind of buggy, well trimmed with red leatherette on the seats and with good long shafts. I noticed that when I led him up and put him under the shafts, he stood very still. Everything I did around him, he seemed to notice. And he would listen and watch for me to put my hands on him —but he never offered to do anything wrong.

I got him hitched to this nice little light buggy and came driving up Main Street in my little home town, driving to the post office. I reined the Rebel Commander in just one building down from the post office where there was a store building with a plank walk in front of it. I reined the Rebel Commander to bring him in at the front of that store, and I dropped the lines—expecting him to stop, like any horse would. Instead of stopping, he drove right on up on the porch of the store where he jabbed both forefeet through the plank flooring of the porch. Then he just stood there and snorted and shook.

I picked his feet up out of the floor—one at a time, very carefully—and talked to him and backed him to the street. His legs were skinned a little.

Now, that morning I had loosened the blinds on his bridle. I had thought they were too close together and too tight. So when I got his feet out of the porch of that store and looked up at him, these blinds were drawn back and there was no reflection of light from that patent leather—and his eyes suddenly looked very dull to me.

I rubbed him on the neck and patted him and talked to him and left him standing while I went in the post office. There was a letter from Baby Belle. She had written me just before she left for finishing school. I could hardly wait to get her letter open, and I tore the envelope up pretty bad and went to unfolding it. It smelled good, and the writing was pretty, and she started off by saying:

Dear Ben,

I am mortified beyond words. This morning I heard Mamma Belle and Daddy Bob laughing in the kitchen, and I heard them call your name. I ran downstairs—I didn't know what was going on—and they were laughing until they were red in the face. I made Daddy Bob explain, so now I have to tell you that the Rebel Commander was *given* to him when the horse ran blind on the track. Those patent leather blinds are on his bridle to reflect light and make his eyes look bright and pretty. . . . The $100 Mamma Belle gave you was bait-money that Daddy Bob gave her to fix it so you wouldn't try to buy the horse for what he was worth. Mamma says he needed to make a good horse trade again—to have something to live for. . . . I just want you to know that I had nothing to do with this scheming of my folks. I hope to hear from you. I don't blame you if you never come to see Mamma Belle or Daddy Bob, but please come to see me.

It all came back—why people were so afraid that the Rebel Commander was going to hurt the Colonel. And why the horse was so perfectly mannered! He was stone blind, and he depended on his driver for every move. At the race, he didn't know whether he was in front or behind, and he was listening to the command of his driver. And the reason Colonel Bob didn't stop when he came through town: he had no place to stand a blind horse without running the risk of people discovering he was blind.

The patent leather blinds—William said I would understand later. It was doubtful that many of the townfolks —or anybody but William—knew the horse was blind. It was a matter kept strictly secret between Daddy Bob and Mamma Belle, and it was a delight to his old black heart that he could cheat just one more horse man.

I had walked very slowly out of the post office reading Baby Belle's letter. When I looked up from reading, several people were standing around Rebel Commander admiring him. I hadn't noticed them around before, and I didn't think anybody had seen my horse go up on the plank sidewalk of the building. But just to take care of things, I walked up to the Rebel Commander and began to unbuckle and take up his bridle.

"He's a little hard-mouthed," I said, "and this bridle is too loose on him for me to keep good control." Of course I didn't mention how pulling those blinds in close put the sparkle back in his eyes.

I got in the buggy—still clutching Baby Belle's letter —and drove the Rebel Commander at a smooth, nice rate of speed right on through town to show that he was a real harness horse with a lot of breeding and a lot of style. I was the only man in Texas who knew that the Rebel Commander was worth exactly what Colonel Bob had paid for him at the track—nothing!

Homer's Last Mule

When I was about fifteen years old, I was a very promising young horse trader, I thought, and was sure that I had already learned the worst and the best tricks about trading horses and mules.

I was riding down the road one afternoon, and an old Ford pickup passed me with a lot of household goods stacked on it—such as cane-bottom chairs, feather mattress, iron bedstead, and a potbellied stove. I looked behind this old pickup, and there was a homemade trailer—in fact, almost all trailers were homemade at that time. The man was hauling a gray mare mule with a long mane and tail, well matted with cockleburrs. He drove up past me a little piece to a shade tree and stopped.

It was late in the summer and pretty hot. As I rode up, the man got out of the pickup and walked back even with the trailer and patted the mule. We passed the time of day for a few minutes, and he asked me where he could sell his mule. His wife stuck her head out of the pickup, stopped the kids from bawling a few minutes, and said: "Homer, you oughtn't to sell that mule. We'll get a mate for her and make another crop. Yore just disheartened, that's all."

"Shut up, Maw," he said. "I ain't goin' to make no more crops. I'm goin' to town and get me a job of public work."

Then he explained to me that the mate to his mule had died, the Johnson grass had taken over his crop, and he was quitting farming and wanted to sell the mule.

All the time he was talking, I was sitting on my horse looking at the mule. I asked him how old she was and if she had any blemishes on her. He told me she was an eight-year-old, was sound, and was a good work mule. I told him that I bought a few mules, and that I might be interested in her if he would unload her and put her on the ground so I could tell something about her. He had already priced her at $75 and had promptly put in that he wouldn't take $200 for a pair like her. We untied the tail gate, took the wagon rods out of it, and pulled the sideboards apart so the tail gate would come out. We got the homemade trailer about half tore down, untied the mule, and backed her out on the ground. She was grass-bellied and fat, weighed about a thousand pounds, and, I thought, was sure worth about $100 to $110.

Every few minutes his wife would holler back from

the pickup: "Homer, you oughtn't to sell the last mule we got."

And Homer would say: "Shut up, Maw."

I decided that I would give $60 for the mule, and he thought she was worth a lot more. But I finally made him see the light—that it was costing him money just to haul the mule around in that trailer. So after he stuttered and stammered a while and rubbed the mule affectionately down the back, he consented to let me steal her for $60. Me being a big operator, I was carrying all the money I had in my hip pocket; so I paid him six ten-dollar bills, which left me an even $10. He threw in the halter and rope and drove off. I started leading the mule to town, thinking about how fast I was going to increase my cash money when I sold that mule.

The general run of horse traders in town shied away from my mule and didn't want to make me a bid on her. I took the attitude that they were just going to try to wear me down and buy the mule cheap. It was Saturday afternoon, so I took my mule home, got my clippers and roached her mane, sheared her tail, and told myself that she was worth a lot more money than what she cost. I turned her out in a grass patch, and late Sunday afternoon I loaded her in a truck with two more mules and sent her to Fort Worth to the auction. The trucker unloaded the mule in Fort Worth at the horse and mule barn, put a number on her, and turned her in the pen with thirty or forty others. There was a long cement trough along the side of the pen that was filled with oats and shelled corn, and there was plenty of prairie hay in the hay rack.

I walked into the horse and mule barn on Monday

morning about an hour before the sale would start. I saw a whole bunch of horse and mule traders and "sweaters" about halfway down the barn in the middle of the alley. Everybody was watching some sort of show, so I walked down to see what the attraction was. There my mule sat on her hindquarters like a dog, swelled up about three times the size of a normal mule, and slobbers and foam pouring from her mouth.

John Yount, who was a partner in the old Burnett and Yount horse and mule barn, explained to me that the mule had eaten some corn and oats and had taken a severe case of colic. He also told me that this mule had been in the barn before and was a chronic "colicker" and could not eat grain. He had called the barn horse doctor for me, and the horse doctor had given her a dose of medicine that had caused her to froth at the mouth in an effort to get rid of the gas. He said that the horse doctor's services would cost me $3, which had already been charged to my account in the office. He explained to me in a very firm and understandable manner that the mule would not be able to go into the auction ring to be sold—and that the last time he sold her, a snide horse trader had bought her.

Well, for a young horse trader with most of his capital tied up in one colicky mule, that was sad news. I said to Mr. Yount: "What can I do with her?"

Sitting on top of the fence was a man who spoke up: "I give ten dollars the last time I bought her, and I'll give ten for her back."

Much to my heart-sickening surprise, it was Homer— the man that had told me he had lost his crop, and that "Maw" had begged not to sell their last mule.

$\mathcal{N}ubbin'$

One spring some horse buyers were shipping several carloads of mares from far West Texas to the Fort Worth
Horse and Mule Market. Their shipping permits ran
too long since the horses had been unloaded, and they
were forced to unload for feed and water at Weatherford, Texas, just thirty miles from their destination.

As I remember, there were three carloads of
mares, neither the best nor the worst
kind of range horses; however, there

were some breedy-looking riding-type mares in the shipment. The water troughs in the stock pens weren't more than half big enough for that many horses, and there was quite a scramble and a fight at the water troughs.

Soon after these mares were unloaded, one of them had a filly colt. I was a thirteen-year-old boy, riding around horseback, and of course I found this stockyard full of horses to gaze at and wish for. When the men came down to the stock pens and found they had a baby colt on their hands, they were unhappy because they didn't have any way to partition off a place for the colt—and they knew it would get trampled to death in the car with all the mares. I heard them talking about it, and I spoke up and asked them what they would take for the colt.

One of the horse traders saw that I had boots and spurs on and saw my horse standing outside. He asked: "What do you know about watering mares?"

I replied right quick that this watering arrangement wouldn't do nothing but get a bunch crippled. He told me that these mares were to be shipped out when the train ran early the next morning, and if I would stay down there and get a stick and keep some of the mares whipped back from the trough and just let a few of them drink at a time, he would give me the colt. I said I'd do better than that, I'd get a whip and ride my horse inside and hold them back and let them come up to water like they ought to.

But first I picked up a gate that had fallen off the hinges and stood it up in a corner of the fence, wired the ends to the fence, and put my baby colt behind it where nothing could happen to it. Their offer sure sounded like a good deal to me, 'cause I imagine at that age I would have watered horses every night as long as I could stay awake for a colt a night.

I kept this dogie colt around my trading pen at the wagonyard and fed it from a bottle, taught it to drink out of a pan, and the milk cow traders would let it suck out a fresh cow ever now and then. This bay filly called Nubbin' soon became the pet of the whole trading yard, but she was also a lot of trouble to everybody.

Holt Brothers had leased out their ranches in Palo Pinto County and moved a big bunch of mares and horses to the wagonyard at Weatherford to sell them and trade them off. These mares were all well bred but unbroke. I broke several mares, and wound up with a good young Holt mare that was heavy in foal as payment for breaking the other horses. The Holt mare brought a colt and lost it, so I was tying her up in a corner every morning and letting the dogie colt Nubbin' nurse.

Early one morning I was in the lot tending to my "trading stock" and had the Holt mare tied up and Nubbin' was nursing when a big old lady who ran a dairy near town stopped her Model T Ford, got out, and walked over to my pen. This old lady would weigh 210, wore men's brogan shoes, ran her dairy, and told her husband what to think and when to shut up. She looked over the fence and saw the colt nursing the mare and said: "What do you want for that mare and colt?"

I told her I wanted $45 for the mare and $20 for the colt; and she immediately told me, "You ain't goin' to split 'em and sell 'em separate. I'll just give you sixty dollars for both of 'em."

I started to try to tell her that the colt didn't belong

to the mare, and as I said: "Mam, you don't want this colt with this mare," she snapped back at me right quick: "Little feller, don't tell me what I want."

That "little feller" made me mad. There I was all of thirteen years old, had been a horse wrangler one whole season on a chuck wagon, wore shop-made boots and had on a Stetson hat that would have shaded a man three times my size, and I sure didn't like to be called "little feller."

Silas Kemp, who ran the wagonyard, mumbled through a crack in the fence: "Sell 'em to her, Benny. Don't try to tell her any different. You won't be lying to her, and she'll be cheating herself."

About that time she snapped at me again: "Are you goin' to just stand there, or are you goin' to take my money?"

I said: "But Mam—"

And she cut in: "Don't 'mam' me. Will you or won't you?"

By this time I was pretty mad, so I answered: "Pay me."

She said: "You'll have to deliver them out to the dairy."

Silas spoke up and offered: "I'll haul them out for you, Benny, while you're gone to school."

The next morning about the same time, here came that Model T Ford; and that big, fat, mean woman stepped out on the ground and hollered at the top of her voice: "Where's that kid?"

In the meantime, my horse-trading friends had schooled me on what to say, because we all knew she would be back, and she was well known as an unpleasant customer to all the traders. I was over the fence in my pen feeding, and I said: "Here I am," in a pretty meek tone of voice.

She yelled: "That colt don't belong to that mare. This morning she kicked it clean over the fence."

I stated: "Yes, that colt does belong to that mare—because I gave it to her."

All the traders were standing around listening, and they couldn't help but laugh. I was a little shaky, but I was determined to stand my ground and get even for her calling me "little feller." She looked around—and would have liked to have killed us all—but had decided to get in her car and leave when I called out and asked her if she wanted to sell the colt. She snapped: " 'Course I want to sell it. I milk cows to sell milk, not to raise colts with it."

I told her I would give her $15 for Nubbin' back. All the horse traders went to shaking their heads and making faces at me as I ran my finger down in my watch pocket to dig out the $15. I paid her and told her I would be after the colt after school.

As she drove away, all my wagon yard "educators" got after me for buying Nubbin' back, and none of them offered to go out and get her in a trailer.

So I rode out horseback that afternoon, and when Nubbin' heard my voice she nickered and begged to come home with me. I knew, then, that I had made a good buy, and I felt much better that I had got Nubbin' back.

*A*ngel

One summer I was traveling the far Southwest. It had been a long, hot day, and I had crossed the desert of lower Arizona and New Mexico and driven into Albuquerque. I hadn't stopped to eat lunch, and it was middle afternoon, so I walked into a hotel coffee shop and sat down at the counter. There were people at a few tables and a few stragglers like me at the counter, but it was far from a busy place. I looked at the menu, and it looked like the last few thousand I had read, so I ordered something and ate it from force of habit. Really, I guess I was enjoying the air conditioning and the rest from the road more than the food. I got up from the counter and walked toward

the cash register in the lobby. I had driven a long way, and I know I moved off from the counter as though I was about road-foundered. Just before I reached the cash register, a young man tapped me on the shoulder and said: "Sir, there is a gentleman back at our table who knows you and would like to speak to you."

I turned and walked back, and as I approached the table where several men were sitting, a young man—slightly gray at the temples with a handsome face and shoulders—got out of his chair and walked a few steps on crippled legs that you would know at a glance were the results of infantile paralysis. He shook hands with me and said: "You're Ben Green."

I answered: "That's right, but I don't remember you."

"I'm Ted . . . Since I see you're still alive, I know you're still in the horse business, and I wanted to tell you about Angel—you called her Nubbin', but after I got her I changed her name."

I still hadn't quite placed him until he went to telling me about "Angel." He related that he had ridden her through grade school, high school, and college. He said: "I wanted to tell you that she was never hungry, she was never tired, and I was never lonely. She passed away in a box stall at my home in Pennsylvania a few years ago, with her head in my lap."

He added further that he would have given away several ponies to children if it hadn't been for parents who objected and didn't understand how much a pony could mean to a child who couldn't run and play.

Then I began to remember the details about his father trading for Nubbin'.

On a rather cold, dismal day in December, not long

before Christmas, I had my regular horses pretty well ridden down for some reason, and I was riding Nubbin'. I was coming through the edge of town, which was not considered the "best" part of town but consisted of the homes of good, honest working people who earned their living by manual labor. Claude, who was Ted's father, waved me over to the side of the yard fence and said: "Benny, I want to trade you out of that filly. She's too little for you to make long, hard rides on, but she's just right for Ted, and I want to get him a pony for Christmas. You see, he needs a pony because he had the fever and it settled in his legs."

I looked down from my horse, and there was Ted hanging from his crutches by his shoulders. He reached out a long, bony, overgrown, callused hand and patted Nubbin' on the shoulder and said: "If I had her, I would never be late to school."

Well, I had been on crutches a time or two for a few weeks in my life by then, and I knew they weren't much fun, and I knew it was a mile to the schoolhouse from where Ted lived. At fifteen years old I couldn't imagine why anybody wanted to go to school, and I thought a boy eight or nine years old who didn't want to be late to school was a rare exception. I did have plenty of other horses that were big enough to carry me and my riggin' on long, hard rides better than Nubbin' could, so I asked Claude what he had to trade.

"I've got that milk-pen heifer that I'll give you for that pony," he replied.

I didn't think that was a very good trade, but when I looked down at Ted a-hangin' on those crutches, I decided that heifer might grow out—and even though I had made a horse trader, I still might have a soft spot left in my make-up—so we had a trade.

We put a halter on the heifer, tied her to Nubbin's saddle horn, and Ted and his daddy followed and drove the heifer until we got to the wagonyard. We turned the heifer in a lot, and I took the saddle and bridle off Nubbin' and put a rope around her neck. Ted handed his daddy his crutches, grabbed Nubbin' by the mane, and crawled up her foreleg. She was a real pet and very safe.

I may have seen Ted and Nubbin' sometime during the following year or so, but I don't remember much about it, and I had changed ranges many times since then and forgotten all about the pony.

While all this raced back through my mind, Ted was telling the other young men at the table about how he rode Angel all through school, and rode her to deliver papers and sell insurance policies after he got up a little older. One of the young men butted in to tell me that Ted was now president of the company he had worked for selling policies.

I asked Ted how he recognized me, and he said that I was older and fatter but I still had that old stiff saddle walk that caused him to know me. Our visit was cut short by the great common American rush to get back to business; so we each got up, shook hands, and told each other good-bye.

As I drove off into the desert, I tried to remember what had happened to the heifer. But as I pondered it all and remembered Ted as he is today and speculated in my mind how much Angel may have had to do with his success in life, I decided that was the most boot I ever drawed in a trade.

Maniac Mule

It was early in the fall, and the horse and mule business had begun to take on new life. Mule buyers were buying young feeder mules, which were mules from three to five years old, broke but not in good condition, that they could put a bloom on in time for the late fall horse and mule market. On this nice brisk Saturday morning, which was

a little bit cool, there were a few scattered watermelon wagons around on the public square, and you could see an occasional wagon with a bale of cotton—cotton picking had just started. You could tell we were about to have a real fall Saturday in Weatherford, Texas.

I rode around the square with nothing particular on my mind, stopped and sat on my horse and visited with a few fellows. While I was talking, I noticed a man driving a good team of mules to a wagon and leading a better mule tied to the back of the wagon. The mule he was leading was a four-year-old mare mule with no harness marks. She was real typey, the kind that would sell for a lot of money. I reined my horse up and rode away from that non-profitable conversation to ride over where that man had stopped his wagon to find out why he was leading an extra mule. It would be supposed that he had brought her to town to sell. As I came near his wagon horseback, I noticed the mule was standing very quietly on a loose halter rope and showing no signs of fear from the people or other teams around her. She was an exceptionally nice-made mare mule, black with a mealy nose, white underbelly, and no scars or blemishes—strictly fancy so far as mules go. In order to conceal my anxiety at seeing such a nice mule, I said to the man in the wagon: "You want to buy a mate for that mule?"

That set up a conversation, and he told me that he was too old to break young mules when he already had a broke team; he had worked this mule some, but she was just green-broke and had just shedded in for a four-year-old. His conversation matched the mule's general condition, and there was no reason to doubt what he said. He had already told me that the mule was for sale "iffen the price was good enuff." After much persuasion, I got him to price the mule—instead of me making a bid on her first. He thought she was worth $135, but that if I had a mate to her the span would sure bring $300. We talked on, and I finally bid him $100. He told me that if he didn't have to spend all day in town trying to sell the mule, he would take $125 for her. I finally agreed to give him $115, and he sold her to me and throwed the halter and rope in. I reached in my pocket and paid him in cash—I never had gotten down off my horse. I reached over and untied the mule from the wagon, dallied the rope around my saddle horn, and led her down to Jim Merritt's barn.

Jim Merritt was an old-time horse and mule buyer who had come to Texas from Georgia. He knew the mule business and was always a good buyer for an exceptionally nice mule, since he had a trade that would buy the better kind of mules. There was not a doubt in my mind but what I had just made $25, and maybe even $35, by leading that mule about three city blocks.

Mr. Merritt wasn't at the barn, but I was so sure this mule would suit him that I led her in, unbuckled the halter, and rode on. Mr. Merritt was my good friend and had always been more than fair in all my dealings with him, and I knew all that was left to complete the trade was to wait until Mr. Merritt got to town to pay me a reasonable profit for my thirty minutes work and, of course, my shrewd ability as a young mule man. I thought of something that I wanted to do and rode away from town for three or four hours.

I came back up the street about the middle of the afternoon, and there was a whole bunch of men standing in front of Mr. Merritt's mule barn—but nobody was very close to the gate. That nice, black, mealy-nosed four-year-old mare mule had kicked and torn down a chute, the partition gate between the barn and the back lot, and was backed up with her hindquarters in the corner of the barn, her mouth open, bawling in an unknown mule tongue. Her eyes were popped out like they were on sticks, her ears were stuck forward, and at the least excitement she would rush against the other side of the barn and knock herself down. She had already peeled and skinned her shoulders a little bit.

All the rest of the horses and mules had gotten themselves into the back lot and crowded into one corner away from her. Nobody knew who the mule belonged to—Mr. Merritt was there, and he knew he hadn't bought a mule like that. I sat on my horse and looked over the crowd at my mule that nobody knew was mine. I damn near didn't want to claim her myself.

I choked, tried to act unconcerned, and said: "Mr. Jim, have you got a mule with the colic?"

He replied, "Colic, my foot. Somebody has turned a mule in my barn that's a maniac."

That started the conversation, and there were two or three people in the crowd who had seen a crazy mule before. I stood up in my stirrups, looked at that mule, and said: "Mr. Merritt, people are the only things that have got little enough sense to go crazy. She must be loco."

Nobody could remember having seen a mule that was loco act like that. Somebody had called old Dr. Justice, a village horse doctor of the old order who had treated lots of horses and mules. He had no suggestions to make, except that he thought something ought to be done with the mule. The mule stood still in one corner for some time, and the crowd finally got tired of watching and began to drift away. I still hadn't gotten off my horse and thought maybe it was best not to, as I rode up close to Mr. Merritt and said: "Mr. Merritt, that's my mule, but she didn't act like that when I put her in there and turned her loose."

He sucked on his pipe a few times, finally took it out of his mouth and said: "Benny, you sure got a booger. If we could get in there and look around on the ground or in that hay or manure, we'd find a ball of cotton that had been saturated with chloroform and stuck up that mule's nose. She was asleep when you bought her."

I looked at her a few minutes and said: "How did they ever get the cotton in her nose?"

Mr. Merritt gave a deep belly laugh and answered: "Benny, that's your problem, but we've sure got to get that mule out of my barn before dark."

I needed help bad. Amateurs and town cowboys weren't going to do me any good. I went on down to the wagonyard, and everybody knew about the mule, but it still hadn't leaked out who she belonged to. I talked to two or three of my advisers, but nobody knew how to put chloroform in a crazy mule's nose without catching her!

After while I found a cowboy friend of mine who was ever bit as crazy as that mule. We took two lariat ropes, and he walked a rafter in the barn, tied the end of the rope to a beam, and dropped the loop down over the mule's neck —which started another mule war. When she choked and fell on the ground, I ran in with another lariat rope, tied her forefeet together, and laced her to the saddle horn on my horse. I had already gone and bought a good supply of chloroform because we figured we'd waste most of it. I had some big wads of cotton already made up in my britches pocket. My wild friend jumped down from the rafters, and I pitched him a wad of cotton. He poured chloroform all over it, grabbed that mule by the ear, and jobbed the cotton up her nose while I drug her enough to keep her feet off the ground. In a few minutes she was lying nice and still. We put a halter with a long rope on her without any trouble. I turned my foot-rope loose while my friend slapped her in the face with his hat and made her get up. She was a nice, quiet mule.

We rubbed all the dirt and hay off her and brushed her while we had her in the dark part of the barn. Needless to say, there was a fair audience at a good safe distance on the other side of the gate. I took several wraps on my saddle horn with the halter rope and asked them to open the gate. My friend Mr. Merritt looked much relieved when he saw we had the mule caught, and he was glad to open the gate and get the people out of the way—which wasn't much trouble when they saw me coming toward them with my mule.

I started across the square for no particular reason except to get the mule out of the way of the people and things before that chloroform cotton came out of her nose. I wasn't sure where I was going or what I was going to do with her. Out on South Main about three blocks from the square, I met a man that I had particular reasons for wanting to become the owner of this nice, quiet mule. He ran a dairy out on the edge of town, and he had a bull tied to the back of his wagon. There were very few trailers or trucks, and it was not uncommon to see gentle cattle being led tied to the back of a wagon. He was bringing this bull to town to be put with some more cattle to be sent for sale to the Fort Worth stockyards.

This good old dairyman was the kind of fellow who starved his mules, scolded and whipped his dogs, bemeaned his family, and made his living by stealing milk from calves. About two years before this, when I was an even younger trader, he had sold me a spoilt-bag milk cow without letting me in on the secret that her bag was spoilt —and since she was a dry cow, I couldn't tell it. After I had sold the cow and took an awful loss on her, he told me that was cheap knowledge—it would keep me from buying another spoilt-bag cow, and he had no remorse for contributing to my education.

As I approached his wagon with my mule and saw that big fat bull tied to the back of his wagon, I wondered if his education was entirely complete. Riding very slow, but without stopping, I said: "What are you going to do with that bull?"

"I would ship him to Fort Worth or I would trade him for that mule," he answered.

The mule was so classy that anybody would like her at a glance, and most anybody in those days could tell she was a young mule without looking in her mouth.

I reined up my horse, and he stopped and began talking. He said the bull was fat and would weigh two thousand pounds and bring five cents a pound, which would be $100—that was all my mule was worth and we would trade even. I knew that bull didn't weigh but fourteen hundred pounds and wouldn't bring more than four cents, but I also knew enough about my mule that I considered it a good trade. I said: "We'll have one more trade," as I stepped down off my horse and tied the mule to the back of the wagon. He went to complaining about having a new lariat rope on the bull and he wouldn't let me have it—but, of course, he wanted the halter that was on the mule. I didn't think it was best to let him get close enough to that mule to smell the chloroform, and I didn't want to be fooling around the mule's head taking the halter off. I didn't want to chum around with Mr. Milkman long enough for me to change and take his rope off the bull and put mine on; so I reached over, untied the bull, and turned him loose.

I said: "I'm a cowboy and horseback. I don't need a rope for just one bull." I stepped on my horse, started driving the bull off toward the shipping pens, and Mr. Milkman turned around and started home with his mule.

This good gentleman had been known to sing awful loud in church and frown disapprovingly at cowboys who didn't attend meetings, but I heard from reliable sources that he almost lost his religion over that mule. I never bothered to ask what actually became of that crazy mule.

Matched Mares

One bright fall morning, with the weather nice and brisk but the sun still shining, I was walking through my horse-trading barn trying to make plans for how to sell the horses and mules I had bought. It was early in the season, cotton picking had just started, and the horse and mule business had taken on new life following the summer lull.

I had a beautiful five-year-old chestnut sorrel mare of good conformation and disposition, and she was well broke to work. She was about fifteen hands high and weighed about 1,325 pounds. In selling work horses there was much to be gained by having your teams well matched in age, size, color, and disposition. A really matched team would bring $50 and sometimes $100 more than the two horses sold separately. This beautiful

chestnut sorrel mare had no mate, and I had bought her cheap because the man who sold her had not been able to match her.

I had her in the back of my barn, and I was sure none of the other traders had seen her because no one had mentioned her. She was a good mare that a trader would have to had made some belittling remark about.

I started walking off down the trading alley where there was a number of other horse traders. I found a trader named Dave in his barn brushing and currying a twin to my good mare. I didn't think he knew that I had one that would match her, and the conversation went about like this: I said "Dave, that's a good mare. It's a pity you haven't got a mate for her. A pair like that would bring a lot of money."

Dave was a-brushing the flax mane and tail of this dark chestnut mare. He didn't stop brushing, he just answered: "I've been tryin' to find another one as good as her for three months, and she's been standin' here eatin' her head off. I guess I ought to sell her for a single and forget about matchin' her."

"I wish you had a pair like her because I've got an order for two, but one wouldn't do me much good."

"What'll you give for her and you try to match her?"

"Nothing. I want a team," I said.

"Would you give $125?"

"No. I'd give $90." I had started out of the barn and I kept walking.

Dave called: "Don't be in such a hurry. Come back and lead your mare off. I've fed her as long as I want to."

I tried to keep a straight face and keep from showing my glee, because I knew she was a dead-ringer for that

75

mare in my barn. I paid him, took the halter rope, and started leading her up the alley thinking about how much money the pair would bring. I tied the mare in front of my barn and started in the barn to bring out the mate and see how they would look together.

Dave and his Uncle Bob were partners, and Uncle Bob had been looking for a mate to that good chestnut sorrel mare, too. As I started toward the back of my barn, Uncle Bob came along and saw the mare that I had just bought from Dave. Uncle Bob originally came from the deep South and had that Southern drawl and also a little bit of a stutter in his speech. He said: "Ah, Benny, ah, thet's a pu'ty nice marh yuh got theah. What'd yuh tek fo' huh?"

I suddenly realized that Uncle Bob didn't recognize his mare, and I thought it would be funny to sell her back to him; so I answered: "Uncle Bob, she ought to be worth $125." I thought putting in that "ought to be worth" would induce him to bid.

He replied: "I can't give you thet fo' huh, but I'd give yuh $110."

I could have made $20 right quick, but I would have liked to make more and make a better story to tell in later years; so I said, "Uncle Bob, I'll split the difference with you"—which was a common practice.

He walked around the mare, looking at her, and said: "I'll raise muh bid $5."

I was holding my breath, so to speak, afraid he was going to recognize the mare after a second look; so I said: "That's too cheap, but since we're good friends I'm going to sell her to you."

Uncle Bob paid me for the mare and quickened his

step as he walked off leading her toward his barn, antici-
pating his delight in telling Dave, his partner, that he had
bought a mate for their mare. In a few minutes you could
hear Dave all up and down the trading alley. Some of the
other traders gathered around him, and everybody was
having a big laugh. I didn't go down to join the party—
I might not have been welcome.

Instead, I went to the back of my barn and caught my
chestnut sorrel mare, led her up, and tied her in front of
the barn. In a few minutes, when Uncle Bob came stomp-
ing back up the trading alley with blood in his eye and
was about to give me a good cussing—before he could get
started—I said: "Uncle Bob, I've got another mare here
you might like."

Uncle Bob blustered: "Plague tek yuh, Benny, I
oughta tek yuh ovah mah knee and give yuh a good
spankin'." (I was seventeen years old, and Uncle Bob was
seventy.)

While he was catching his breath to start over, I
calmly stated: "Uncle Bob, I've got the mate to that mare."

His anger began to subside as he went to walking
around this mare of mine. He asked in a still irritated but
interested tone: "How much fo' huh?"

"$125," I replied.

Uncle Bob turned around and in a loud, bull-like voice
called to his nephew Dave to lead the other chestnut sorrel
mare out in front of the barn. Dave led the other mare
out. Several traders were standing around watching as
Uncle Bob looked down the alley and saw Dave holding
this other chestnut sorrel mare. Uncle Bob turned around
and bellowed at me: "I'm fo sho this is a different one, and
I'm goin' tah buy huh, plague tek yuh, Benny!"

The Rockcrusher and the Mule

When I was a wild, rough young horse trader, I rode into Mineral Wells's trading square on second Monday. A building was being constructed adjoining the trading square, and a rockcrusher was crushing rocks to put in the foundation. On the off-side of the rockcrusher, out of the way of the men working on the building, there was a big, black, mealy-nosed mule tied to its wheel. He was a good stout mule, and his hair was in good condition. He was standing there perfectly gentle in spite of all that noise and the fog of dust that was being made by the rockcrusher.

I had an old horse-trading friend that I was partnerin'
with, and he had brought a bunch of horses and mules
into Mineral Wells the night before by leading them behind a wagon—which was the custom of the day. Among
them was a nice little fat brown mare. She would work
and ride, was gentle, and she looked good. I had traded
for her a little while back; after I got her, one day I rode
her pretty hard and discovered she had a pretty fair case
of the heaves. I fed her some wet bran and turpentine, and
put bluing in her water, and used all of the other well-
known and respected remedies that good horse traders
used. This little mare breathed perfectly normal as long
as you didn't run or trot her or try her wind.

As I rode up to the wagon—where the horses we were
going to trade on were tied—I glanced around. There
were lots of other horse traders' wagons with a good
many horses tied up, and it promised to be a fair day for
swapping.

A long, tall snuff-dipper walked up to the wagon and
looked around and picked out the little brown mare. We
talked about her good and bad points; he looked in her
mouth and didn't ask her age, so I supposed he could tell
—and it was no use my telling him unless he asked. He
said he had a boy going to school that needed a horse to
ride, and he had brought a mule to town to trade for the
mare. I started following him afoot to look at his mule,
and I said to myself that I'd sure found a sucker. He must
be some farmer who didn't know enough about horse
trading to untie the little mare and run her to try her
wind. We went up to the mule that was tied to the rockcrusher. I was afraid to untie him and try him for wind,

because that might cause the man to go try my little brown mare.

He asked me $25 boot, and I offered him $5. We finally traded by me paying him $10. The mule, from all outward appearances, was worth about four head of the little mare, and I said to myself that I was making a real horse trader.

We went back to the wagon, and he untied the mare and started leading her off. I sent my old horse-trading partner to get the mule. As soon as the mule was a little away from the rockcrusher, you could hear him making some strange, loud, sickening noise when he breathed. The sound coming from that mule had begun to scare all the horses tied to the wagons that he passed. He would wheeze and whistle when he breathed, and a strange rattle came from his throat. The farther he got away from the rockcrusher, the worse he sounded. The horses we had tied to our wagon began to shy and try to break loose as he got closer.

I walked out and stopped my old friend that was leading him and said: "What have I got?"

"He's a rattler," he answered.

"I can tell that," I said, "but where did he get it, and what caused it?"

Of course, my old horse-trading partner didn't know any more about the anatomy of a horse or mule than I did in those days, but he tried to explain that this mule's windpipe had been injured and that he would never be any better. The reason he was so nice and fat was because all he did was eat and drink water and stand around. My partner asked: "What do you think we ought to do with your new stock?"

I thought a minute and told him: "Take him back and tie him to the rockcrusher!"

Later that afternoon I traded this mule for two old wore-out, mossy-headed, buck-kneed, big-ankled, bog-hocked, cow horses—both worth about as much as the $10 boot that I had paid. And my almost-good little brown mare was gone, gone.

Poor Heifers
— The Judge
— Wild Mules

During the worst cold spell in the now historical depression that occurred during the thirties, I went into a country store a few miles out from Weatherford, Texas. I had a pasture leased nearby and had been out to feed my herd of heifers. I had gone broke in the big-steer business and

had been buying, trading, and working for some little bitty, sorry, cross-bred, various-colored heifer calves and yearlings. I had about fifty of these little heifers; there were no two of them alike, their value was low, low, low, and I had a pretty low feeling every time I poured out feed to them. Money was scarce, and feed was hard to pay for.

I had left my horse tied to the south side of the country store, come in the back door, and was hovered up against the stove when some fellows stopped in front of the store with a truckload of horses. The horses were saddled, had sweat dried all over them, and showed that they had been used on some kind of a hard drive. Two of the boys came in the store while the old man was filling up their truck with gasoline. They bought up some of the common things you could get in a country store to eat—canned pork and beans, crackers, canned salmon, a few cookies, and so forth. While they were poking around getting what they wanted, one of them saw me sitting over by the stove. He walked over, warmed his hands, and looked at my boots and spurs. I didn't have on two-toned boots, wasn't wearing double-seated britches, and my riggin' didn't give off much glamour; so this town cowboy had to ask: "I guess you're one of the local cowboys?"

Along about then was one of the few times in my life that I wasn't necessarily proud of that fact. I answered: "I guess so. Looks like your horses have been stayed with pretty hard."

"Yeah. We came out from Fort Worth to pen that Fort Worth lawyer's mules up in the mountains, but we didn't have any luck."

I had vaguely heard of the lawyer's wild mules, but I had never been given a firsthand report on them. With a little persuading, this town cowboy gave me a full report on how wild the mules were, how big the pasture was, how thick the cedar brush was, and how deep the canyons were. He added his personal opinion about what he thought of anybody who would let his livestock business get in the shape that the lawyer had by letting a bunch of wild mules take his ranch away from him. I listened carefully and culled this city cowboy's conversation for what true facts there might have been in it. I walked out to the truck, humped up in the cold, and looked at the horses. They were a nice bunch of over-fat, wrongly shod, beautifully rigged, soft town horses that had been rode about half to death—and nobody had caught a mule.

After they drove away, the old country storekeeper came back to the fire. He and I sat there watching the blaze through the open door of the potbellied stove. He finally broke the silence and asked: "Reckon that lawyer in Fort Worth will ever get them mules gathered so he can get his pasture back to where he can put cows in it?"

"I don't know. How come him with those wild mules?"

Then my storekeeper friend related the story of how, about three years before, the Fort Worth lawyer had staked a would-be-rancher nephew to buy yearling and two-year-old mules to stock a section pasture—640 acres. After the mules were turned in the pasture, the nephew had lost interest in them and decided to be an automobile salesman or something in town. The mules had kept the grass bit down close, killed a few calves that had been put in the pasture—which mules will sometimes do—and the judge wasn't too happy with his nephew or with the "stock" in his pasture.

All of this time I had been sitting there peeling pecans and eating them and hitting the door of the stove with a few of the hulls. I closed my pocketknife, stood up and shook the pecan hulls off, and started toward the back door. The old storekeeper said: "You must have run out of conversation. Come back when you get recharged."

I got on my horse and jogged up the road. The weather was cold and the wind was high. My little heifers were *pore*, the grass was short, my spendin' money was getting awful low, and I just thought to myself that from a promising young rancher—before those steers went down—to pouring out feed to those sorry, bad-colored heifers, I sure had slipped since I quit the horse and mule business. It was time for me to take a fresh start.

It was thirty miles to Fort Worth, horseback or on the bus. You could ride horseback for nothing; it cost ninety cents to ride the bus, so before daylight next morning I counted my money and rode horseback. I left my horse over at the Burnett and Yount Horse and Mule Barn, rode the streetcar to town, and went way up in one of them tall buildings to this lawyer's office.

As I entered the stiff-looking legal establishment, a very precise, not too young lady glanced at my saddle-marked britches and unshined boots. As she sized me up, I took my hat off, and my head didn't show that it had been exposed to a lot of brushin' and curryin', and I could tell by the tone of her voice that she didn't think I was a client of the honorable attorney. In a crisp business voice she asked me who I wished to see. I told her I wanted to see the lawyer. She had her note pad in her hand, asked me my name, and said: "What do you wish to see him about?"

"He may want to see me much worse than I do him, 'cause I might help him with his mule troubles."

I didn't much more than get the word "mule" out of my mouth until the judge was standing in the doorway of the next office looking at me and saying: "Come in, come in."

We shook hands and I told him who I was. He smiled and said: "Have a seat over there."

He motioned to one of those big soft chairs, and I kind of sat on the edge of it rather uneasily as he said: "What do you know about my mule business?"

"I know about your mules, but I wouldn't call it business—the way you've been handling them," I replied.

He showed a weak smile, but he didn't seem to think my remark was very funny. It was about noon, and he said: "You could probably talk better over some food."

I didn't hear grub called food very often, and it took me a minute to answer; but anyway we went to a nice place that had linen tablecloths and napkins and real silver to eat some dinner. The judge ordered up a batch of stuff and along with the meal we discussed his mule business. He explained to me that he knew how to handle cattle and could hire people who could tend to them, and he would like to get rid of these mules. I told him I had a bunch of heifers I'd trade for his mules, and that I'd gather the mules and then deliver the heifers. This sounded real good to him, only I could tell he didn't much think I could gather the mules.

About that time somebody passed the table, slapped

me on the back, and said: "Ben, what are you talking to the judge about? Are you in trouble?"

As he reached across the table to shake hands with the judge, I was glad to recognize an old friend I had worked lots of steers with. He had some other people with him, and as he started back to join them he laughingly told the judge: "If you ever get to be as good a lawyer as Ben is a cowboy, I'll take you on as my attorney."

That made me feel real good, and you could tell it wiped some of the doubt out of the judge's mind about me gathering the mules. He began to show more interest in the heifers I had to trade, so he asked me about them. I told him they were mostly Jersey, Holstein, and mixed breeds of various colors, shapes, and sizes, and that they were all pretty *pore*.

He laughed and said: "You don't paint a very good picture of your heifers."

"No, but I know where they're at, and I can gather them, too," I replied.

He asked me did I owe any money on these heifers. I told him I was pretty dumb, but I wasn't dumb enough to borrow money to buy that kind of heifers. As an afterthought I said: "Judge, do you owe any money on them mules?"

He laughed and said jokingly: "No, Ben. I never could get anybody close enough to them to make a loan on them."

He was already cheated, because he couldn't gather his mules. He told me he would rather have that bunch of heifers that he could see—provided I could gather *all* the mules.

We talked about the weather being bad; and it being

the dead of winter, I agreed to feed the heifers until I delivered them. We decided that I ought to be able to finish the whole trade in not more than a month's time.

I went back to the stockyards, and it was too late to start riding back home, cold as it was, unless I had to; so I spent the night at Mrs. Brown's boardinghouse. I saddled my horse and left for home early the next morning. By the time I was halfway home, various ideas had crossed my mind about trapping, setting snares, or getting enough men to relay the mules for two or three days in order to run them down; but everything I had thought of so far either would not work or would take too many horses and men.

I was still pondering my problem when I crossed the Clear fork of the Trinity River, about ten o'clock in the morning. There was an old Frenchman who had a little house on one side of the road and a barn on the other side. As I came up, he was crossing the road afoot. We stopped and visited a few minutes. His horses had their heads stuck over the fence, looking like they wanted some more feed, and I noticed that one of them was a gray mare with all the hair gone off her back and the upper part of her shoulders and around the top part of her neck. There was some pink skin that anybody could tell was scar tissue. I asked the Frenchman what on earth had happened to that mare. He explained to me that he had gotten her out of the Fort Worth Horse and Mule Barns after the big fire which had occurred a few years before. He said that she was one of the many that were to be destroyed because there was no hope they would recover from their burns. They had given her to him, and he had brought her home and healed her burns; but the skin was so light where the collar and harness rubbed that he had never been able to work her. I said: "Sell her to me cheap and I might could use her for a broodmare."

The old Frenchman said in broken English that they had given her to him, and he would be glad to give her to me.

As I led her away behind my saddle horse I noticed that her feet and legs were good, she was in fair flesh, and, in spite of the hideous scars on her body, in good condition. I put her in the back lot at home where my daddy happened to look over the fence and see her. He asked what I was going to do with her. I just grunted and told him I had my plans.

In a few days the rumor got around that I had traded for the outlaw mules. All of the cowboys and old men had lots of advice to give me, but nobody wanted to go with me and help to gather those wild mules. The judge's pasture was about twenty-seven miles from town. Friday afternoon I left when school was out with a little pack of grub on the back of my saddle, a small bedroll, and leading the gray mare. Everybody who heard about the mules and saw the gray mare had decided that I was not the promising young stockman they had thought me to be.

I spent the night with a farmer friend of mine who lived about ten miles from the mule pasture. After supper when we were sitting around the fireplace visiting, he told me how come the mules were so wild. It seemed that all the teen-age boys for miles around had been gathering on Sunday afternoon, when the weather was pretty, and had been running the mules for fun. The corral at the pasture was on the north side, and you had to cross the canyon and go through the densest part of the cedar brakes. He said it was in this canyon and in the cedar brush that the Sunday cowboys always lost the mules, and nobody had ever been able to drive these wild mules through the dense brush.

That night I slept in a nice warm feather bed at the farmer's house and had a big country breakfast the next morning. After thanking the farmer's wife for the night's lodging and breakfast, I saddled my horse, caught the gray mare, and started on to the pasture.

The south side of this pasture ran along a public road for about a quarter of a mile, and there was a little open prairie spot at the south end. I had wrapped a big bell with a leather strap on it in a tow sack and tied it to my saddle before I left town. After I got into the gate into the pasture, I buckled this bell around the old gray mare's neck and took a piece of baling wire and tied the buckle where it wouldn't come loose. Then I turned the old mare free and proceeded to drive her up into the cedar thicket.

Mules will naturally come to a gray or spotted horse and will very readily take up with a gray mare. I left the mare in the thicket, grazing on the grass and ringing the bell, and took off to ride around the outside of the fence and try to get acquainted with the pasture. After several hours of riding, I had a pretty good idea as to how the pasture lay and had determined that most all the land joining the fence was in cultivation. Since there was no brush over the fence to graze or hide in, the mules had never tried to get out.

About the middle of the afternoon I rode down in the canyon, got on the sunny side of the bank, built a small fire, fried some bacon, broke open a loaf of bread I had tied on my saddle, and had a feast. I had discovered on my round of the pasture that there had been a good many cedar posts cut on the back side, and there was quite a lot of dead cedar the judge probably didn't know about. More than likely the post-choppers had helped themselves and told no one about it. I went on back to town and spent the next few days going to school and begrudgingly pouring out feed to that sorry bunch of little heifers.

About two weeks went by and nothing much happened. On a Saturday afternoon late, I unsaddled my horse and went into the front room as the radio was giving out the weather. This "radio weather" was kind of new stuff and we didn't set too much store by the report it gave; however, I stopped to listen. The announcer said there was a blizzard on the way, coming out of the Panhandle, that would be in Wichita Falls by midnight and would probably strike the Fort Worth area by two o'clock in the morning. The Fort Worth area was us.

I went in my room and started to getting clothes. It wasn't cold enough yet to put them on, but I wanted a batch to take with me. As I headed toward the barn with a batch of extra britches and leather jackets, my daddy drove in the driveway and called: "Where you fixin' to spend the winter?"

I told him I was fixin' to have a little mule drive. He thought my mule trade was very foolish but had been too kind to say so. I knew he thought those heifers would be grown cows and have calves before I got the mules caught.

I had two good horses in the barn—well fed and shod and drawn down hard from constant use. Old Beauty was my standby; I felt she had more sense than most of my schoolteachers at that time and understood me better than my family did. Charlie was a big bay horse with a scar on his forefoot that didn't hurt him. He was a head-nodding fox trotter the same as Beauty and a big, stout, hard, using horse but not too trustworthy. I saddled him and started out leading Beauty. She didn't need much leading, as she would travel right up even with your saddle horse and not even tighten the halter rope. As I rode out of the front yard, my dad stepped out on the porch. By this time it was nearly dark, and he hollered at me that if I got in trouble to turn that old mare loose. The reason he said this was because Beauty would come home—and in a way that would spread the alarm, and he would know to come and see about me.

I sat pretty straight and tight in the saddle and kept old Charlie headed north. I wanted to make it to the pasture before the norther hit. It must have been about eleven o'clock at night when I reached the fence-line on the south side. I took my horseshoe nippers off my saddle, tore the barbwire off the posts, and laid the fence back for about two hundred yards in the southeast corner of the pasture. I tied old Beauty across the road on a loose rope where she could graze a little and poured some oats I had brought in a sack on the grass for her. Then I rode Charlie to the far north side of the pasture.

I knew that the sound of burning wood and the smell of cedar smoke would strike terror to the heart of the old mare who had been in the barn fire. It was my plan to set fire to the dead cedar where the north wind would blow the smoke through the canyon, and the old mare would lead the mules to the south side of the pasture. A cold front always moves in with a lot of high wind which

I needed to fan the flames, and when I heard on the radio that the norther was coming, I knew it was time for my mule roundup.

I rode onto the spot where the dead cedar was, but I needed to pile it up some to where it would start a big fire. I slipped the bit out of Charlie's mouth and poured the rest of the oats on the ground for him. I loosened the cinch so he could eat and rest while I piled the dead cedar and started a fire. When the flames began to jump about twenty feet, I knew I had a real brush fire started; so I tightened my cinch, rebridled Charlie, and got ready to ride.

The wind was against the mules and the mare, and from where I sat I couldn't hear her bell. There was a little trail around the fence toward the pens, and I brought Charlie out in a dead run. As I rode into the west side of the pasture, I could hear the bell a-clanging, and I heard the old mare nickering in a loud tone that was almost a scream. The mules were braying and the stampede was on.

I found a clearing and rode to the southwest corner as fast as I could. There was a ditch at the road which I knew would slow the mules and the old mare up a little, and I wanted to beat them to the road to be sure I turned them toward town if I could. As I jumped my horse across the ditch, Beauty had her head up and began to nicker at all the excitement. I held her still until the old gray mare came into view—followed by the herd of mules with the flames behind them lighting up the northwest. I turned Beauty loose toward town and dropped back to make sure the mules didn't go up the road in the wrong direction.

After about three or four miles, the mules quit running. The old mare had begun to give out, and Beauty was in the lead in a long, swinging trot heading for home. When you handled wild mules, the thing to do when you started to drive them was to run them until they winded themselves; then they were easy to drive. By daylight, these mules drove like they were gentle. I jogged along slow behind them, let them graze, and gave my horse time to rest a little and water where a creek crossed the road.

About the time that all the good people were out on the street in their Sunday best going to church, here came the renegade of the community down the main street of town, wrapped in dusty chaps and leather coats with two tired saddle horses, an exhausted gray mare, a roadful of not-such-wild mules, and obviously not on his way to church.

I missed a couple of days of school because it took that long to drive the judge's heifers to the pasture and put the fence back. I roached, sheared, halter-broke, and sold mules until spring. It may seem strange to modern-day livestock operators that a man could be shearing a mule's tail and feel like he had struck a gold mine, but these mules were selling for $100 apiece and more, and by spring—after selling the fifty-four head of mules—I was almost rich, compared to my low ebb during the winter when I was in the heifer business.

A Road Horse for a Broodmare

One brisk November evening just about dusk—the weather wasn't cold but it was nippy—I had gone to the pasture and driven my pet mares that were bred for fall and winter colts into town. I was bringing them into the barn in town to give them some special attention through the winter.

As we started up the slope toward the barn, I noticed the outline of a man standing leaning against it and holding the reins of what was bound to be a broodmare, also outlined against the barn. As the horses neared the gate, I hollered at the man to open it for me.

After we got the mares inside the pen I wanted them in and got them some good hay, we began to visit a little. My horse was pretty well ridden down since I had left town that morning about daylight. This fellow was tall and looked like a horseman. You could tell that he, too, had ridden a long way, and his mare—a good bay, heavy in foal—should not have been ridden as much as the dried sweat on her indicated she had. The fellow told me he had crossed the Brazos River late in the afternoon, had stopped at a country store called Tin Top, and had had a talk with Matt Sisk about trading for another horse.

Matt Sisk was a member of an old pioneer family and had been quite a cowboy in his day. He had settled down to keeping store many years before this and was looked upon more as an institution than a man. He gave out good information and advice and seldom, if ever, repeated anything that would be damaging; consequently he had the confidence of all the natives along the river.

Matt Sisk had told the fellow that if, when he got to Weatherford, Texas, I would let him have one of my own riding horses, he would get a horse that would be sound, hard as iron, and a good traveler. Matt went on to describe a black horse that I had ridden past Tin Top a few days before, while driving a roadful of mules. He said there was no danger of this horse's not being able to stand the ride he had in mind, because I had probably already given him plenty of chance to road-founder from distance.

When this fellow got through telling me the story about what Matt had told him, I got the black horse out of the stall. He'd had two or three days rest and was in shape for a long hard ride.

Being more curious than Matt Sisk, I had to ask him a few questions about where he was going and what was his hurry. He explained to me that he'd had a little misunderstanding, and that he felt like if he could put a few hills and valleys—and especially the Red River, which would put him into Oklahoma—between where he had been and where he was going, he would probably winter with a greater peace of mind.

His mare was a good six-year-old bay and was bred to Joe Bailey, so he said. I could readily decide that she was worth as much money as the black horse, but she was not in fit condition to carry a man seventy miles, cutting across country, and beyond the Red River by morning.

There was a little something about the black horse that neither Matt Sisk nor very many people outside my family knew about. After a day's rest, I always would have to have my daddy come out and ear this horse down and hold him in order for me to be able to get on him. He wasn't bad to buck, but he was hard to get on. And he was a big stout horse, and I was a short-legged teen-age boy. A few mornings before this I had gotten my dad out of bed before daylight in the cold to ear down this horse, and he had told me either to grow up to the horse's size or ride him down to my size, that he was tired of having to get up to see me off on these early morning rides.

Of course, feeling sorry for my friend who was in trouble—or was trying to avoid trouble—I felt like I should make him a fair proposition; so I told him I would take $100 boot between my grain-fed, fresh-shod, good-traveling black horse and his weak, grass-fed broodmare. The old boy walked around a little, then stomped and said he had a $100 and needed the horse—but he just couldn't give me all of it. He'd give me $85 and ride on. Not wanting him to be clean out of grub money, I consented to take the $85 and the mare; so he saddled the black horse and rode away.

He was a big stout fellow about thirty years old and didn't have any trouble getting on this horse—and I sure was glad he didn't have any trouble before he had gotten out of sight.

Even though I was a seasoned horse trader, I was just a boy in high school. About a week later Mr. Grandstaff, who was principal of the school, came to the room where I was attending class, stuck his head in the door, just crooked his finger at me, and said: "Ben, come in my office."

It wasn't exactly a pleasant tone of voice nor a welcome invitation, but Mr. Grandstaff was a fine fellow and a great friend of mine, and I didn't have much fear of whatever he wanted to see me about. When I walked into Mr. Grandstaff's office there was a short, fat, big-bellied, past middle-age man sitting in an armchair holding a great big hat in one hand. There was a great big star on his big fat chest. We shook hands and he told me he had been by my barn, where there was a good six-year-old, heavy-with-foal bay mare in my lot. She belonged to a good voting citizen of his county who said the mare was ridden away without his knowledge or consent by his son-in-law who was in a hurry. The sheriff had come to get the mare.

I choked and felt a little sick about my horse trade

and asked him if he could identify the mare. He said that she had a small wire scar on the inside quarter of her right back foot, and this was the only blemish on her—which I knew. He said that the father-in-law of my passing friend was waiting at my barn and was ready to haul the mare home.

Mr. Grandstaff said that I could take off from school to go help load the mare. I was glad to go, but I told Mr. Grandstaff that it wasn't to help load the mare—it was to be sure that only one mare was loaded!

Cowboy Trades for a Wagon 'n' Team

The summer had been very enjoyable. I had been to lots of ropin's, horse races, and all day picnics. And during the time I was having all this "growin'-up" cowboy fun, I had made several good horse trades.

It was beginning to get late in the summer, and trading on saddle horses had dropped off some. I had about twenty nice, smooth, medium-sized, gentle riding horses of good ages, all sound and most of them shod. I knew I didn't need that many saddle horses to make the winter on, and I knew it was time that I should try to turn some of them into money. The crops were good all over the land, and it would not be hard to sell riding horses if you knew where to take them.

One morning I packed a bedroll and some supplies on a couple of packhorses, turned them into the road with the rest of the horses, and started driving them away from town. I hadn't fully made up my mind where I was going, but I felt like the farm country might be the best place to sell these good, sound kind of usin' horses that were gentle for farm boys. I drifted over into the blackland part of Texas. It was a while before cotton-picking time; I didn't get many takers on these good ponies, and nobody wanted to give enough for them.

About the fifth or sixth night away from home I rode onto a road construction job where there were a good many teams and a big camp. I fed my horses in one of their corrals, ate supper, and spent the night with the mule skinners, who were driving the fresnoes that were being used to build the highway roadbed—much of which was done in those days with teams.

During the night's visit, sitting around the cook's campfire, one of these old boys thought that the Washita Valley up in Oklahoma would be a good place to sell the kind of ponies I had. Well, I didn't have any better information than that, so I decided it ought to be all right.

I crossed the Red River close to Marietta, Oklahoma,

and in a few days drifted up near the town of Paul's Valley. Sure enough, that country was prosperous and my horses just lasted a few days. Of course I always kept one good horse—to keep from being afoot and to have a way to carry my money.

By this time I had been gone about three weeks, and the weather made a man glad that he was living outside. It was the early part of Indian summer, and I didn't feel like hurrying home too fast. I was carrying a good deal of pack on my saddle horse, since I had sold my packhorses, and everywhere I found a good wagonyard or good livery stable I'd rest my horse and visit a day or two. After all, a man shouldn't rush through a fresh country that he hasn't been in before. A good many of the country roads were not infected with so many automobiles as they are now, and it was easy to stop in the middle of the road and talk to whomever you met or visit with somebody who was plowing and came up to the side of the fence. These people who didn't have any more sense than to stay home were all right to pass the time of day with. They always had watermelon patches, ripe peaches, and other forms of country hospitality that would make the modern-day drive-in seem like an empty eggshell.

I stopped in Decatur, Texas, and it was trades day. I decided it was a shame to be that close to home—thirty miles—and go back with just the horse I was riding. The best-looking horses on the trade ground happened to be a team of beautiful blood-bay, matched geldings with black mane and tail. They were exactly the same size, appearing to weigh about fourteen hundred pounds; their hair was short and slick, and they were carrying just the right amount of fat to make them purty. They were hitched to a new wagon, which was painted green with red wheels, and the wagon bed and wheels were trimmed with bright yellow stripes. The team was harnessed with a flashy set of harness—brass spots all over the leather breeching and big brass knobs on the hames. The bridles had long, flowing tassels about the color of corn silk and just as shiny.

I don't know what made me think I needed a wagon and team, and I suppose the reason I wanted to buy them was because I was carrying too much money.

The man sitting in the spring seat and holding the lines was dressed up like a gentleman farmer. He was talking to some people on the ground. I rode up and listened a while and was really surprised to learn that a team and rig like that was for sale. He was telling somebody else that he had moved to town and the team was just standing in the lot eating; and his wife and kids had been naggin' and beggin' him to sell the wagon, team, and harness and buy an auto, and that was the only reason they were for sale. The conversation around among the lookers was that they were too high priced for anybody around there to afford for just common farm work. One old man commented that the team ought to be hooked to a railway express wagon or a dray wagon.

I finally broke into this conversation by asking the man how much he wanted for them. He made me quite a speech about how good the set of harness and new wagon was and how hard it was to find two horses so perfectly matched. I got down off my horse and looked in their mouths. At a glance their mouths looked to me like they were eight years old. (Now, thirty years and two hundred thousand mouths later, I realize they were eighteen years old and their mouths had been worked.)

He asked $600 for the whole rig—to just "get down and hand me the lines." I told him that was enough money to buy a farm (of course, I didn't want a farm) but that I might give $500 for the rig. He acted like he was highly insulted and just wasn't going to think about it anymore, so I rode off.

There was a chile joint on one corner close to the trade square where I ate dinner. There was a feedstore close by where I bought some oats and fed my horse on the corner of the store loading-dock. My horse had about finished eating, and I was brushing and currying his back and getting ready to resaddle him, when this old gentlemanlike retired farmer drove up with his wagon and this good team of blood-bay horses. He said that I was the only bidder he had had, and if I still wanted the team he would take $550 for them.

Of course I was a real smart boy and knew when I made the offer that my bid didn't have to stand after I rode away the first time. So I told him I had changed my mind and didn't think they were worth more than $450, and we were still $100 apart.

He said: "Young fellow, you just think we're $100 apart." He crawled out of the wagon, stood on the ground, and handed me the lines.

I tried not to show much eagerness, but I didn't waste any time digging into my pocket and coming up with the money.

I tied my saddle horse behind the wagon and started home. It still hadn't dawned on me that I didn't need a wagon and team. This nice big fat team walked about half as fast as a man would ride horseback. By dark I wasn't much more than out of sight of the town, and had begun to wonder if riding in a wagon was worth the time it took.

That night I camped by the side of a creek. I had bought a sack of oats and a couple of bales of hay; I fed my newly acquired team out of the wagon and tied my saddle horse up toward the front of the wagon bed and fed him. I staked these nice fat horses out on each side of the wagon where there was plenty of grass and gave them some hay. I crawled in the wagon bed, spread out my little pallet, and went to sleep about dark.

When I hooked up the team the next morning, they seemed a little listless and moved off slow to the wagon. I noticed it but thought that was just the difference between work horses and saddle horses, and it didn't bother me much. By noon I got to Springtown, Texas, and this pair of nice big fat horses had lost at least two hundred pounds apiece. They walked up to the public water trough, drank as much as an elephant, and began to sweat just a little. I still thought everything was fine—that this was just a pair of big fat horses the man had kept in his back yard, and it would take them a day or two to get drawed down and used to traveling.

By dark they looked like a pair of skeletons—they had lost so much bloom—and were barely moseyin' along to that wagon. My saddle horse was following along behind the wagon, enjoying the rest, and looked like he was gaining weight.

I got back to Weatherford the following day, which made two and a half days to come thirty miles, and by then the horses were almost reeling in the traces. I un-hitched them at the wagonyard, put them in a pen, and rode my saddle horse on home.

I guess my folks were middlin' glad to see me, but nobody seemed to be bothered about whether I had had a good trading trip or not. My citified brothers didn't ask to borrow any money or offer to loan me any. My mother commented that she was glad all the horses were gone out of the back lot and that I didn't bring any home with me. At supper my daddy commented: "I see the Indians didn't set you plumb afoot. You still had a horse to ride home on."

Next morning I went to the wagonyard, and my big, high-priced pair of work horses were barely able to stand. This was the first time I really appreciated that new wagon, because it looked like that was what I had for my $450.

Several of my old horse-trading friends came by, looked at my team, and smiled to themselves, but offered no advice or comment, and walked away. (I learned later that they didn't know anything about my horses and had no advice to give.) I knew I had me *somethin'* in that pair of horses—but I didn't know what. They had lost their appetites for feed, drank very little water, ate very little hay—and any horse trader knows that's not the habits of a big horse.

I stayed away from the wagonyard all day, because I didn't want to answer questions about what I was going to do with my wagon and that set of harness. Late that afternoon I rode off out to the edge of town, where an old-time road trader lived. He had long since been out of the horse business because of his age and his inability to see. We set a spell in the front yard on some old hickory-bottom chairs, and I told him my troubles.

When I got through with my story he sat a while; then he said: "I didn't know there was anybody left that could do that good a job of doping a horse."

At that stage of my life, "doping" meant putting salve on a sore; so I told him the horses didn't have any cuts on them and hadn't been doped.

He said: "Ben, this is a bad piece of experience for you, because you'll never be able to use it again." Then he explained to me that these horses had been fed arsenic. He told me how a road trader could take a sound but wore-out old horse and put him on arsenic. A man would start putting arsenic in a horse's feed, measuring it on the point of a knife blade. The first dose would barely be enough to cover the point of the blade, but in three or four weeks he would be feeding the horse as much arsenic as would stack on the knife blade from the point back to the handle.

He explained that if you didn't kill the horse, you could "puff him up," and the arsenic would also cause him to have a good appetite and eat enough to make his hair look good. He told me it was a wonder that my horses ever lived these four or five days after they had been cut off from their "knife-blade medicine."

The old man stopped talking and we sat in silence a long time. I finally choked and in a very meek, whipped-like voice asked him what I must do with my horses. He sat a few minutes longer, finally stomped his walking cane on the ground, and said: "I've still got a knife with the right size blade in it—give them to me."

I went back to the wagonyard that night, led the

horses out of the back gate, took them and turned them in the old man's back lot.

A few weeks later I rode by and saw a beautiful, fat pair of blood-bay horses standing under the shade tree back of the old man's barn. I never asked him what he did with them—and he never told me. To my knowledge, I've never seen an "arsenic fiend" horse since.

*H*orse from
*R*ound *R*ock

Round Rock, Texas, is known and remembered by most people because Sam Bass, early-day gunman and horseman who owned the Denton mare, was hemmed up and killed there during a robbery. But when I think of Round Rock, it reminds me of a horse trading experience that I am not likely to forget.

It was in the early fall, and I had driven a herd of mules and horses from West Texas down to Gonzales and Caldwell County, south of Austin. I had sold the herd

to the native farmers, who were mostly of German descent, for cash and was riding a good seven-year-old horse
named Tom, a blood-bay with black mane and tail. He
was shod, hard fat, and a real good road horse.

I stopped in Round Rock a little before noon and
found a feed and mercantile store, where I bought my
horse some oats, led him out under a big live oak tree, took
the saddle off of him, and poured his oats in a pasteboard
box that I had got at the store. There was a Sam Bass Café
in town, and I thought I'd go up and eat some dinner
while my horse ate his oats and rested in the shade of that
live oak tree.

When I came back to my horse, there were three or
four men standing around looking at him and probably
admiring him, but they didn't say so to me. One of the
men finally spoke up and said he had a mate for that horse
—the same size, height, and color and ever bit as good a
horse. Well, I was carrying a batch of tradin' money and
would always buy a horse as good as Tom, so I told him
I would be interested in buying his horse. He said he'd
rather trade him because he was hard to catch and a little
mean to handle, and that he would give me some boot.
I was a long ways from home and on a good horse, so I
wasn't going to be put afoot by that kind of a conversation. I told him I could use two horses, and I'd rather buy
him than to swap mine off—if his horse was worth the
money.

We got in a Model T Ford and drove out of town for
about a mile to a creek-bottom pasture where there were
several horses; and sure enough, the man had a good bay
horse, rolling fat, with a few cockle burrs in his mane and
tail. As we got close to him in the car, the man said to his

friend, who was with us sitting in the back seat: "Those kids must have been down here riding those horses, and that bay horse has gotten away with one of their belts around his neck."

Sure enough, this bay horse had a good leather belt around his neck at his throat latch. This fellow got out of the Model T with some ears of corn, shucked an ear or two, hollered a few times, and the horses came up to him. He eased around and caught ahold of the belt around the bay horse's neck. He said: "I guess he broke loose from those kids, but that belt made it handy for me to catch him."

I had brought my bridle and saddle along in the car and had left my horse tied with a rope. We saddled this horse, and he seemed to be gentle, but the owner warned me that he was a little spooky—which along about then didn't make no never mind to me. He held the horse by the bridle and I stepped on. When he turned him loose, the horse humped a little bit but he didn't really try to buck. He did show to be a nickel's worth snorty, but I think back now and that could have been because he was rested. He was a good eight-year-old horse, with good feet and legs; he had a nice running walk, a good fox trot just like my horse Tom, and I thought how nice it would be to have two horses that good and that much alike. When I looked in his mouth I noticed his teeth were a little brown, but the man said it was because he had been running in the field eating cotton stalks. I didn't know whether cotton stalks would turn a horse's teeth brown or not, but it sounded reasonable.

The man asked me $125 in cash, or, he said, he'd pay me $25 difference between this horse and mine—just be-

cause he was a little afraid of this horse. I wasn't in any
bind for money, and I never did have enough good horses,
so I offered him $100 for his horse. He hemmed and
hawed a little bit, while he stood kicking the dirt around
with the toe of his shoe and looked at the ground.
Finally he looked up at me and said: "I'm going to sell
him to you because I'm *afeared* of him."

That made me feel awfully good because I could buy
the horse cheap and because I wasn't afeared of him.

I rode back to town, stopped at the blacksmith shop,
and had my new horse shod. I picked the cockle burrs out
of his mane and tail while the blacksmith shod him, and
there never was a gentler horse. I remember now that the
blacksmith said he knew the man was trying to sell the
horse, but he didn't know what his reason was.

As I rode out of town on my new horse, leading Tom,
I heard somebody holler at the man I had bought the
horse from: "I see you got rid of that cribber."

Well, that didn't disturb me any. I had heard horses
called oaters and hay-burners, and I thought cribber was
another name for horse feed. That night I made camp,
staked Tom out on some tall grass, and told him how
lucky he was that he had somebody to do part of his work.

Then I turned around to stake my new horse out. He
had ahold of the top of a fence post with his teeth and was
leaning back sucking air with all his strength. I hit him
with the stake rope and said: "You old fool, there's grass
to eat on the ground. What are you trying to bite a post
for?" I staked him out on a long rope, made down my
bed, and went to sleep about halfway between my two
horses.

There was an awful noise woke me up in the middle

of the night, and I could see by the moonlight that this horse had ahold of the fence post, groaning and pulling. I squalled and threw rocks at him, then laid back down and went to sleep. He must have repeated the performance several times that night, because I saw the bark knocked off a stump and that post top was bit—which were about the only two things he could reach. His teeth and gums were sore in the front part of his mouth.

I saddled Tom, took up my camp, and led the other horse. Up in the morning, I stopped in the little town of Jarrell just to loaf and visit a little, drink a coke, and pass the time of day. I tied my horses to a hitch rack behind the grocery store. I was sitting in the back of the grocery store eating some ginger snaps and drinking a coke, when I looked out the back door and saw that my new horse had ahold of that wooden hitch rack with his teeth and was setting back groaning like he was going to tear that hitch rack down. The old gentleman running the grocery store looked at me and looked at the horse, and I asked him: "What makes that old fool do that?" Then I told him about the way the horse had acted the night before when I had made camp.

The old storekeeper laughed and said: "Young fellow, you've got a stump sucker."

Then I remembered about the man hollering and using the word cribber; so I asked the old storekeeper what was the difference between a cribber and a stump sucker. He said: "There ain't any difference in the vice—the difference is in the location. If he's in Kentucky, he's a cribber —and if he's in Texas, he's a stump sucker."

The old gentleman went out and looked at his mouth

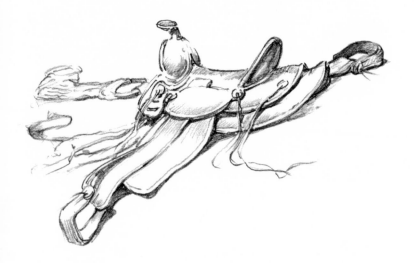

and saw that his teeth and gums were bloody. He said:
"You'd just as well buy you a leather strap and buckle it
real tight around that horse's neck at the throat latch, because then he can't swell his neck to bite and suck wind.
That will keep him from getting his mouth sore. Anytime
you tie him or turn him out, you better have that strap
good and tight around his neck."

I sat down on a sack of salt at the back of the store. I
was about half mad, but still it was funny about the man's
belt and his story about the kids letting the horse get away;
so I told the old storekeeper, and we had a good laugh.
When I got up to leave and started to pay for my coke
and cookies, the man said: "Young fellow, the treats are
on me!"

As I rode along that day, I wondered what I was going
to do with that stump sucker. I was on the road several

days, and I kept a tight leather strap around the horse's neck every time I tied him or staked him to graze. Two or three days later I rode into Hillsboro and went to a livery stable with my horses. Of course, I knew enough to take that strap off the horse's neck before I got close to town. There were several horse traders around the livery stable, and I noticed a Fort Worth buyer with a big diamond horseshoe stickpin and a big diamond ring. He was highly dressed, was entertaining the crowd, and was buying a good many horses and mules. He immediately bannered me to sell him a horse.

I had ridden the stump sucker part of the day, so he had dried sweat on him which showed he was a saddle horse—and he was shod. I told the man I might sell him the horse I was leading 'cause I couldn't ride both of them. He said: "Saddle him up and ride him for me."

So I took my riggin' off Tom and saddled the other horse up. He had a good fox trot; he reined good and was a nice-looking horse. This fancy horse and mule buyer didn't want to get his hands too nasty mouthing a horse, so he just opened the horse's lip at the corner and saw that he was open in the corners—which meant that he was eight years old. Another nice thing about it was that a stump sucker doesn't damage his corner teeth as much as he does his front teeth.

After a short conversation with everybody listening, my dressed-up horse buyer offered me $110. Of course I had asked a lot more, but I remarked: "You ought to know more about what the horse market is than I do, so I'm going to sell him to you." I unsaddled the horse, and he paid me and said: "Turn him in that lot back at the end of the hall of the barn."

As I started to lead the horse off, he said: "Just a minute. Of course I'm going to resell this horse, and if he has any bad habits I'd like for you to tell me about them. I've already paid you for the horse, but I'd just like to know if there's anything wrong with him."

I didn't answer the man. I just turned around, took a strap off my saddle, buckled it around the horse's neck good and tight, and turned him in the lot. Nearly everybody in the livery stable knew what that strap was for, and they just about died laughing. The horse buyer took it good humoredly that he had been cheated by a kid.

Easter Lily

When I was a young man about sixteen or seventeen years old, Mineral Wells, Texas, was considered by many—and especially by the people in Mineral Wells—to be quite a health resort. People went to the Crazy Hotel to drink Crazy Water and take Crazy Baths and listen to the Crazy Hotel radio broadcast advertising Crazy Mineral Crystals and the Crazy Hotel, and maybe do some crazy things.

It all may have helped their health some, but I think the principal good they got out of it was bolstering their ego, adding to their social prestige, and giving them something to talk about when they went back home: what they did when they were at the Crazy Hotel in Mineral Wells.

Of course, these people had to have a place to go horseback riding. There was a Mr. Cush Wise who had a

very elaborate and elite public livery stable. He rented horses to people who were at Mineral Wells on vacation, and also stabled horses for people who lived there. Occasionally some real horse person would come from afar to the wonders of Mineral Wells and bring his own private saddle horse with him. And of course there was only one place where any horse could be kept with distinction and pride in Mineral Wells—Cush Wise's livery stable, which was on the south end of the main street, down close to the trade square.

Mr. Wise had been some kind of higher-up in the cavalry of World War I, and it was hard for him to overcome it. He wouldn't hesitate to mention to you what they did in the cavalry. He still wore the pantaloon cavalry britches and hard-top boots with low heels. He stayed well dressed and well groomed and had a military air about him, and in all respects was probably a good horseman. However, he led you to believe—in fact, he was ready to confess—that he was a gentleman of the highest order and horsemanship and horses were not a business with him, but a love; a part of his life that he couldn't do without. That was the real reason for his being in the horse business, and not because of any money that might be connected with the running of a livery stable and the buying, selling, and trading of horses.

This kind of angle on things was sort of a new breed of animal with me. I thought horse people were in the horse business because they had to be or because they wanted to be, and since I was a small boy I've more or less considered the horse business not a business but a disease. The thing a horseman ought to do was to learn all he could about the disease, so he could live with it without its totally ruining him, financially and otherwise.

Anyhow, I rode into Mineral Wells one day on a nice dun horse with black mane and tail that weighed about eleven hundred pounds and had a nice way of carrying himself—a six-year-old, stylish enough, about as nice as western horses came. It was in the dead of winter and the usual tourist crowd had gone home, and the livery stable business was rather dull. Mr. Wise was having trouble passing the time of day. However, he always had a horse or two crosstied in the center of the hallway, with somebody brushing and currying them while he stood by with his hands in his pantaloon-britches pockets, waiting to tell them how it ought to be done and how it was done in the East and how far western horsemanship was behind eastern horsemanship. None of this ever made him too popular with the cowboys, but I guess it did make a hit with the people who came to Mineral Wells to enlighten themselves and build up their ego and ride a-horseback from a fancy stable.

I rode into the barn and stepped down off my horse, and Mr. Wise walked up and stuck his hand out and shook hands with me, and his hands were soft as a woman's. He was shaved and smelled good, had a pretty little snapbrim hat on, and those hard-top, flat-heeled boots. He introduced himself and told me he was Cush Wise. Well, I'd met him before, but I didn't see any use in embarrassing the man and embarrassing myself by making a point out of the fact that he didn't remember me; after all, there wasn't too much about me to remember.

I hadn't been in the cavalry and I hadn't been East and I didn't know all those things Mr. Wise professed to know above and beyond what a cowboy knew about a horse.

Finally he got around to asking me what he could do for me, and I told him I was going to be in town overnight—it was the middle of the afternoon then—and asked him if he could put my horse up for me. He very graciously said he'd be glad to. As I slipped my rigging off my horse, he commented that I was riding a nice horse that was well balanced and had a good back, and I must be one of the better kind of Texas cowboys since I didn't have any cinch sores or kidney sores or saddle sores anywhere on the horse's back. He also commented that my horse's feet were properly shaped and properly shod, and that except for the fact that I, like all Texans, hadn't brushed or curried his mane and tail, he showed he had been well cared for and properly fed, and there was a possibility that if I had the opportunity he had had I might make a horseman.

Well, I listened to all this, but I didn't believe a whole batch of it. I picked up a bucket and got a little cool water and washed my horse's back off while he began to eat his oats. Mr. Wise continued to entertain me with the finer points of horsemanship: the proper thing to have done was to have washed the whole horse off and then to have blanketed him; and, of course, never curry a wet horse but wait until he's dried, then curry him and brush him. Well, he didn't know how little of that was soaking in on me, but it looked like it was giving him a lot of relief to get it off his chest, and I figured somebody ought to listen to him once in a while. It wasn't bothering me, so I didn't talk back to him, I just let him talk on. I finished with my horse and Mr. Wise stepped out of the doorway of the stall, and I came out and closed the stall door and hung my bridle on the door. He had a nice, big, long barn with a brick floor in the hallway and lots of fancy tack rigging hanging up and down the sides of the wall. Of course, I didn't see any lariat ropes or hackamores or halters or tiedowns or any walking W's, things that would help a cowboy handle a rough bronc. Everything I saw there was for a horse that already had the rough took off him.

As we neared the back of the barn, I saw a great big stall, about twice as big as the other stalls, and a beautiful dapple-gray mare standing at the hay rack just sort of nibbling at some hay that she didn't want. She put her ears forward and looked at us like she might have some consideration for the human race, but not much. I mentioned that she sure was a pretty mare, and that was all it took to tap Mr. Wise off to tell me why that was a pretty mare. He went into a long rigmarole about her many illustrious ancestors, and called off names—Denmark, Rex Peavine, Stonewall, and a lot of others that sounded like he was describing people instead of horses. (I had owned a Denmark horse who was the grandmother of Beauty, the best horse I ever rode, and that had some Rex Peavine blood, but I didn't tell him I knew what he was talking about.) These were all American saddle blood, and this was an American saddle-bred mare that had been shipped out of Kentucky by a very elegant horsewoman. I didn't know what his "elegant" meant, but I could tell by the way he said it that this sure must have been quite a horsewoman he was talking about. He said that while she was in Mineral Wells she had ridden this mare around the streets some, but mostly in the small pasture behind the barn. She'd come down in the morning and ride the mare a few rounds and then go back to the hotel. He told all about how her people in Kentucky had fine horses and had bred this mare, and she had brought her to Mineral Wells with her while she enjoyed the vacation wonders of the Crazy Hotel.

I could tell at a glance that this mare hadn't been ridden in a long time, so I asked: "Well, where's the lady now? Evidently, the mare ain't been rode in some time."

He said the lady had gone back to Kentucky or to some other vacation resort, and that she'd left the mare there, and it would be a long time before spring and before there'd be anybody to ride the mare, and that the mare was for sale. Well, she was a beautiful mare with clean, straight legs and an intelligent eye and a handsome set of features, only I didn't know what business I had with her. She was worth a lot of money to somebody; but it didn't look to me like she could catch a yearling or drag a bronc horse or snub a wild mule for a man to harness, and I couldn't think right off why I'd have any need for her.

Mr. Wise thought this was a little bit funny, and he had a sort of sarcastic smile on his face when he said: "If you should ever have the privilege of riding a mare that moves down the road as this mare does, your life wouldn't be complete until you owned her."

He went on to tell me that she could move at ten or twelve miles an hour in a nice swinging fox trot or some other saddle gait and that an egg wouldn't fall off her back, she'd be moving with such rhythm in motion and such smoothness. You'd hardly know that you were gliding across the country at such a terrific rate of speed. All of this sounded very interesting to me, but still it never dawned on me that I had any business with the mare.

But I looked her over, just the same. She was a beautiful mare. She had a nice deep body, a beautiful topline, a good-looking hindquarter for a mare of such breeding, and good legs. She couldn't have been more than about an eight-year-old, judging from the dapples and the amount of dark hair that was still in her coat. (You know, gray horses are born black with a few little gray hairs in them, and as they get older they get lighter until when they are old they are white. When they are from six to ten years old, if they are properly cared for and brushed and curried, they have just that beautiful gray dappling around over their bodies; and their legs, from their knees and hocks to the ground, are usually very dark. They'll have black manes and tails and a little tip of black on their ears. To me, this is about the most beautiful color you can have on a horse.) Of course, I know color doesn't make much difference with horses; but it just happens I've had some good gray horses, and so I'm partial to the color. But I still didn't entertain the idea that I was able to afford to own such a mare. So I told Mr. Wise that I was going uptown to loaf and visit around, and I'd be back in the morning. He said he'd have his man give my horse plenty of hay for the night.

I reached down and untied my little roll that I had tied on the back of my saddle. It was the proper way for a man to travel, to have a little roll like that, maybe with some extra clothes or some extra money, maybe a six-shooter or something he thought he might need on a trip across the country on horseback. I had another shirt in mine, and maybe something else.

I found a rooming house that wasn't too close to the Crazy Hotel. They weren't offering Crazy Baths, but they would sell you some Crazy Mineral Water, if you'd buy it. That didn't appeal to me; I'd always thought that spring water and windmill water and even good clean pool water wasn't bad, and I couldn't see the point of drinking that Crazy Water. I was afraid it might make me act like some of those people I'd seen who'd been on it up at the Crazy Hotel.

This rooming house was good enough. My room had a good bed and a great big bowl and a great big pitcher of plain, common water. The pitcher might have been cracked and the bowl was chipped, but as far as I was concerned it was luxury, and I knew I could make the night in a stall that was rigged like this one. I rinsed my face and hands and took my britches legs out of my boot tops and let them down over my boots, and got a jacket that was sort of new out of my bedroll and went out on the street and walked up to the Crazy Hotel. I stood around against one of the big pillars in the lobby and watched people play games and visit and talk. I'd see men kind of squire around and stand on one foot and hold their hat just right in the curve of their elbow. And some of the fancy ladies would come through the hotel with high-heeled shoes on, and they'd kinda trill one of those heels across that tile floor. Of course nearly everybody would look up, especially the menfolks. There were some old white-headed men and ladies sitting around visiting. The men were carrying walking canes, and the ladies had some eyeglasses hung out on the end of a stick, and you'd see the old men kind of straighten their mustaches and rub their bald heads and think of something nice to say. Every now and then somebody would glance up and see me, and you'd see them take a second glance; they wondered if I was one of the guests of the hotel or something wild that had just struck the town, and I hoped they decided the latter because I sure didn't want to be one of their crowd.

I moseyed into the dining room, which was a great big place with an awful lot of trimming in it just to serve chuck. I ordered up a batch of stuff and ate it, and it was good. There must have been a chuckwagon cook in the kitchen.

When I walked out onto the street it was better than dark and getting pretty chilly. I wandered around a little while and watched the bright lights, then went back to the rooming house and went to bed. I got kinda wallowed out into that bed and thought it was time to get unconscious. That was never any problem with me, but that night I rolled and tumbled a little bit. I could see that long, wavy, black mane on that gray mare, and every now and then it'd kind of pass through my mind how she looked standing in that stall and how clean her legs were from scars or blemishes, and that dappling color kind of fascinated me. I finally got around to wondering how much a mare like that was worth; it just dawned on me that I'd never asked Mr. Wise how much she would cost. I got to wondering if, in the dead of winter when there was no riding season, maybe she was in a range I could afford. The more I thought about it, the less I could sleep.

I got up and put my boots on and dressed and walked down to the livery stable. There were a lot of lights up and down the hall of the barn, and it wasn't locked up. I walked down the hall, and the mare was standing with her head over the stall door. I rubbed her and talked to her and ran my fingers through her foretop and noticed how soft her ears were and how nice and big her eyes were and that they were out on the side of her head where they belonged. I sure got to wondering how it would feel to ride a horse like Mr. Wise said she was. The more I thought about it, the more I got to wondering about her price. I'd had a pretty good year and I was carrying a lot of trading money. So I thought, well, I'll go back to the rooming house and go back to bed, but I'll look into this gray mare business a little more in the morning.

Of course, I woke up awful early. I had been raised to believe it was a disgrace to be found in bed after daylight. I unrolled my little roll and took out what clothes and money I wanted, and rolled it back up and tied the strings around it good and tight. Country-like, I had paid for my room when I came in the night before. Nobody was at the desk, so I just took my little bedroll and went on back to the barn. About halfway down there, I stopped in a café that had opened up and ate a batch of stuff and waited for daylight before going to the barn.

I glanced in my old horse's stall and saw he was all right. He was living just about as fancy as he ever thought of; he was lying down in the stall with deep straw in it and had all the hay and grain he wanted. I guess he was wondering if some horses lived like that all the time. The sun was coming up and began to warm things, and the horses began to nicker, and sure enough, here came Mr. Wise with his man to feed and tend the horses and open up for the day's business. I saw them coming, so I got in the stall with my horse. I'd picked up a brush in the hall of the barn, and when they got there I was rubbing his fetlocks and his knees and ankles a little bit, and letting on like I'd listened pretty close to what Mr. Wise said the night before.

He came in and spoke and stood around a minute and said: "Well, I see you're trying to give your horse a little better attention. You know, with the proper schooling, somebody to show you and tell you, you could make a horseman." Then he told his man: "Bring out Easter Lily and clean her off before you do anything else."

Well, I didn't know who he meant, but I looked up and saw his man bring out the gray mare. That was Easter Lily! He brushed and curried and combed her mane and combed her tail, and I stepped outside my horse's stall and stood and watched. The more I looked at her, the nicer she got.

Mr. Wise said: "Ben, if you should ever own a mare like Easter Lily, you will know what it means to ride and own the finest in horseflesh."

Well, ordinarily I'd have thought this was a sales talk, but he'd made such an impression that he wasn't in the business to buy and sell horses, that it was just a love, a part of his life, that I couldn't believe he was getting ready to sell me that Easter Lily mare. I finally stumbled around and said: "I never saw too many horses in the class of this mare, and I ain't too well posted on what the going price would be for a mare of this kind. Just for my edification, what is this mare worth?"

"Oh," he said, "she could be worth several thousand dollars, if the right person came along. It will probably be summer before somebody comes along that will truly appreciate her and pay what she's worth. I suppose I'll keep her through the winter, take care of her, and have her ready for some real horse-person to enjoy the coming riding season."

That still hadn't told me what he wanted for the mare, so I turned around and picked up my saddle and kind of shook it around and knocked some of the straw and dirt off the sheepskin lining, like I was getting ready to get my horse out of his stall.

He said: "Are you riding out so early today and leaving me?" like it was hurting him to see me go.

"Yes, sir," I said, "I guess I spent about as much time here as I ought to. I think I'll drift down on the Brazos River and see if I can buy some horses or mules."

He looked real surprised and said: "Why, I didn't know you bought horses!"

I said: "Well, I do, such as they are. I don't buy any like the Easter Lily, but I buy some good horses; sell them to people that's got a use for them." I thought I'd just cut him a little bit, so I said: "I don't generally have any trouble getting people to price the kind of horses I'm interested in buying."

He gasped his breath a little and said: "Oh, Ben, I didn't realize you were asking the price of the Easter Lily mare. I would dearly love to see you with a mare of this quality; she'd be something you could ride and enjoy and brag about, and cherish and remember all your life."

I said: "Well, that may not be sales talk, but it sounds pretty much like it. You still ain't give me no price on this mare."

He said: "Well, you wouldn't think she is worth what she is, and I had no idea that you'd buy her. You really wouldn't have any need for a mare of this quality; however, just for your information, a mare like this is worth about five hundred dollars in the winter and about twice that much in the summer, when there are buyers around."

Of course, I knew enough right off to know he was kind of baiting me, to let me know I could get a bargain by buying her in the dead of winter. So I said: "Well, I don't know that she ain't worth that, so I couldn't give you any argument. But I wonder, just as a favor to a country boy, would you let me put my saddle on her and ride her?"

"Oh, Ben," he said, "I'd be glad for you to ride this mare. I'd just be delighted. And you'd feel better in your own saddle, so go ahead and put your saddle on her."

He went to helping me get her saddled. Then he looked down at my spurs and said: "I think you'd be better off without those spurs. She won't need them."

I glanced up and saw the way he was looking at me, like I was going through military inspection before he would allow me to ride the Easter Lily. So I pulled my spurs off, wondering whether I was going to have to go get my britches pressed or get a shave and comb my hair before he'd think it wouldn't be too disgraceful to let me ride her. I never did like to get on a horse inside the barn, so I turned to lead her out the back door and he said: "Just ride her off down in that little pasture yonder."

Well, the gate to the little pasture was open, and it was a nice spot that was used to exercise horses in, and I thought it would be all right to comply with the man's request. After all, it was his mare, and it was fixing to be my rare privilege to ride her. I stepped on the mare, and she stood perfectly still. I got my reins in hand and sort of shook myself a little bit and sat down real comfortable, and she still hadn't moved. I reached over and stroked her on the neck and spoke to her, and she just started off in a nice straight walk with her head a little above the level and her ears standing out looking at the world, taking an interest in everything that was about her. By the time I got to the pasture gate, she'd eased into the nicest fox trot you ever felt under you. She moved beautifully, and she didn't jar you, shake her head, or pop her neck around, and she wasn't wringing her tail. Mr. Wise had told the truth: she did get you across the world without much effort on your part or, seemingly, on her part.

The little pasture probably had twenty-five acres in it. I rode her around the outside fence. She never crow-hopped with me or hit the ground crooked or made any kind of half-hammer motion. I brought her to the center of the pasture and figure-eighted her along in a little fox trot. Then I eased her up into a little more speed, and she very easily shifted into a sweet rack, and that mare could rack as fast as the average horse could run. I didn't want to get her too hot—after all, this was a guest ride I was making—so I reined her up a little. I thought: "Well, this will make her cross her legs and do the half hammer," but sure enough, just with one stride and one motion, she dropped into that easy natural fox trot, touching the ground as light as a thief in the dark. I knew then that this was one of the good mares of all the horse kingdom. I hated to go back to the barn with her, but I rode in a walk back to the barn so she would cool off a little. I hadn't noticed Mr. Wise watching me at all. If he had been, he was watching through a crack in the barn. As I came into the barn, I stepped off the mare and he stepped out of his office.

He looked up at me, smiled, and said: "Well, young man, now you've been horseback!"

I said: "Yes, sir, and I believe all you've said about the mare is true. I suppose she's worth $500, but I don't have any way of knowing because I've never been on a mare like this before."

He said: "I'd probably have more need for the horse you're riding, and more opportunities to sell him than I would this mare, between now and spring. If you're really interested in her and feel you can afford a mare of this kind, we might have a trade."

I knew then that he'd already looked at my horse while I was gone, and had sneaked into his office just for a blind. I began to decide this Mr. Cush Wise was a horse trader. I decided that it was the dead of winter, he had a good many horses on feed, and I didn't know how much money he had in the bank. I thought: "Well now, I might own this gray mare before this session's over."

I set out to tell him how good my horse was—how much substance he had, how much riding he could stand, what a good horse he was in a tight when you had to rope something or pull a bronc horse or cross a bridge or catch a wild mule in the pasture. "Well," he said, "I'd hardly have any need for the horse for these things myself, but there are people in this country besides you who use horses, and I'd have some occasion to sell him, provided I could own him at a modest figure."

I wasn't quite used to this word modest, in place of cheap, but I did savvy that they meant the same thing. So I asked him: "What do you think this modest amount would be?"

He answered: "Oh, I'd have to do some things to your

horse before I could sell him. He needs quite a bit of finishing up to knock off the rough edges, but I suppose I could allow you $125 for him if you chose to buy the Easter Lily."

Well, my dun horse was a good horse and worth a little more money than that, but not a whole lot. I said I couldn't afford the mare at that price, but that I thought my horse was worth $200 and I'd give $300 difference if he wanted to trade.

He said not to be ridiculous, that the mare was worth several times more than he was asking for her to begin with. So then we started to wrangle, and it went on quite a long time. Finally I started to saddle my own horse, and I was about to put my foot in the stirrup when he said: "Well, now, Ben, don't rush off. Just because you're a nice young man and I want to do you a favor, I'm going to trade with you for the $300."

It had been my idea for about thirty minutes that that's what he was finally going to do. I had just wondered how long he'd hold out. So I smiled and looked back through the barn where they were cleaning the mare off after the little ride I had made on her. I could hardly keep from jumping up and down. I said: "Well, Mr. Wise, that suits me if it does you."

So I unsaddled my horse and took my bridle off him and turned him loose, and reached down into my pocket and shuffled and came up with some money, and paid Mr. Wise his $300 in twenty-dollar bills. He looked at it, smiled, and said: "Well, you're a man that carries your money with you."

Rather than show my hand any, I said: "No, I'm a

man that *did* carry my money with me. You've got it now."

He gave a nice sociable kind of laugh at that remark and called to his man to bring the Easter Lily up to the new, proud owner. When the man came leading the mare up, I could tell that he was well pleased that she had been sold, which was sort of a surprise to me. He handed me the halter rope, and I slipped the halter off, put my bridle on her, fastened the throat latch, and proceeded to saddle her. My little traveling roll was on the back of my saddle, and I thought it helped her looks a little to have a working man's rig on her.

Mr. Wise said: "Ben, you'll get home so quick on your new mare that the folks won't think you've been gone."

We both laughed, and I waved good-bye to him and started to ride the mare out into the street. I had to ride across the street the livery stable was on and up another street about a block, before I turned on the road that led out of town. I got across the street; Easter Lily was moving nice. I was just thinking that I was about the luckiest man in the world when all of a sudden she snorted and squatted and turned back suddenly and nearly lost me. If I hadn't been riding a good saddle, I couldn't have stayed on. She grabbed the bits between her teeth, dashed across that paved street and right into the hall of the barn, and stopped. It all happened so fast I hadn't had time to figure it out. This mare had action, and could whirl completely around and face the other direction as quick as the winter wind could flip a leaf.

Mr. Wise looked terribly surprised. The barnman was

nowhere to be seen. Mr. Wise said: "Well, something must have bothered her. She's been feeling good, standing in the stall eating. Let me lead her back across the street for you."

Well, that was sort of an insult to a cowboy. Nobody ever had to lead any horses for me, and I told him so. I said: "I haven't swapped for no leading stock—she's supposed to be a riding mare. So I'll just ride her back across the street."

I reined her around and rode her back across the street, and she put on the same performance. This time she turned her ears back a little bit like she was mad, and she went around the side of the barn and into the back, right next to where her stall was. She was frothing at the mouth, and she'd grabbed those bits and I couldn't jerk them loose from her with both hands—and I was a pretty stout young cowboy. When she decided to go back, that mare had the hardest mouth I'd ever felt.

"Perhaps you ought to ride her around back there," Mr. Wise said, "and get acquainted with her."

So I reined her and went back down to the little pasture and she rode like a dream. No mad, no nothing, didn't do anything wrong, didn't take the bits. But I said to myself that I couldn't take that pasture home with me just to have a place to ride the Easter Lily.

I came back to the barn and Mr. Wise said: "She's probably over her spell now, Ben; just ride her on off."

I thought this time I'd go around the side of the barn. About halfway up the side she threw a walleyed fit and turned back. I pulled on her, and she didn't stop. When she hit the hall of the barn, I stepped down off of her and unbuckled my spurs off my saddle and went to putting them on; they were long, heavy spoke rowel spurs. The spokes were dull and wouldn't cut the mare, but I sure could make an impression on her with them. At least I was fixing to get her attention.

Mr. Wise said: "I just can't imagine what caused this mare to act so horribly. It's just not like her at all. I'm sorry she's doing this, and I think you're horseman enough to ride her, but I hate to see you put spurs on her."

"Well, Mr. Cush Wise," I said, "maybe you'd better look the other direction, because I'm damned sure fixing to put my spurs on."

I was getting about half mad, and at that age it didn't hurt for me to get mad. I knew I could eat that mare, figuratively speaking; she couldn't throw me and she couldn't do anything to me that I couldn't stand. I stepped back on her, reined her out of the hall of the barn, and started around the corner. This time she decided to have her fit right next to the barn door. When she started to whirl back to the left, I caught her way up in the shoulder with the big spoke rowel spurs. You could tell it was quite a shock to her sensitive nature, and she wheeled the other direction. I caught her in the right shoulder, and that unnerved her beyond expression. She jumped forward, bawling real loud. Her breeding had robbed her of her natural instinct for being able to get rid of a man, and even though she was barn-spoiled beyond description she didn't know how to buck. I jabbed her down the side a time or two with the spurs. That got her mixed up enough so that she shuffled her gaits a time or two, clicked her forefeet with her hind feet; then she straightened out to a fox trot and headed for the little pasture. That wasn't going to suit me. I pulled her around to the right with one rein, and she turned her neck, but not her body. I stood up in my right stirrup and slapped her in the jaw with my left leg, and that turned her around good. She started fox trotting back to the barn. When she got there and started to dive in, I caught her again and jerked her around. That made her lose her balance and she fell to her knees. She hadn't been trained to fall, and wasn't supposed to fall; this was accidental. I got ready to get off her in case she tried to roll with me. It wouldn't be a new experience; I'd met some of that kind, too.

For the last several minutes, Mr. Wise had been standing in the hall of the barn with his hat off, begging and squalling and beseeching. "Ben," he said, "we could make some kind of a trade and I'd take the mare back before I'd see her ruined."

I got the mare to stand a few minutes; she was shaking and trembling all over and blowing her nose pretty bad. She had her ears cocked back at me like she was trying to think of something else to do. I said to Mr. Wise: "What kind of a trade did you have in mind?"

"Well," he said, "you can't ride her away from this barn—*no one else ever has.* The experience ought to be worth $100 to you."

I told him he'd made a little mistake about who was fixing to get the experience, and it might not be worth $100 to her. But I was going to make more than $100 when I rode the Easter Lily away from that barn. Money wasn't too plentiful with me, but worse than that, my reputation was at stake. I'd been *took* by one of those smart military cavalry horsemen, and that wasn't setting too well with me. But before I threw too big a fit I said to Mr. Wise: "Well, maybe a little later up in the day, after she gets over her mad spell, and I've had time to get better control of my spurs, I could ride her off. Would you mind if I just put her back into the stable with my saddle on her while I go uptown and rest? Maybe I'll come back around noon."

"Oh," he said, "that'll be fine, Ben, fine. You just put her in there now and we won't bother her, and she'll be all right. You're going to unsaddle her?"

"No," I said, "I don't want to unsaddle her."

"Anything you say," he said, "but now, before you ruin the mare, why don't you admit you can't ride her and take your horse back; and after all, you should pay for your education."

I just shook my head and put the mare in the barn, with the bits still in her mouth and the reins done up on the saddle horn. Then I moseyed out of the back of the barn and around the side and started back up toward town. I had sighted the stableman up in the loft looking out the end, watching the show. I wasn't out of good earshot when I heard him slide down out of the loft and him and Mr. Wise have a good laugh. He told Mr. Wise not to worry about the spur marks on the Easter Lily; he would brush and curry them off in just a few days. The hair would grow back, and I hadn't busted the hide on her.

As soon as I was out of sight, I quickened up my pace a little bit. I walked up to the lobby of the Crazy Hotel, where there was one of those built-in long-distance phone booths over to one side in a big mahogany cabinet. I went in and called Lester Lewis, a man I knew in Weatherford, where I lived, that had a truck. It was one of the little trucks that were all they had in those days, and it would haul two horses. I didn't tell my friend all my troubles; I just told him I was afoot in Mineral Wells and wanted him to go to the wagonyard and get Beauty and bring her to me at Cush Wise's livery stable, and to borrow an extra saddle for me and bring it too. I said if he was here now, he'd already be late. He said he thought he could be with me in an hour and a half. While I waited, I walked up and down the back streets and tried to stay out of sight and out of conversation with anybody, because I was mad. A young cowboy isn't very good company for himself, much less anybody else, when he's mad.

When I saw my friend coming, I got in with him and rode back to the barn. He took his endgate out and backed up to a little ditch, and Beauty jumped out. She nickered to me, and I was glad to see her, too. She was always my friend and my standby, helping me out of whatever I happened to get into with bad horses or wild cattle. It was heaps better than sending for some of your folks, because they'd scold you if you got into some kind of trouble. All Beauty wanted was to help.

I saddled Beauty up with the rigging Lester had borrowed from a friend of mine at the wagonyard, and went in and took the breast collar off my saddle and put it on Beauty. Then I led the gray mare out into the opening. Mr. Wise was becoming perplexed. I guess that is a good word for a man of good social standing, prestige, and ability in horsemanship.

He said: "What are you going to do, Ben?"

I said: "I'm fixing to ride the Easter Lily."

"No," he said, "what *are* you going to do, Ben? Load the mare and haul her away?"

I said: "No, sir. I don't think this mare was bred to

haul and you didn't mention her loading qualities. I'm fixing to ride the mare. If she's barn-spoiled the way it seems she is, hauling her won't break her from it."

"Now Ben," he said, "before you do something foolish, it would be wise of you to reconsider the proposition I made you. You can have your horse back and the $200."

I said: "It could be, but I don't think I could resell that experience, and I don't want to be out the expense. It might be worth something to you, Mr. Wise, to find out about the way cowboys break spoiled horses. Of course, I'm sure it ain't horsemanship, but it might be something you could use sometime, so you just watch and keep your damned mouth shut."

By now I had Beauty rigged up and I'd put a halter on the Easter Lily underneath her bridle. I took a good silk manila lariat rope and put it around her neck. I tied it where it wouldn't choke her and ran it down through her halter, tying it to her halter ring so she would be pulling on her neck and her head at the same time. I double half-hitched this rope to Beauty's saddle horn, with just enough room to make her have to lead up about halfway on Beauty's side, so she would be able to get behind her and tromp my good mare's hind feet with her forefeet.

Mr. Wise asked if my friend who had brought the bay mare in the truck was going to ride her. I told Mr. Wise: "She's all the help I'll need, without a rider."

By that time, something else had developed. The barnman wasn't in the loft, he was standing on the ground looking excited, and his mouth was open and his eyes were crossed a little bit. He was watching Mr. Wise, and Mr. Wise was watching me, and you could see a kind of sickish expression crossing both of their faces. The Easter

Lily showed no excitement, but you could see in her ears and her eyes the firm determination not to do what was right.

In the meantime, Mr. Wise had explained to me that the lady had ridden the mare only in the little pasture and she'd never been up and down the streets, and that she didn't like to leave the barn. I told him I was fixing to get her over that. Beauty had the saddle, blanket, and breast harness on and no bridle, and that looked a little odd to everybody concerned. I stepped on the Easter Lily after I had her tied hard and fast to Beauty and had taken Beauty's bridle off; she was standing perfectly motionless and right where I could reach over and pat Beauty on the hips and talk to her and she'd know what was going on. I'd snubbed no telling how many bronc horses, I'd drug mules, I'd done everything to Beauty and with her, and she wasn't the least bit excited; however, she was chewing a little bit and watching me closely and had one ear turned, and had her head turned enough to bring the whole picture into view on the eye on the left-hand side.

I spoke to Beauty and I spoke to the Easter Lily and we rode off beautifully; the Easter Lily rode on a loose halter rope until we crossed the road. When we crossed the road and started up the street she started to throw a fit, but she'd waited a little long for that fit, and this was the last one she was fixing to throw, and I thought she better get the full benefit of it. I didn't ever spur. I reached over and patted Beauty on the hindquarters and spoke to her, telling her to go on. She'd get a little closer to the ground and pull a little harder. The Easter Lily's hind feet were marking the gravel road where Beauty was dragging her, and she was moving her forefeet forward

one at a time, just fast enough to keep from falling. She'd
begun to bawl a mournful, hard, mad, hateful bawl, but
that didn't excite me nor Beauty. I reached over and spoke
to Beauty again and spanked her on the hip. By this time
she had such a grab on the Easter Lily, and had her scoot-
ing so bad when she was trying to pull back, that Beauty
struck a little, hard, deep-pulling trot, and when she did
she unnerved the Easter Lily to the point that she had to
go to moving her hind legs as well as her front ones. Then
I spoke to Beauty to pull back to a walk. The Easter Lily
was walking with her feet in front and behind, very re-
luctantly, and was pulling hard on Beauty. Beauty was
having to lean forward and way over to the right, since
I'd snubbed the Easter Lily to the left.

Mr. Wise had gotten in his long automobile and had
his barnman with him. He was coming up the street behind me. My truckman was out in front of me a little
piece and had already decided that everything was going
to be all right, but it seemed he wasn't going to run off
and leave me until I was outside the city limits.

Mr. Wise drove up in front of me and jumped out of
his car. "Ben," he said, "I hate to see you abuse that mare.
Let me give all your money back and come and get your
horse."

I said: "I don't have a horse. He's yours, and it's not
my money, it's your money. And don't worry about me
abusing this mare. It so happens I traded for her, and with
my wagonyard background, I'm not thinking about back-
ing out or trading back even, or any of those vulgar things
which a man of your background might be inclined to
suggest that I do."

Anyway, by now he was having to trot to keep up

with me, because Beauty was moving pretty brisk and the Easter Lily had begun to weaken, and was just walking at a lean instead of pulling back so hard. He'd jump in his car and drive a little piece, and then he'd jump out of his car and trot a little piece, and then he'd jump back in his car and drive a little piece, and we were nearly out to the edge of the town. We got out of the city limits of Mineral Wells—at that time there was a red brick paving along the main highway out there, and I was off that paving and over in the ditch, and Beauty was going along good, having to pull a little on the Easter Lily, but not too much. My trucker friend had decided to drive on and leave me. Evidently he thought everything would be all right. Mr. Wise was still following me, still driving his car and jumping out and walking, and I wasn't stopping to talk to him. Beauty was as hard as iron and had the lungs a horse ought to have, a deep girth with a short back and powerful hindquarters, and good forelegs, and she could pull that mare from daylight to dark and not give plumb out. I knew she wasn't hurting and the Easter Lily was weakening, so I began to relax a little bit and enjoy part of the fun.

Mr. Wise finally drove up past me, stopped his car and jumped out again, and said: "Ben, would you take a profit on the mare, *sir*?"

I said: "Thank you, *sir*. The only profit I'd take would be that summer price you was discussing, of $1,000."

"Well," he said, "if she was cured of being barn crazy, she'd be worth $1,000."

I said: "If she ain't cured by the time today's over, she'll be cured by the time the week's over. Good-bye, Mr. Wise, don't bother me any more. I've got work to do."

He didn't turn around, just stopped and sat in his car until I was over the hill and out of sight. I don't know whether he cried there or cried back at the barn, or how much remorse and grieving he went through, but I rode on toward Weatherford on the Easter Lily.

In a little while, the Easter Lily quit pulling very much, just occasionally, and she was traveling on a loose halter rope. Beauty was fox trotting along a little bit, and every once in a while she'd get a chance to stop and take a bite of grass. She didn't have any bits in her mouth, and I didn't care if she grazed a little along. We walked and poked along and got to Milsap. By now it was getting about 3:30 in the afternoon. I hadn't made very good time, but I was accomplishing a lot, reconstructing a saddle mare's ideas about what distance was and how to act on the road. I was bringing her to realize that life wasn't a constant round of good hay and good feed and brushing and currying and little short rides in the little pasture behind the stable.

Well, I rode into Milsap and stepped off the Easter Lily. I was afraid Beauty might drift around a little bit and graze or get into somebody's yard or something, so I put her bridle on her (it was tied on her saddle horn) and hitched her to the hitch rack. I untied the Easter Lily. It's not fair to your saddle horse to tie him to a hitch rack and leave another horse tied to the saddle, that might pull him and get him in a strain and cause the bits to hurt his mouth, or make him have to break his bridle rein or do something he knows better than to do. So I untied the Easter Lily from the saddle horn and tied her to a post separately. She had lather all over her. She was wringing wet with sweat from anger as much as from exertion. She dropped over on three legs and breathed a long, hard breath of relief and just stood there.

I loafed up and down the streets a few minutes and went into a little eating place and ordered me a batch of steak and 'taters and all the trimmings. I got through and had a piece of mince pie sitting in front of me (this was before they found out there were more than four pieces in a pie) when I looked up, and there was Mr. Wise, out near where my horses were tied. I wasn't fixing to go off and leave that pie, so I picked it up and went to shoving it in my mouth and eating it and walking, and paid the woman as I started out the door.

Mr. Wise started to walk up to my mare, and I said: "Mr. Wise, don't bother my horses!"

He reached up and took his hat off and brushed his long, white, beautifully kept hair back, and he said: "Ben, I've mistreated you, and it hasn't been my custom in life to do a thing like that. You're a young man, and I can tell you've been greatly disillusioned. I feel I should make some amends for having traded you a barn-spoiled mare. That's the reason the woman couldn't take her back to Kentucky. She'd gotten barn crazy, and the little pasture was the only place anybody could ride her. I see now that she can be ridden elsewhere, and that you're very likely to break her of her bad habit."

I said: "Yeah, could be she's seen the light, too; and you're fixing to lose a horse that's been making you a little money along. How many times you sold her to people who couldn't leave with her?"

He said: "That's beside the point."

"Well, might be," I said, "but this labor of love that

146

you've been engaged in—not for the money but for the sheer pleasure—selling the Easter Lily could be the way you've been helping pay the feed bills on them horses you stand around there with their manes sheared and their tails pulled, looking like a cross between a jackass and a bull because society thinks they ought to look different than a natural horse. For the sake of society you wouldn't mind messing up a good horse."

"Oh," he said, "those are things you don't understand. I'd be willing to take the mare back and pay you a reasonable price for the trouble you've been to; and of course, you'd take the horse back in the trade."

I said: "Mr. Wise, that's a nice big old dun horse, and he looks good, and he's gentle. Society idiots and small children can ride him—and old men like you. He won't hurt you, I don't think. But he's not a good active horse. He's a little slow on the uptake and a little slow heading a yearling. He can do a lot of things it takes stout horses for. Could be—no better than you're getting along in the horse business—you're going to have to make a crop, and you ought to keep him. He'd work, I think, if you put a collar on him; and I don't want him back."

This seemed to be some sort of a shock to him, and he said: "In that case, I'll pay the $500 that I priced the mare to you, and keep the horse."

I said: "Well, that's nice of you, but I'm thinking about that summer price. You said she was worth about $1,000."

He said: "I doubt there would be anybody with money enough to afford a thousand-dollar mare in this area, but there are places she might be worth that."

I said: "Well, you can't tell. That might be my barn."

"Oh," he said, "I don't think you can ever get $1,000 for her."

"I don't think so either," I said, "but it's going to be fun to ride her after I get her over being barn crazy."

He asked: "How do you break a mare from being barn crazy?"

And I asked back: "Didn't they learn you that in the cavalry, or in the East, wherever that is? If they did," I added, "it looks like you didn't do so well, so I'm going to try my hand at it, Texas style."

By that time I'd finished eating my pie, and I went back into the café and got a drink of water and reset my hat and shook myself a little bit, and said: "Well, Mr. Cush, I believe I'll rig up and leave."

He stepped back away from my horses—didn't open his mouth. His lip was quivering a little bit and he was sort of pale around the corners of his mouth.

I said: "You look sick. I don't know what's the matter with you, but maybe you can take a pill for it."

Then I tied the Easter Lily back to Beauty's saddle horn and stepped on her. I really intended to ride Beauty and lead the Easter Lily the rest of the way, but for his benefit I thought I'd better ride her. I untied Beauty and took her bridle off and put it back on her saddle horn, so the bridle reins wouldn't get in her way, and spoke to her; she started moving. The Easter Lily started to move, but all of a sudden she had a lapse of memory. She started to whirl and pull on the rope. I squalled at Beauty and she pulled the rope tight. The Easter Lily flopped on the ground and started to sulk. In the meantime I managed to get off. By that time the twelve or fifteen people that were in Milsap had gathered around. The Easter Lily was lying on the ground moaning and groaning. Beauty had the halter rope pulled so tight that her neck was stretched hard.

Mr. Wise rushed up to the Easter Lily. He was reaching over to Beauty's saddle horn, and he said: "I'm going to untie that halter rope before she hurts herself."

In his hurry he tripped (maybe over my boot toe) and fell in the dirt about halfway across the Easter Lily's neck. This brought her out of her sulking and made her fight her head enough to keep Mr. Wise off balance, and he couldn't get off the ground. I didn't think he was going to hurt my mare any more, and I didn't try to get him up. Two men rushed up and got hold of him and dragged him out of the way and helped him to his feet. He had dirt and scare all over him.

All the time I was trying to buy the Easter Lily, I never had looked at Mr. Wise very close. I was always looking at the horse. If you want to get a real picture of a man or a horse, get him in a tight and see what he does under the stress and strain. This was the first time I had taken a hard look at Mr. Wise. He had the starch knocked out of him, and his face was about the color of an eggshell. His eyes had sunk into his head and he was real ghostly looking. This was the first time I had noticed that he was so narrow-eyed you could punch both of them out with a hairpin without spreading the pin. Without that fancy shoulder-padded coat, he would be about half as long as a wagon tongue and not as thick. As I stepped between him and the Easter Lily, I thought to myself: "The cavalry was bound to have heaps better men than Mr. Cush Wise, or we would have lost the war."

This time the Easter Lily rode off like she was supposed to. I got home late in the afternoon and fed my other horses and unsaddled Beauty and kind of rubbed her around a little bit and fed her good. She hadn't had a very hard day's work, as far as she was concerned. She could drag two or three mares that far. I didn't feel like I had mistreated her any, and she didn't either.

My barn had four stalls in it, a feed room, and a saddle room. I took the Easter Lily and started to put her in a stall, and she almost tried to run over me to get into the stall. All of a sudden it dawned on me that that might be a mistake.

I led her into the back lot and gave her a drink of water and about half a block of alfalfa hay. I didn't give her a bite of grain. The next morning I saddled her up and started to ride away. She threw a fit and tried to go back to the barn. I let her go, then led her into the back lot again and left her where she could get water. That night I gave her a little hay.

By morning she looked pretty drawed. She was hungry, and she nickered when I was feeding the other horses. When I led her through the barn she tried to smell at the feed troughs, but I led her on like I thought she had been in the land of plenty all the night before. I rode her off, and she got in the middle of the road and started to throw that fit. I jabbed her about twice with my spurs, and she hit that fox trot and rode on away—but she showed the signs of no feed and hard riding.

I rode her out into the edge of town, where I had a little pasture with some more horses and a little doghouse-looking place where I kept some feed. I got out about a half gallon of oats and poured them out onto a slab of concrete, took the bits out of her mouth, and let her eat that feed. It wasn't much, and she was hungry; but when I rode her back to town, she did have the nicest fox trot anybody has ever ridden on a horse. I put her in the back lot with a little bit of alfalfa hay, but not very much, after I had rubbed her back and tousled her ears with my bare hands—this was my way of telling a spoilt mare when I was ready to make peace if she was.

Next morning I had some horse work to do, and I saddled one of my other horses and went to move some mules eight or ten miles out in the country for a horse trader friend of mine. He was putting them out in an oat field—the oats were green this time of year. I got back to town late in the afternoon. It was a pretty winter day, and I saddled the gray mare. This time I took time to brush and curry and clean her up pretty good, and then I sad-dled her and led her out in front of the barn and stepped on her. I had put about a gallon of oats in a towsack and rolled it up and tied it on the back of my saddle.

When we hit the middle of the road, she didn't offer to fly back or look back at the barn or do anything nasty. She stuck her ears up and started off to ride on down the road. When we got close to the little pasture in the edge of town, she looked up and started to turn in the gate, and nickered a little bit. I reined her past the gate and rode her on down the road. It was about thirty minutes before dark, I guess. I stopped beside the road and scratched a place in the grass; I took the oats off the back of the saddle and poured them on the ground. I took the bits out of her mouth so she could eat oats. This time she was getting about a gallon of oats, which was the most feed she'd had now in three days. She finished the feed and ate the grass down. You could tell she was sure hungry, and she'd gotten a new lease on life and a change of disposition.

I rebridled her and rode her back to town. This time I went downtown with her for the first time. I rode her across the square and tied her to a big telephone post down by Hudson's drugstore. I got off her and walked up and down the street and went to a picture show and came back late, about ten o'clock. Then I got on her and rode home and put her in the back of the lot, and this time I gave her a whole block of alfalfa hay. And of course she could get plenty of water.

The next morning it was a bad cold morning; I didn't much want to get out in the weather, but along about that time I did need to keep schooling my mare. So I fixed me up some feed and tied it on my saddle and rode out another direction from town. I found a windbreak behind a little hill in the curve of the road and stopped there and poured the feed out on the grass for the Easter Lily.

I kept up this kind of practice for about thirty days. I got the mare to where she was getting all the feed she needed and had begun to mend, and the skinned places on her were getting real well and the hair was coming back. Her disposition and outlook on life had changed considerably. Her hair was a little rougher and a little longer, because I hadn't been stabling her. The Easter Lily had always associated that nice big stall with feed, water, and hay, and with brushing and currying and petting; a barn was a place where you were looked after and cared for, bragged about and admired. The little ride she'd been used to in the small pasture behind the barn never had been for very long and never had kept her out in the sunshine too long, or away from feed and water, so she hadn't objected to that. Well, I brought her to realize that a barn didn't mean much; it just meant she'd stand outside with a little hay. I had made her realize that any time she was being ridden, somewhere down the road she'd get fed. And that had made her decide that traveling wasn't such a bad thing after all, because the feed was at the end of the road and not back at the barn.

I rode the mare most of the winter, a little off and on, and sometimes made long, hard rides. Her disposition had changed entirely. Her body and legs had hardened, and she was even better looking than she'd been when she was so soft. I'd fed her just most anywhere by then, and in the wagonyard, but I had never made a practice of giving her an undue amount of attention at home. I let her discover that home or barn wasn't just the haven of rest she'd thought it was when she was in Cush Wise's stable at Mineral Wells.

Occasionally, I would learn that Mr. Wise had been inquiring about my mare, and once in a while I'd see somebody from Mineral Wells, and they'd ask me how I was getting along with the Easter Lily. She was a delightful mare to ride, but she didn't have much stock sense. She didn't know how to drag a mule or catch a wild calf, and the fact that she was a gaited mare kept her from having any speed at the run. I really didn't have any great use for her when I was working stock, and sometimes she would go for several days without being ridden.

The winter broke and spring followed, and the grass got green and the mesquite leafed out. It was a nice balmy time of year, not yet quite hot weather. I rode the Easter Lily on special occasions, and everybody did think she was a beautiful mare. She created a lot of comment. People would stop on the sidewalk when we passed and look around and watch her. She had a beautiful way of going. I'd gotten her mane and tail combed and all the dapples back, and she was looking like she did when I first traded for her.

One afternoon I'd been out in the country moving some stock, and was riding Beauty. I came into town late in the afternoon, and when I stopped at the drugstore they told me there had been a lady in there looking for me. That was rather unusual; the ladies, young or old, didn't look for me much. I asked what she looked like, and they told me she was a nice-looking lady with a chauffeur driving her around. They said she had spent some time there that afternoon, but they didn't know whether she'd gone or not. Well, that aroused my curiosity, but it didn't dawn on me that it was the elegant horsewoman from Kentucky. I thought maybe it was somebody who owned some land around there and wanted some stock moved, or wanted to sell some horses or steers or something of the sort. I dismissed it from my mind and started on down to the wagonyard. And sure enough, I met a long black automobile with a beautiful woman in the back seat.

The car stopped, and the woman stuck her head out of the door and asked: "Are you Ben Green?"

I said: "Yes, ma'am."

She said: "I understand that you have my mare."

I said: "No, I don't guess so. I haven't stole any mares lately."

She had a nice bubbling-spring kind of a laugh, and she thought that was funny, and she said: "No, the mare that Mr. Wise sold you."

I said: "Oh, the Easter Lily!" Of course, I'd already

figured that out in my mind.

She said: "Yes. I'm told that you have cured her of her bad habits."

"Yes ma'am," I said, "I think I have, and I'd like to know how she got such a habit."

She said that she hadn't ridden the mare much while she had her in Mineral Wells, the year before, but she'd left her there at the stable and thought possibly Mr. Wise might have spoiled the mare some. And she probably spoiled her too, because she didn't ride her out in the countryside or around town. She'd usually go down and just ride her for a few minutes in that little pasture. Possibly, she said, everybody had contributed to the mare's being ruined, by not realizing that they were doing it.

I said: "Well, I guess she's realized she's cured."

She laughed about that and asked: "Where is she? I'd like to see her."

I told her where my barn was and that I'd come on horseback and she could drive on down there. When I got there she was waiting for me at the front of the barn. I brought the Easter Lily out of the lot at the back and brushed and curried her a little and petted and rubbed and talked to her.

The lady said: "You know, this is a very well-bred mare. I still have her papers."

Along about then I didn't know papers came with horses, and I had never thought to ask about her papers when I bought her.

"I think," the lady said, "that whether you sell her to me or keep her, the mare's papers should be with her. I want you to know in the beginning that I'd like to buy the mare back, but if you don't choose to sell, I'll give you the registration papers; then she may be kept as saddle or broodmare, or be shown in her own right. After all, her breeding does belong to her, and her papers aren't any good to me without the mare. I just felt you should know, in all fairness, that I have come to buy her if you care to sell her, or give you the registration papers if you don't. She was born on Easter morning—that's why I named her Easter Lily."

I didn't let on that I hardly knew what registration papers were, but I thanked her and told her that was nice of her. And I told her that Easter Lily would be better off with her than she would with me. I said that I didn't really need her; I'd enjoyed riding her as a road horse, but other than making a long trip straight down the road I didn't have a whole lot of use for the mare. Since she had been so fair in telling me that she wanted to buy her back, and since I felt the mare would do her more good than she would me, I'd try to sell her to her.

I asked her if she was in Mineral Wells for the summer, and she said she was. I told her that if she'd promise me she'd stable the Easter Lily somewhere besides Mr. Military Oversmart Cush Wise's barn, I'd consider selling the mare back. She thought that was rather funny, but she said she supposed there was some other barn in a place that size where she could keep her mare; and if that would give me any personal satisfaction, and if it was one of the conditions on which she could get the Easter Lily back, she would agree to it.

By this time I had the Easter Lily saddled. The lady had riding clothes on, and she mounted the Easter Lily with the greatest of ease, sat beautifully in the saddle, held the reins in her left hand, and rode off on the Kentucky-bred mare. You could tell that the pair of them belonged together. She was gone maybe thirty minutes and came back in a walk. The mare was just warm, and there was just a little bit of moist hair up and down her neck, but she hadn't broken into a sweat. I had her good and hard, and she wouldn't be subject to sweating and fretting and getting nervous, as she would have when she was soft and fat.

The lady was aware of that too, and she said: "You have her in excellent condition. She'd be a pleasure to ride, since she has so much more stamina than she used to have when I kept her in Mineral Wells last year."

Everything she said was in the vein of fairness and complete understanding of the fact that I owned the mare. Finally, she approached the subject of purchasing her and asked me how much money I felt I was entitled to for having rehabilitated the Easter Lily. That was a new word to me, but I had an idea what it meant because of the way she used it.

So I said: "Well, if you think I've done a good enough job on her, I think I should have $750 for the mare."

She stroked the mare on the neck and walked around her and smiled at me and said: "That wouldn't be too much for the Easter Lily, if you'll deliver her to Mineral Wells."

I thought it best then to tell her how I'd managed to change the mare's mind. I explained the strategy I'd used, feeding the mare somewhere besides the barn, brushing and currying her on the outside, not giving her the idea that a barn was a lap of luxury for fine useless horses to spend a life of idleness in. She thought this was all very odd and unique, and she had never heard of such a thing before. She didn't know that horses thought or realized what their surroundings were, and she appreciated my telling her and giving her these details. She assured me that the Easter Lily wouldn't have the opportunity to take up bad habits again. She gave me her check and thanked me very much and climbed in that long car and drove away.

When the elegant lady from Kentucky said: "That wouldn't be too much," she meant what she said. I have sold her and her friends and family horses through the years. And now, more than thirty-five years after the episode of the Easter Lily, I have an order for a pony from the elegant lady's granddaughter.

Mule Colts

One early fall in the thirties there was a good demand for mule colts, yearlings, and two-year-olds. Most of the fellows that wanted to buy these mules intended to feed them through the winter, and in those days we had a class of mules that was spoken of as "feeder" mules. Farmers would buy these mules, run them on oat fields through the winter, feed them a little grain, and sell them as two- and three-year-olds, depending on the age of the mules, in the coming spring or following fall.

I was in Fort Worth one night, sitting in a café at the Cattleman's Hotel on Exchange Avenue, and got into a conversation with some fellows sitting close to me about young mules being so high compared to some other classes of horse stock.

There was a half-Indian looking character sitting on a stool next to me, that followed me out of the café onto the sidewalk to give me a "real good" piece of information. He said he knew where there was sixty good young mares, and every one of them had a great big mule colt following her, and he knowed I could "shore buy 'em cheap 'cause the fellow was in a tight over some gamblin' debts and needed the money."

After a considerable visit with this character, he sold me on the idea that I ought to go see these mares with mule colts. They were located away out West, on the Pecos. My hook-nosed, high-cheeked, newly made friend said he was busy and couldn't go with me but that he knowed they was there 'cause he was "rite fresh from the Pecos."

The next morning I saddled up a brand new four-cylinder Chevrolet and headed for the Pecos, because it sounded like I could "steal" these mares and their mule colts. I bedded down somewhere on the way for part of the night, but I was driving hard because I was afraid someone else would find them first. I drove into Pecos, stopped at the Bell Garage, and inquired about the man that supposedly owned the mares with mule colts. They told me he lived about forty-five miles northwest of town, on the Carlsbad Road.

I didn't have too much trouble finding the place, and the man was home. I drove up, got out of the car, shook myself, and asked for a drink of water. I will tell you now that water wasn't very good—it was a little salty, a little gippy, and a little sulphury—but if you was dry enough and tough enough you could drink it. I swallowed it without making a face; I knew better than to make fun of a man's country.

We passed the time of day, talked about the weather, and he asked me where I was from. I told him I was a horse and mule buyer from Fort Worth. To this remark the old man brightened up a little and said: "What kind of horses and mules you buy?"

By then I was a pretty smart young trader and replied: "You generally buy the kind of horses and mules the people have got for sale. They don't sell you their good ones."

He smiled and said: "That's pretty good thinking, but I'll tell you a little different case from that. I'll sell you all I've got 'ceptin' two saddle horses."

Then he described his mares and mule colts to me and told how good they were and how young the mares were. He told me frankly that they were all unbroke, which was common in that day. Most everybody could break a mare or mule to ride or work, and that didn't depreciate the price as it does today in this world of softies.

He had a cowboy and a half-grown Mexican boy saddle up the two saddle horses that he didn't want to sell, and go out into a big greasewood pasture and round up these mares and mule colts and throw them up in a corner of the fence. He explained to me that he didn't have a corral that would hold them and that unless I was sure I wanted to buy the bunch of mares and colts there wouldn't be any use driving them to the stock pen, which would be about forty-five miles. We drove out into this big pasture, to a windmill that was down near the only draw running through the pasture. This draw was covered with mesquite trees about as tall as a horse's back and was the only break in the scenery from a greasewood desert.

In about two hours we saw a trail of dust boiling up across the pasture, and here came the mares and their mule colts—sixty head of mares with sixty head of mule colts. The mares were all fat, and he hastened to explain that there had been a good mesquite bean crop and that all the horses in the country were fat, and that the colts were old enough so the mares had about weaned them. These mares were of fair size and good dark colors. The mule colts were almost as big as the mares, with shaggy manes and foretops falling down over their eyes, and, of course, long mule tails that had never been sheared. They were a very uniform bunch of young mules. I could just see how good they would look cut off the mares, with their manes roached and tails sheared.

The mares were snorty and so were the colts, and they kept trying to break out of the corner of the fence. As I tried to walk up closer to them, they made a break for that mesquite thicket and I got a glimpse of them as they ran into the brush.

The owner said that he needed the money for some urgent business, and if I would take them all, he would sell them for $65 a pair, meaning $65 for a mare and a mule colt. Well, I knew that the colts were worth from $60 to $80 and that the mares would be clear profit. We discussed how to get them shipped, and I made a fast trade with him before he backed out. Realizing that it would take two or three days to round them up again and get them out in the public road to drive them to the stock pens, he assured me that he would ship them for me and I could go on back to Fort Worth. Being a trusting young horse trader, that sounded good to me. I paid him and headed my four-cylinder Chevrolet back East.

I had made the trip so fast that I had hardly been missed around the mule barns, but I had made such a good trade that I couldn't help but tell some of my close friends about my mule colts that would be in town in a few days.

One morning I went down to the horse and mule barn, and my mares and mule colts had been unloaded. My friend in the West had separated them and shipped them, and in those good, high, close pens, I got a real good look at my mares. They were just about as they had appeared in the corner of the fence, weighing from nine hundred to a thousand pounds, and of decent quality. However, I couldn't help but notice that none of the mares were suffering from the colts not having sucked, and I didn't hear from the next pen any colts braying for their mammies.

As I looked over the fence at my mules I had to face the sad realization that these mule colts had been colts about three to six years before this, far south of the Rio Grande River, and were the smallest sort of little fat Mexican mules. The rancher west of the Pecos River had done a real good job of keeping them mixed up with those mares, and had let them break loose and get away into that mesquite thicket just before I could get close enough to them to realize their true age and identity.

These cute little Mexican mules were next to worthless on the market, and the mares sold for a little more than half of what they all cost. I learned in later years that the "friend" in Fort Worth who gave me that "real good piece of information" also had an interest in the mares and mules!

Mine Mules

That same winter I was staying in town more than common, and the main reason for it was that I had my hook hung on that bunch of cute little fat Mexican mules.

These nice little, fat, young, hard-twisted, ill-tempered, unbroke Mexican mules were getting in bed with me, so to speak, because they were worth about $17 a head; I had been feeding them about two months, and I had a little more money than that in them to start with, not counting the feed bill. I had tried all the tricks that I

knew to get these little mules sold, and I had gone to my
old mule-trading friends, and none of them knew where
you could ship these little five-hundred-pound mules and
get them sold for anything or something, much less a
profit. I had given up on the idea of a profit, but I thought
my banker would have greater esteem for me as a horse
trader if I could get the money back out of them, and I
was trying awfully hard.

I had taken so much hurrahing about my little mules,
and about them being sold to me for colts, that it was
almost unpleasant to live over on the north side of Fort
Worth around the mule barns and stockyards. It had
ceased to be too funny since those little mules ate grain
twice a day and hay all night, and were working hard to
run up the overhead. I was staying over at the Texas
Hotel in big town Fort Worth, where there were fewer
mule men, and I was enjoying a reasonable amount of
relief from being hurrahed. However, I was more or less
ill at ease and out of place in that great big hotel.

I was sitting in the lobby, bogged down in one of
those big plush chairs with my big hat pulled way down
over my face to where I was just peeping out from under
the brim, and had my boot crossed over my knee so everybody could for sure tell I was from way out West. I was
sitting there watching the people, when here came an
unmistakable old Southern gentleman. He was wearing an
old Kentucky black hat, raw-edged with a wide band on
it and pushed back off of his face, which was proof to me
that he hadn't faced much sunshine and was living in the
shade or he would have had that hat pulled down over his
eyes. He was wearing a double-breasted blue serge suit
that had been his Sunday suit for a good fifteen years, and

he had on a soft-toed pair of black shoes. He walked up in the lobby and stood looking into the dining room; then he'd look back across the lobby and I could tell for sure that he was off of his home range and wasn't too sure about where to feed and water. Having a fair idea how he felt, I got up and stretched and moseyed up close to him to get acquainted, because I knew I looked country enough that he would ask me whatever it was that he was trying to find out. He turned around and looked at me a few minutes, and I turned just enough to catch him out of the corner of my eye and said: "Howdy."

In a soft, lonesome Southern drawl he replied: "How do yuh do, suh," and moved over a step closer.

We talked a minute or two about the weather and Fort Worth, and he mentioned that he would like to have something to eat, that he had just come in off a long trip and got a room in the hotel, but he didn't know whether that dining room was the proper place to eat or not. Well, it suddenly occurred to me that the old man might not want to spend as much money as it cost to wipe your chin on the fine linen napkins in that dining room, so I told him I hadn't had a chance to eat either and that I knew a good place to get lots of grub and not too many frills for a fair price. He said: "Well suh, I'd be obliged if yuh'd show me around some, 'cause I 'spec I'm goin' to be here for several days, and I needs to know where to get somethin' to eat." I told my Southern friend that it wasn't far and we could just step out the side door here and walk and get a bit of supper.

I knew of a family-style eating place where you just sat down to the table and "pitch 'til you win" that was run by some good old women. That night they had everything on the table that looked like it was good to eat, and my Southern colonel (I was by that time calling him Colonel) made himself right at home and ate way more than my money's worth. When he got up and left the table, and I had paid the boardinghouse woman, you could tell that he was well pleased with the feed ground and was liking my company pretty good.

When we stepped out on the street it was good dark, and a norther had struck which made it a little uncomfortable; so the Colonel and I hit a decent sort of a fox trot back to the hotel lobby. I looked around, and there wasn't many people in the lobby, and it was going to be a long black night, so I suggested to the Colonel that we set a spell before going to bed, and that was the master stroke. The conversation led off to his business and mine, and he confided to me that he had come to Fort Worth to buy some small mining mules to ship back to his native West Virginia. I tried not to show any excitement or pleasure in his statement, but I said to myself that those cute little fat Mexican mules were about to get introduced to the hardships of the life of a mining mule. The Colonel told me that he hesitated to buy mules at the auction and that he had gotten to town two or three days ahead of the auction day, hoping that he could buy mules without having to go into that crooked old auction and bid against them "professional" horse traders. Well I didn't want to booger the old man, so I worked up slow and easy to telling him that I had some little mules. I first asked him how many of these little mules he needed, and he said that they actually needed about a hundred in West Virginia but that he had no hopes of buying that many in one place. I finally told him that I had sixty of these little

mules that were fat and young and not too big, as he had
cautioned me that he had to have a small mule. I told him
that these little mules were unbroke but sound and in
good flesh and would stand shipping a long way. I explained to him that I didn't like auctions either, and I had
these little mules in some pens way back behind the auction barn, and I had been dreading the thought of letting
them professional horse and mule traders steal them from
me.

The Colonel was right interested in the mules and
wanted to see them first thing the next morning. I told
him that I'd meet him for breakfast, and he said that he
got up early and would see me about daylight. He
stretched and moved around the edge of his chair and
finally got off toward the elevator, and I told him good
night and that I'd see him in the morning.

He didn't know how bad off I was to sell these little
mules, nor how little I slept that night, and how easy it
was for me to be up at daylight. I was standing in the hotel
lobby when he got off the elevator the next morning,
about 5:30. It wasn't nearly daylight, but I was afraid that
he might get down to the lobby or even to the stockyards,
and that he might get caught by one of those "professional" mule dealers.

We stopped on the way out to the stockyards and ate
breakfast. Then we were on the old streetcar going out to
the stockyards, and I reached up and rang the bell, and
we got off about three blocks before we reached Exchange Avenue. I told him I knew a short cut over to
the pens and we wouldn't have to go through the auction
barn, and he and I could look at the little mules without
anybody being any the wiser.

We walked down a back alley and across the creek
and crawled over the fence into the mule pen. The Colonel
walked around among the mules a few minutes, and kind
of waved the tail of his overcoat at them and made them
jump and shy. It was still pretty cold and just daylight,
and the mules were blowing a little fog out of their noses,
and he turned to me and said: "Ben muh boy, these are
just what I want. Now how much will yuh have to have
fo' 'em?"

It had developed in our conversation that he was buying these mules for himself and some other mine operators,
so I thought I should play it real honest with him. So I
said: "Colonel, there's no use in me trying to rob you and
your other miner friends, and I don't believe that you'd
try to steal these mules from me. So why don't you tell
me all that you can give for them per head, and represent
your own interest and be fair to the other fellows at home
that you're buying these mules for. If I can stand it at all
I'll sell them to you, and you and I won't have any hard
feelings if I can't take the price. That way there won't
be any bidding and dickering and hard words among
friends."

He told me he thought that was the fairest way to
trade and that he was going to give me every dollar that
those little mules were worth in "West Virginy," less
what the freight would be; and he asked me if I knew
what the freight would be per head by carload on these
mules. I told him that the freight would be about $25 per
head and if it was more than that I'd pay the difference.

He studied a few minutes, walked around the mules,
and I was insisting that he cut out anything that didn't
suit him, and he told me they all suited him. He looked at

them a few more times, and I was about to lose my breath thinking he might not ever tell me what they were worth in "West Virginy." He finally turned, spit off into the ground, and said: "Ben muh boy, these mules are worth $100 apiece in West Virginy, and that'd amount to $75 apiece here, and that's all I can give yuh for 'em. If yuh can take it, we'll go call the folks back home and see if the deal is all right with 'em, befo' I give yuh a draft fo' the mules."

I stood real quiet a few minutes trying to keep from shouting, and when I finally had control of myself I said: "I guess it's worth something to sell them all in one bunch, and I feel like you're being fair, so I'm going to sell them to you."

For fear that somebody else might see him, we walked back up the alley to North Main Street and I hailed a cab instead of waiting for the streetcar. We went up into my room at the hotel, and in those days it took a long time to get a long-distance call back to West Virginia, and it seemed like an awfully long time. He finally talked, and he painted a glowing picture of these little mules and what a good man had them and he wasn't having to buy them through the auction, and they decided to close the deal.

He hung up the phone and we went to his room, and he got out a long checkbook and wrote me a check for the mules. Then I called the railroad office and ordered a forty-foot car to ship the mules in that day (the trick in shipping mules was that there were very few forty-foot cars and the railroad would have to furnish you two thirty-six-foot cars at the same price). I found that the mules couldn't be loaded until the next morning, and I was dying to get over to the bank with that check; so I told him I would go out and see about the car and what time we could load them, and that he could stay around the hotel and rest up a little. I said I would be back in time for us to go to dinner, and that suited him fine. He immediately pulled off his soft black shoes, took off his coat and necktie, and was lying down on the bed when I left.

I hurried over to the bank, and they wired on the check, and it was good as gold. I warned my banker not to tell a soul about my Colonel from West Virginia until I got those little mules loaded.

I entertained the Colonel the rest of the day, and that night I took him to the old Majestic Theater to see a stage show which he thoroughly enjoyed.

We loaded the mules the next morning. Then I took the Colonel to the train, told him good-bye and, as the train whistled and left town, went by the bank and got some spendin' money. Then I set out to the stockyards to tell my dumb, "professional" horse-trading friends that were handling big mules the going price of little mules.

When Big
Horses Went
Out of Style
— Almost

The spring movement of big steers to the Osage
grass country of Oklahoma and Kansas was
getting into swing. Every year, big
steers were wintered in Texas,
then moved north for
summer pasture.

Somebody went with these cattle to take care of them while they grazed the bluestem country. Cow men would lease these big pastures that didn't have any improvement on 'em other than grass and water and some kind of fence —and some cowboy would go along with the steers to take care of them through the summer and ship them out fat in the fall.

This year, hands were kind of scarce—the kind that would leave home and go to the bluestem to camp out in the pasture with a bunch of steers—and a couple of steer men out of Fort Worth made me a proposition to go up and spend the summer with their cattle. Well, I'd had a good winter; it was going to be a long hot summer in Texas; and I just decided I needed to see Kansas.

We shipped out eight hundred head of steers and a few over in the early part of May. It was still a little chilly when we unloaded them off the railroad in Kansas, but the grass had started and the bluestem was green, and it looked like it would be a good summer.

Around this pasture we had a few neighbors that were in the farming business; they had bad fences and worse dispositions. But outside of a little farmer trouble that goes with any cow operation where them clodhoppers join your pasture, the summer was mostly peaceful and not much work. We had some good rains and the cattle got fat. I had a good camp close to a windmill under an old shed—plenty of water, enough wood to cook with, and not too far from a little country town where a man could lope in and get some conversation, store-bought grub, and find out what was going on in the rest of the world.

In the same stock cars with these steers, I shipped up

some good saddle horses that belonged to me to ride during the summer. Of course they got fat and did good through the summer, and I didn't ride them too hard. When we shipped the cattle out in the fall, it wasn't to my liking to get rid of these good horses and come back to Texas afoot. It would be too expensive to have a boxcar or a stock car on the railroad to haul five head of horses, and trucks didn't haul cattle and horses like they do now.

We shipped our cattle out in the fall after they were fat; I drew my summer wages and the world looked pretty good; it wasn't too bad a-weather yet, and I just decided I would start out for Texas, using my horses to ride and to pack my camp. I had a packsaddle to carry my bedroll and stuff on, and I just thought I'd ride along and change about on my horses and get home before winter set in—with plenty of time to get into some kind of a stock deal at home for the winter.

These infernal combustion machines called tractors had begun to get kind of plentiful in the plains country and open country in Kansas and Oklahoma. Work stock had gotten cheap. Great big broad-hipped, good kind of sound, beautiful-headed, heavy-bodied Percheron and other draft-type horses weren't much in demand. Every tractor trader had a penful of them somewhere around the edge of every little town, and they were hard to sell. There weren't too many mules mixed up with them in that country, and very few saddle horses were ever traded in on a tractor. I camped along the way, and I kept noticing that every town I'd come through with my saddle horses, there was an awful lot of good draft horses around these traders' pens and around these farm implement warehouses.

These were kind of a new breed of people to me. In my country, when I was growing up, farm implements was a sideline to a general hardware store—not a major business. But after tractors got started in the country, they got to be all the vogue. Implement dealers and automobile dealers thought they were just as good as any horse trader. I never did share their opinion about that, but I might have been wrong. There got to be more implement dealers and less horse traders as time went on.

I rode into Liberal, Kansas, late in the afternoon, and found a trade yard with an empty lot and plenty of feed and water. It was next to a lot where one of those implement dealers was stacking in draft-type horses and a few mules. I couldn't help but notice there was a lot of nice dapple-gray horses—some a little lighter, showing a little more age, but a few young mares were just dark iron grays—good feet and sound legs on them, and good deep bodies. Most of them would weigh about sixteen hundred pounds apiece. Generally speaking, in work horses blacks and grays were mostly Percheron breeding. (Sorrels and red roans were usually from Belgian breeding.) These horses were gentle and well broke and as nice as any man had ever seen.

I just couldn't stand the thought of riding by all these good horses and not taking some of them home with me. I thought surely there would be somebody in Texas that would like to have some good work horses, and the more I thought about the deal, the better I liked these horses. I decided I'd gather me a bunch and bring them back home with me to trade on through the winter.

It was pretty late in the afternoon, and I had my

horses put away and fed and watered. I took my little roll off the back of my saddle and went up to the country hotel, registered in, and got a room in the house for the night. I took a bath and shook myself, put on a clean shirt, took my britches out of my boot tops, and went down to supper. This supper table was one of those big long tables in the middle of a big old dining room. Two or three good women were a-going around waiting on the table, and you just sat yourself down and pitched 'til you win. There was lots of grub on the table, and a few farmers and a few business men and a few other working people from town were eating there that night. I just casual-like brought up the conversation about all these nice big horses.

I said to the bunch at supper that surely the people were making a mistake. These tractors couldn't be here to stay. They're just a passing fancy. Some morning the folks were going to wake up and be out of work stock, and wouldn't be able to make a living with these put-put machines a-trying to work the soil. Didn't seem like there was anybody agreed with my opinion much. Some of them laughed a little bit, but there wasn't none of them stopped putting grub in their mouths to give me any back-talk: until an old boy sitting down the table from me—I didn't think he looked too bright, and he wasn't a sure-enough Westerner, he'd been shipped in from somewhere it seemed to me—he said: "Why don't you buy some of these horses and take them back to Texas with you, so the people won't get out of work stock?"

I told him that looked like a pretty good proposition and the next morning I might try my hand at owning some work stock.

He looked up real wise and said: "That's my pen down there, next to where you turned your horses tonight. In the morning I'll be glad to give you a look for free. Maybe you'll find something you'll buy."

I got down to the lot next morning 'way before he did. I went through his stock and looked at their mouths to see about what ages they were, looked at their feet and legs, lined them up for blemishes and scars, and decided there were about fifteen or sixteen head that I wouldn't mind driving in front of me on down to Texas. I just knew I'd find somebody would think more of them than people did in that country. After I had pretty well made up my mind what I'd try to buy and was ready to listen to what he would take for them, I got out of the pen and walked off catty-cornered across the street about a hundred yards to a little country café—where I could see the trading pens—and ordered me a batch of breakfast.

I ate kinda slow and looked out the window. About the time I finished my grub, I saw him a-coming to the pens. I let him catch his horses, brush and curry them, and throw out some bundled feed. He stood around, and I'd see him look back over the fence toward the hotel and back toward town. I could tell he was thinking I had give him the cold shoulder and wouldn't show up. I noticed, too, that he hadn't caught the kind of horses that I wanted to buy. He was a-brushin' and a-curryin' the wrong end of his bunch, so far as I was concerned. It looked to me like he was getting ready to sell me the tailings and him keep the best ones.

I also noticed that sitting around were several good wagons with broad tires, and in good shape. There were wagonloads of good leather harness with heavy tugs, good jumbo collars, and brass knobs hames. You could tell that, so far as that open country was concerned, work horses and good harness were going out of style.

I watched him through the window of the café till it looked like he was going to give me out, then I started moseying up the street. I saw that he had caught me out of the corner of his eye—he went to dusting his hands and dusting his britches and trying to get that horsehair off him like he thought it wasn't clean. That's the way with those fellows in the implement business. They didn't mind getting axle grease or oil on them. That was fine, that was a characteristic of the trade; but some sure enough good horsehair they seemed to think would contaminate them.

I walked in the front gate of the trade grounds and just kinda glanced over his way and waved at him, and went over to where my horses were. I had already fed them when I was there the first time, and they had finished eating. I went in and caught my best horse to brush and curry him. I picked his feet up and cleaned them out with my pocketknife and acted like I was getting ready to saddle up and start out of town.

He came moseying over to my fence and said: "I thought you were going to try to buy some work stock this morning to take back to Texas with you?"

I told him I wasn't plum out of the notion, but looked like as plentiful as they were, I could buy them farther down the road and closer to home, and wouldn't have so far to drive them.

He said he didn't think there was any use of that, when he had a bunch right there that would sure be good for me to take home, and he would sell them to me to where they would make money.

I said: "Well, maybe I'd better take a look at your stock. You might have some in there that might do to drive home for a profit." I went to asking him what he wanted for his horses.

He pointed out a good team of brown horses that was about half big enough, a little age on them and a little moss around the ears. He said it was a good farmer's team, and he would take $100 for both of them.

I thought I would lead him on. I said: "That ain't much money. What else you got to show me?"

Well, he picked on another pair. They weren't exactly mates. One was kind of a slim-jim, roman-nosed horse with a big rough ear and a straight shoulder, coarse across the hips, and a little thick in the hocks—not exactly unsound, but far from being an ideal horse. The mate was a little squatty and a little short, not gaited to the other horse. He might have swapped for them together, but they didn't belong together—of course a tractor man wouldn't know that. He said he would take $125 for that pair.

I said: "Well, I wouldn't be too interested in them, but keep a-talking." I was still waiting for him to pick out a good horse.

He never did show me one except those he had been brushing and currying before I got there while I was watching him out the café window. He priced another odd horse or two by themselves for $60 to $85. I said to him: "I guess, then, that you are figuring these horses at about $60 a round."

He said, "No, but if a man would take a bunch of them, they ought to be worth around $75 a round."

I whittled and looked off over the fence and said: "Oh, there's plenty more horses between here and Texas. I don't believe I'll try to do no business with you. I guess I'd better pack up my riggin' and get on down the road. It's getting fall of the year, and it might be winter afore I get home, at the rate I'm going."

He came back with the idea that I never had said which horses I wanted, but if I would pick out some, he would make me a price on them.

I told him I guessed I'd pick out about ten head at $50 a head. I threw in the fact that I never had farmed much, and I didn't know much about farm horses, and that my picking might not hurt his bunch very much.

He said that was too cheap, and he didn't feel like he could do much business on $50 a head, but that he would take $65 for some. He would pick half of them, and I would pick half of them.

Well, I related to him that that didn't suit me too good, because I didn't like for another man to do my picking when he was using my money. Of course, I was trying to get a price per head, and then I was going to pick these good deep-gray mares, and even some of those that were nearly white, and a pair of black horses that was in the pen that sure were good'uns, and a light sorrel pair that had flax manes and tails.

We whittled up two or three planks on the fence between us. Finally, he said he would take $75 a head and let me pick whatever I wanted. I thought about that for a while, kicked my toe around in the manure, went back over toward my horses, and told him I guessed we couldn't do business.

He said he guessed that was the best he could do; then

he started back up to a tin shed where he had all of those put-put tractors and stuff. It looked like the day's work was over.

I walked back up to the main part of town, stayed a little while, and came back down where my horses were. I passed this implement shed of his afoot, but I didn't look off or give him no truck. I just kept a-heading for the trade yard like a dry steer that had smelled water. I didn't much more than get to the gate than I saw him come out from under that shed just like he was going to tree me. He was stepping pretty lively.

By the time he got to the pens, I had walked inside my pen and was shaking out a bunch of ropes and halters and getting ready to catch my horses. He came up and said he believed that I ought to buy some of his horses at $75 a head.

I studied about it for a while and told him that they might be worth it to him, but that they wouldn't be worth it to me. We visited on a bit without either one of us showing the other one a great deal of courtesy. Finally, I told him I'd seen he had lots of harness there that would fit these horses—that he couldn't eat and he couldn't swap off—and it wouldn't go on one of those tractors. If I could get a set of harness for every horse, and one of those good wagons to hook a team to so I could carry some feed and some rigging, then I guessed I would give $75 a round for sixteen head.

I saw this made him awful nervous. He turned around a time or two and reset his hat on his head a couple of times. You could tell that I'd caused his dandruff to begin to itch a little bit. He opened his pocketknife and forgot what he was going to do with it, closed it back up and put it in his pocket. Finally, he said he couldn't use all that harness—just like I said—and it didn't fit any of his tractors. If he let the horses go, he wouldn't need the harness—so he believed he would trade with me.

I told him it looked like I was cheated again. That's what I got for popping off when I was away from home in a foreign country, but I guess I'd just as well go to picking out my horses and getting the harness that fit them.

Now that I had a price of $150 a team with harness to fit and a wagon to hook one team to, I decided I would buy some stock. I told him to hold the gate between the two pens, and I'd cut out what I wanted. He went to pointing out which ones were good and giving me the history on them—who had worked them and how they'd never been hurt and one thing and another. Every time he would point at one of them, I would look off. Now and then I would tell him to let a certain one through the gate—or I would walk up and catch one by the mane and lead him through or drive him through. In a few minutes I had sixteen head of the best horses that ever walked. They ranged from three-year-olds to ten-year-olds, and there was a set of harness over there in those wagons to fit every horse I had picked out.

I sure had left him a bunch of culls. He began to get pretty sick and told me that he couldn't let me have that many, that I was a-robbin' him, that he didn't know that I was going to pick this pair and that pair, and so on. And he went to telling me how much trade on a tractor he'd allowed old man So-and-so for that team. I wasn't interested in his troubles. I told him I would either take sixteen head of horses with all the harness and one good wagon, or I would turn them all back and let them mix up with the snides—for him to just make up his mind. After all, he had been telling me how good all that bunch was that I was letting him keep, and I supposed he had rather have them. I explained to him that I felt like he was so attached to them that he wouldn't mind keeping them. These others that I was cutting out, he hadn't bothered to mention. I just supposed he didn't care much about them.

He paid me a pretty big compliment along about then. He said he believed I was a better horseman than I looked like I was. And just a kid, too. I had cheated him, but he needed to get rid of some stock; so he was going to sell them to me, he said, and go on back up to the implement shed and sell a man a tractor.

It took me two or three hours to rig up and fit out that harness and get the right collars on the right horses, with good leather lines and tugs, to where I wouldn't be ashamed to show this stock after I got back to Texas. I had eight teams of horses all matched and standing out there, and all the harness that fit them. I picked out a pair of good old gray horses and hooked them to one of the best wagons; it had full sideboards and the paint was still new on them. The wheels were tight, and the tongue hadn't been broke. I threw my saddle and my pack and all my stuff in the wagon.

In the meantime, while I was picking out these horses and fitting this harness to them, there was a misplaced cowboy came up and saw what I was doing. He helped me and furnished some conversation and told about being out there working on the farms after being a cowboy all his life. His boots were run-over and patched, his hat was worn out in front and water could leak in at the top, and you could tell that farming hadn't been too good to him. I asked him if he wanted a job helping me get out of town with my stock. He said he would be glad to help me as far as I wanted to go.

I felt like this would be a pretty good deal if I kept him on two or three days, until I got all my horses road-broke to where they would follow the wagon. He could help keep them out of the fences until I found out all about them; then I could get along with them by myself. He said he would be glad to get $3 a day, but he would have to go down to his boardinghouse and check out—and he wondered if I could let him have $10 so he could leave town. The boardinghouse wasn't very far, the town wasn't very big, and he was a pretty good kind of a fellow. I didn't think he would run off with that $10, so I let him have it.

He came back in about thirty minutes with a tin suitcase loaded up with his life's belongings, a pair of old spurs on his boots—old-timey kind of loose-rowel spurs that wouldn't cut a horse—and said he was ready to change his range. I told him to get in and shake the lines and get used to the rig. I was going up to the sheet-iron shed to pay the man for his stock, and we'd be on our way.

I had the money on me, and I paid the man in United States cash. He seemed awful glad to get it, but at the same time he kept whining and complaining about how I had cheated him. I told him if he really felt that way, it looked like he would change his way of making a living.

We started out of town about one o'clock. We drove down to a crossroads about eight or ten miles out of Liberal. Where the roads forked, there was a wide place where the fences didn't come together and there was lots of tall grass. Our stock had watered good before we started out, so we pulled out to the side and made camp for the night. I'd bought a wagon sheet and some bows up at the hardware store, so we could cover the wagon in case the weather got bad.

This old misplaced cowboy that I had picked up wasn't too bad a fellow. He'd just got misled to working on those farms. He was a good teamster, and he knew how to stake out horses. He tied the mates out together where they wouldn't be nickering for each other in the night. He was good to help make camp, and we just gathered up wood and built a nice enough fire to cook supper —and sure enough, he turned out to be a real good cook. In a few days we passed through Perryman, Oklahoma, and stocked up on pots, Dutch ovens, and stuff. That old boy could make sourdough biscuits that would raise the lid off a Dutch oven.

That little strip of Oklahoma that separates Kansas and Texas isn't very wide, and we were in Texas in a few days. These horses were all sound and good travelers. I rode along and he drove the wagon; then we would take time about and let him feel a horse between his legs. It looked like that was doing him more good than the money he was going to be paid for the trip.

It was nice kind of cool fall weather when we rode in close to Canadian, Texas, early one afternoon, and stopped by the river out north of town to make camp. I rode in to town to see if there was any conversation around about the horse business—and if anybody might be interested in some good big draft horses. I visited around Canadian in the local cafés and up and down the street. I saw cowboys loading a bunch of cattle at the stockyards, so I went down by there and talked a while. Didn't arouse any interest in my horses. Nobody seemed to want to farm, and if they did—they wanted to do it with tractors.

Anyhow, it wasn't very popular conversation, so I came back to camp pretty late in the afternoon, and my old horse-wrangling friend had made a big pot of stew. This was sure good cowboy stew. I ate a batch of it and went to bed and didn't let the horse market bear on my mind too much.

For the next few days we were passing through farming country, headed south, and I began to inquire around if anybody would want to buy some good big horses. I began to build my sales talk up pretty good, because every time I brought it up, anybody I was talking to had three or four good reasons why they didn't want a great big horse. Some of them would tell me they ate too much. The next ones would tell me they didn't need that big a horse to work in sandy land. Then the thing that was always a thorn in my side—they were constantly telling me that they thought maybe the country was going to tractors. None of this increased my feeling for the farming industry. I was proud of my big horses and the good harness and the trade that I had made. I knew my horses should bring a lot of money, but I was having a hard time finding anybody else that thought so.

We didn't try to travel too fast. We grazed along the road and our horses stayed in good shape. We fed them a little grain at night. When we would come through a town and find a feed store, we'd buy a few sacks of oats and maybe a few bales of hay—just for the horses that we were going to keep up for night horses.

In about ten days we got down to Childress, Texas.

By now I had begun to try hard to sell some horses. I had even gotten to where I would suggest if they had something to trade . . . but nobody wanted to talk to me very long. They would just kinda brush me off, or tell me they had plenty of horses, or say they weren't going to buy any more horses—they were going to buy a tractor. I began to worry a little bit about my horses. In fact. once in a while I'd wake up at night. In cowboy conversation: "They was gittin' on my piller with me." I'd had these horses two weeks—nearly three weeks—and hadn't sold one. It looked to me like people didn't realize what a good proposition it was to have a big draft horse.

We made camp on the outskirts of Childress. I was going to circulate around the next morning and see if I couldn't find somebody that needed some big stout work horses. In the meantime, I'd nicknamed my traveling partner "Cookie," and we weren't having a bad trip. He was such a good cook, and the horses followed the wagon good, and the weather was nice and fallish. But we weren't having any business, and this began to get on my mind.

I saddled up a good horse the next morning and rode up into town, around the edges and down the square. I saw four or five pens of horses and mules that farm implement and tractor dealers had been accumulating in trade for those noise-making, iron-wheeled machines. I rode back to camp to take on a batch of chuck and ponder my next move.

Cookie was a nice kind of man who didn't burden you with his troubles, and he didn't have much to say. But that afternoon he said that if I was going to stay around the wagon and look after the stock, he believed he would mosey up town and get a haircut and visit a little while—

see what the town was like. Well, he had been awful good help, and I didn't see why he shouldn't go up and look this town over and maybe daub a little red paint on it somewhere. It would have been all right with me if he had, but he came back about four o'clock in the afternoon. His conversation had brightened up considerably, and he had gotten a fresh haircut and a shave and bought a new shirt.

He told me he had been in a place to eat somebody else's grub—a nice little chile and stew and short-order place, he said. It was just off the edge of the square, and the farmers kinda hung out there along with the working people and the cotton pickers. He had got into conversation with the man that owned the place. This fellow had a hankering to get out of the chile-joint business and had bought a little piece of land out in the edge of town. He saw that my friend Cookie might be a prospect, so he set out to sell him this café. Well, Cookie was looking for a place to squat. He wanted to settle down some good place to make the winter, and running that good café sounded like an awful easy thing to him. It was a way to make money and not have to work too hard for a living. There was a little batching quarters in the back of the café where he could sleep.

He came back to the wagon telling me all of this, and I was waiting for him to tell me how much it cost, but he didn't get to that. Directly I said, "Well Cookie, why didn't you buy the joint?"

He said: "I didn't have any way to pay for the café— but I shore b'lieve I could make a go of it."

It kind of dawned on me that this might be the place to start a man who wanted to farm with a team of horses; so I told Cookie to go back the next morning and see if he could swap a team of horses for that café. I would just put him in the chile business.

Well, Cookie got the night's dishes done up and the fire chunked up, and reached over and got his jacket and put it on, and said: "I b'lieve I'll go back up there and talk to that bird tonight."

He took off in a storm, and he came back a little after bedtime—but he couldn't lie down and go to sleep. He chunked up the fire again, cleared up his throat and coughed around, and lit a cigarette. I knew I was going to have to get up and listen to him. I rolled out of my bedroll and pulled on my boots—moved over by the fire and said: "Well, let's get it off your mind so we can get a little rest."

Cookie said he had sat around and watched business— and that old boy was doing pretty good, according to the way Cookie saw it. He finally got around to talking to him about buying him out. Seems this fellow was a country boy at heart, and he wanted to sell out pretty bad. He was tired of waiting on people, and he didn't much like the café business. Cookie had got him to make a price to him —$300 for the whole café.

I asked: "Did you offer to swap him a pair of horses?"

"No," he answered, "I'm not much of a trader. I thought we'd just wait till morning and go by there, and you could do the tradin' with him. If you'd trade with him for me," he said, "you could be full pardners with me till I got you paid back, and then I'd pay you for the horses and have the place to myself—if that'd be all right with you."

Well, that was all right with me because I never had any aspirations to fry hamburgers all day. So we went to bed. Cookie I don't guess slept very much, but it didn't bother me a whole lot. I rolled back up in my warm bed-roll and waited for sunrise.

We got our camp broke up and our horses rigged up and hitched, and drove out. We had our horses all tied to-gether and tied to the wagon, going into town. We didn't want them running loose up and down the streets. We pulled up in front of, and across the street from, this little café that Cookie had on his mind, stopped our horses, tied up our lines, and went across the street to the eating joint.

The old boy was just opening up. He had the fire going and was ready to start business. We ordered break-fast. Didn't anybody come in for a little while, and we had quite a talk with him. I told him that Cookie had told me that he wanted to sell out and go back to the farm. I told him the first thing he would need on a farm was a good team of big, stout horses and a good set of harness, and that I had plenty of horses out there in front. We'd pick him out a good team and sell them to him for $450. We'd take the café in on the trade.

I saw Cookie turn a little pale, but the café fellow didn't flinch too much. He looked across the street at our teams, and he commented that we sure had some good horses. I could tell right off that he had been so busy fry-ing hamburgers and stirring stew that he hadn't heard about those tractors. It looked like we might do some business.

We finished eating our breakfast and he rolled his apron up. He stepped out across the street and walked around our teams and looked and looked and talked and talked. He picked out a pair that kinda suited him. They weren't the best and they weren't the worst we had, but he sure bragged on them. He was a country boy at heart, and he just thought how wonderful it would be to have a team of horses like this out there on this piece of land he owned, out on the edge of town.

I had begun to wonder if he had enough land to raise enough feed to fill that pair of horses—whether he made a living at it or not. But that wasn't any of my business, so I didn't bring it up. Somebody went in the café, but he just glanced over that way and never did quit talking. He said that he couldn't afford to give $150 boot between the team of horses with a set of harness and his café—but he went on to tell how good a business he had going.

I told him I never had swapped a team of horses for a bunch of chile bowls and a stove, but that if he would give some boot, I would try to trade with him. Cookie never had opened his mouth. Maybe he thought I was trying to drive too hard a bargain and that there wasn't a chance.

I went on to ask him if he owed any bills. He said no, that he paid for his groceries and did his cooking himself. The rent for the building was $12 a month, but that was paid up for the rest of the month—which wasn't but another week or ten days. It seemed like his business was in order. Finally, he said that he would give the café even— for the team he had picked out with the harness that was on them.

I looked over and saw that Cookie was getting a little weak and had to lean against the wagon wheel and look off in the other direction. Maybe he thought we had it done—but I told this café operator that this sounded like a pretty good proposition for Cookie, but it wasn't much for me. I asked how much cash was in the cashbox.

"Enough," he said, "to make change with—probably about twenty dollars."

I told him if he would just hand Cookie the keys and leave the cash in the cashbox, he could go in there and get his hat and his coat, along with whatever personal belongings he had there in that back room. I would hitch that team of horses to the post there, right in front of the café. He could drive them home.

He smiled a big smile and said: "Well, I shore am glad to git that done. I just been afraid you wasn't gonna trade with me."

I looked over at Cookie, and he was all smiles. When we walked back into the café, two customers were sitting at the counter. They both seemed to know this ex-café operator, and they said: "Joe, where you been? You can't make a living out there looking at them stock."

Joe said: "You just think I can't. I've got a team of horses hitched to that post out there in front. You'd better give your orders to the new proprietor." And he waved his hand toward Cookie.

Cookie threw his hat under the counter, reached over and washed his hands under the hydrant, and said: "Gentlemen, whatcha have?"

Cookie was a man that fate predestined to be born of lowly station. Mother Nature had not laid a kindly hand on him to give his stature or his features a pleasing appearance. Dame Fortune had never dealt him a winning hand in this life's game. But for all this, Cookie was glad to be alive and have any kind of a chance at survival. He stood in the presence of men without bitterness or complaint of his lot, said nothing unkind of his fellow man, and never abused a dumb animal. This breed of man would do for a friend when the trail was rough. You could bet that he would pay back favor or money—and he did, many times over. I was always glad I swapped that team of horses for that bunch of chile bowls and that cookstove.

Well, I bid Cookie adieu and started on south with my stock. I drove my wagon and let my saddle horse follow behind. These horses were all handling nice, and they weren't any trouble for one man to get along with on the road.

In a few days I made camp out of Aspermont, on the bank of the Brazos River, about ten or twelve miles down from the Double Mountain fork. It was getting on late in the afternoon, and there was a blizzard blowing up. Looked like it was going to be a rough night. The road ran north and south, and on the east side of the road there were some high, rough, cedar-brake hills. I made my camp on the south side of these hills—on a bluff overlooking the river, close enough to the road that I could see it and the bridge.

I got my horses back up in this cedar brake, tied and fed and fixed for the night, and I got my wagon sheet up on the bows. I was in behind a hill and out of the north wind, but this blizzard was coming down pretty bad. I had a few bales of hay left after I fed, and I stacked this hay on the north side of the wagon bed and made my roll down on the south side of the wagon bed—trying to get it as warm and tight as I could. I had a good bedroll with a cowboy's tarp on the outside of it, plenty of Navajo blankets to put around my feet, and plenty of other blankets to cover up with. I wasn't counting on being uncom-

fortable during the night, but I just wanted to get fixed
for it.

There was plenty of dead cedar and some live oak.
I got off away from the wagon about twenty feet, and
built me a big fire and rounded it up good. I let it burn
a while and get down to coals; it was just about dark when
I started cooking me some supper.

From my camp on the bluff, you could look up the
river and see the bridge and see the road on both sides of
the bridge. This was a new road they were building, and
it was kinda muddy. There had been a rain a few days
before, and on both ends of this nice bridge were big
mudholes. However, I hadn't met or passed anybody
much, and I just didn't figure there would be any traffic
on a new road in bad weather like this. In fact, I hadn't
given it a thought that I was likely to have any company,
because of those bogholes. Just about dark, I saw a wagon
down in the flat across the river. Four mules were hooked
to the wagon, two abreast, and a man up on top of a big
load of something in that wagon was popping a line over
those mules. They were in pretty deep mud and they
were pulling with all they had, but the farther they went,
the deeper the wheels were getting into the ground. It was
getting late, and I couldn't see what-all was going on, but
I watched as long as I could make out the outline of
things. The wind was against him, so I couldn't hear him
or the team. Finally, I just moved back over by my fire
and sat there to make out until bedtime.

Like I said, there was a big wind blowing, and it was
getting cold fast. I was thinking I was pretty lucky to be
in behind that big hill in a good cedar brake, with my
stock all fed and a nice warm bed in a wagon with a sheet

over it. I was full of grub, my horses in good shape for the night, and I was just kinda sitting there feeling sorry for the poor folks.

Directly I heard a little noise off to the west side of my wagon a good piece—a little bit of a whistle going on. That would be the way for a man to come into your camp in the West at night—make some noise, hum or whistle or sing, or do a little something to let you know that it was a human being coming in and he didn't aim to cause any trouble. At the same time, by making a little noise 'way off first, he wouldn't booger whatever stock you had around your camp.

The norther was blowing hard but the sky was clear, and it was getting colder with every gust of wind. This stranger came up to where I could begin to see his outline from the light made by the fire. I said: "Come on up to the fire."

He said: "I saw your fire from down on the river road, and I sure was glad to see that there was somebody around that had a camp."

Well, it was several miles in any direction to a ranch headquarters or a farm where anybody lived. I felt sort of lucky to be camped out there by myself. (It just shows how people's thinking has changed and how times have changed.) Sure enough, this cowboy was the man that was driving that four-mule team to the wagon. He told me he was stuck down there in the bottom. He had left his team hitched to the wagon and come up to see what kind of camp this was—or what was afire. He said he didn't have much hopes of getting out down there that night.

He ranched off close to Double Mountain, and he was

freighting his cottonseed cake for his cattle out from Hamlin Oil Mill. He was a little late getting out with some of it. The roads had gotten so bad they couldn't get a Model T Ford or a Chevvy through there, so he was having to bring some cake in a wagon. He said he had on a big load of cottonseed cake, and he was working some light-boned, half-Mexican kind of mules that weren't heavy enough for the load. He said that he knew he was going to have a little trouble; this was the reason he was working four-up instead of a single team. He just didn't have enough mules to get through that mudhole on the other side of the bridge.

It was about a quarter of a mile down to where he was stuck, maybe a little farther. I said: "Well, let's get on a couple of my saddle horses and go back down to the wagon and unhook your team. You can bring them up here and camp with me for the night. And," I added, "I've got some other horses here that can probably get you out in the morning."

He said he sure would be much obliged for that kind of a proposition, and he was glad I had a camp made there. He didn't have anything to camp with because he was intending to get home that night. If the roads hadn't been so heavy, he would have made it.

We saddled up—I didn't see any use in walking a quarter of a mile in the mud and the cold and the wind a-blowing. So far as I was concerned, walking was all took up when I was born. Horses were made to carry people around in the weather, anyhow. We went down and unhooked his team and led them back up, unharnessed them, and threw the harness over by the wagon. I got some hay out of my wagon, and some oats. He tied his mules up away from my horses, fed them good, and we sat down by the fire. I stirred him up some hashbrown potatoes, bacon, and scrambled eggs. He sure got around a batch of it. He was cold and hungry.

He was a sure-enough rancher and a sure-enough cowboy and a good fellow to visit with. We sat by the fire and listened to the wind howl and talked about handling stock. I told him I had been to Kansas and summered a bunch of steers. He said he went to Kansas once, but he hit a drouth and didn't do so good. He said he had been ranching over there at the Double Mountains a while, and he guessed if he could make the winter and get into spring he would have a good calf crop. We finally ran out of conversation and began to get sleepy. I told him I guessed the best we could do was both of us get in that bedroll of mine in the wagon and try to make the night.

He was agreeable to that, so I got the rest of the saddle blankets and stuff I had laid around. We piled it on top of us. Of course, men who have lived outdoors don't bother to take off too many clothes in a blizzard. We just slipped our boots and our jackets off—and our hats—and kinda undone our belts and got comfortable. Before you know it, we were both sound asleep.

The next morning when the sun came up, it was cold and clear. That sun didn't change the temperature of the surroundings much, but I had rustled plenty of wood the night before, so we got a good fire going and fixed a good breakfast. Needless to say, I'd already decided last night that he was in bad need of nice stout work horses that could pull a load of cake out of the mud. He couldn't see my horses in the cedar brake in the night—and he didn't know what kind I had. I didn't bother to tell him, and I had gone out and fed the horses while he was getting breakfast ready.

After we ate a batch of hot grub, I said: "Well, let's pick out a team of horses that can hook up and get your wagon out of the mud."

He walked out through the cedar brake with me and his eyes jumped out. He said: "Why I didn't have any idea there was this kind of horses in the world—much less camped up here by the side of the river last night when I got stuck!"

I just kinda laughed and told him that I fell in love with them up in the bluestem and had drifted down and brought them with me. I said I was started home where I thought I'd use them.

The oldest pair of mares I had were big gray mares, nearly white from age. They weren't but about ten years old, but gray horses get white by that time. They were sound and clean and well shod. I knew they would pull with all they had and until they give out. They were the kind of horses that helped take the West. I just knew when I hooked them to that load of cake, something was going to have to give. I was hoping the doubletree and singletrees were plenty stout, because I knew that pair of big mares would sure bring that rig out of the mud. While I was getting them harnessed, he harnessed up the mules and took them back down there with him. I jumped on my saddle horse and led my mares. I couldn't help but hurrah him a little bit, and I asked him what he was taking those mules along for—did he figure they would want to ride on the wagon after they got a team that could pull it?

We laughed a little bit, and he admitted they were

awful small mules for the thing he was trying to do with them. But they were mules, and that was all the mules he had, so he was working what he had and doing the best he could. "But," he said, "I shore would like to own a pair of those great big nice horses, iff'n you didn't need all of them at home."

I said: "Well, we'll wait and see if they can pull your wagon out. You might not want them at all."

By this time we were down close to his wagon. We had crossed the bridge and saw that nobody had come along in the night. Hadn't anybody pushed him out of the road, and there wasn't anybody behind him waiting. If anybody had come up, they had turned around and gone back before they got into the worst of it—or else they would have stopped and come to our camp for the night.

Well, I got this good pair of gray mares hooked in to his wagon, and I told him I would use them for the wheelers. He hooked the heaviest team of his mules on in front of them for the lead. I told him if he didn't want to get those mules' feet muddy, he could wait until I got the wagon out. He knew that was kinda funny, but he said they might help that pair of horses some; he believed he would hook on—just in case.

We got all rigged up, and I had the horses move up and just tighten their traces a little bit. Mud and ice had frozen around the wheels during the night, and I knew it would be a hard pull. He was driving his mules, so he stepped off to one side. I had stepped off to one side and held the line on the horses. I asked him if he was ready. He said: "Yeah."

I spoke to this good pair of gray mares and slapped them a little with the lines, and then I just pulled enough on the lines to steady them. A pair of good pulling horses, they go down in front with their heads and necks and lay their weight against the collars. If you just pull enough to steady them, they can do a lot better job of pulling and are not as likely to go to their knees.

Those big mares laid in there and you could hear them grunt a little bit. They just kept laying and getting closer to the ground and closer to the ground, and directly that wagon began to move. I squalled and hollered and told him to get his mules out of the way—that I might have to run over them. Of course that was just a joke. The mules were pulling all they could, and they were live, active kind of mules, and they were 'way on out in front.

We pulled the wagon across the bridge and out on dry ground. I started unhooking my mares, and he said: "Now wait a minute before you go unhookin' that team of mares. I've got a proposition I want to take up with you. I don't know how many horses you've got up there in that cedar brake, but you've got enough you could spare me this pair of mares."

I said: "Well, I had plans for these horses and I kinda hate to split 'em up. This is one of the best pullin' pairs I got."

"That's why I want 'em," he said. "I need 'em all this winter. I can freight this cake all up and down this road with 'em, and I can use my mules out in the pasture to pull my feed wagons—when I'm just putting out enough for a day's feeding."

I didn't want to seem too anxious about getting rid of this pair of good pulling mares, so I said: "Well, I don't know whether a man ought to sell a pair of mares like this or not. With a mudhole like that, and the winter just startin'—I might just stay here and make the winter."

We both laughed pretty big. He knew I didn't mean it, so he asked: "What would you have to have for this team of mares, and let me buy 'em from you?"

I just thought I'd try him for size. I didn't know whether he knew anything about the horse market or not, so I told him that the mares ought to be worth $300.

He said he thought so, too, but he wasn't able to give that much for them—but he sure would like to buy them. He said he had more mules at home of a smaller size and brand, but this pair of bay mare mules that he had and was using for leaders were nice little mules. They weren't as heavy as his wheelers, but they were about seven or eight years old and clear of blemishes—a little snorty, like Western mules were—but clean-typey kind of little mules. He told me if I would take $150 difference, he would swap me that pair of lead mules and pay me the $150 boot, and that I ought to be able to get $150 out of the mules. That would make my $300, and he would have a team to do heavy work for the winter.

I told him it looked to me like he was looking after his interests better than he was mine, but that I guessed it was a pretty good trade, and I believed I would swap with him. The harness on his mules was just as good as the harness on my mares, but of course the collars fit the mules and the collars fit the mares; so I suggested he let the collars go with the mules and I'd let the collars go with the mares.

He hooked his heavy mules, that had been his wheelers, up in front of the mares. We visited and gave each other our addresses and shook hands. I told him if I was ever back I would come visit him. And he said if he ever got down in my country, he'd look me up. We'd made a good trade and had a good visit and parted friends.

I had begun to think that maybe I wasn't too unsmart when I bought that bunch of horses. I had an interest in a café, $150 boot, and a pair of mules clear. It looked like I might not have such a hard winter after all.

I led my mules back to camp and tied them to the wagon wheel and sat around by the fire and stayed warm. The wind had died down in the night. It was still awful cold, but the sun was getting up higher and it had begun to warm up. I decided that I would rig up my horses and pull on out across the river and head for Anson, Texas. I didn't know much about this pair of little mules; they might try to run off or break loose or something. I had put a pair of black horses to the wagon—real good horses that I knew could pull it all right—and I just thought: "Well, that pair of mules might give me as little trouble up there as leaders as they would tied to the wagons."

So I hooked them up for leaders and made me a four-up team, and in a few minutes I went across the bridge and hit the mudhole. I spoke to these horses a few times and held a tight line on the little lead mules. We got through the mudhole without much trouble, pulled out on the other side—it had been a pretty long pull—and I let them rest a few minutes to get their wind. Then we started on down the road.

For the next several days the winter was coming on. At night it was cold and in the daytime it didn't warm up too much. I went through a farming country where nobody wanted to buy any horses, it seemed, and you'd see those trade lots full of horses and mules around those tractor places. The trip was sorta uneventful for several days, and then I pulled into Albany, Texas.

Down on the creek—out of town a piece after you came down the mountain from Fort Griffin, and before you got into town—there was a little glade that had always been a campground. I pulled out there and got my horses sort of fixed for the night. I watered them at the creek, gave them some feed, and got my camp laid out pretty good. It lacked a little while being dark, so I stepped on my saddle horse and rode on up to Albany.

Albany was then and is now and always will be a nice kind of West Texas cowtown. I ate supper in a café for a change, loafed around the drugstore and drank a coke, and visited a little bit. I let it be known that I was camped out there in the edge of town with a bunch of horses, and that I was going back home from being up in Kansas with a bunch of steers. I ran onto two or three fellows that I knew either by reputation or personally; then I went on back out to my camp about dark so I'd be there around my stock. After a while I went to bed. Nothing much happened.

Next morning I got up and thought: "Well, I'll harness my horses up here and get hooked up and pull on up in the edge of town somewhere—stop and eat breakfast instead of building a fire and cooking."

I pulled up on the square where there was plenty of room and stopped my horses and my wagon and all, got out and went across the street to the old hotel about a block down. I was sitting there on a stool eating my breakfast when a great big rough fellow came in and said: "Wonder who that bunch of big horses belongs to up there on the square."

I raised my head up and looked at him—you could tell

he was an oil-field man—and I told him they were mine.

He asked: "You want to contract some dirt work?"

I said: "No sir, I'm not a dirt work man. I'm started home with those teams."

"Where's home?"

I said: "Over by Weatherford."

"Well," he said, "we need some slush pits dug out here around some oil wells, and the weather is bad and wet, and these boys haven't been able to do it with machinery."

I told him that I understood his problem, but that I didn't have any fresnos to dig holes with—or turning plows or nothing—and I wasn't rigged up to do dirt work. And anyway it was getting winter and I was trying to get home. I'd rather just take my horses and go.

He asked: "What business you got with so many big horses like that if you ain't doing dirt work? Are they good for anything else?"

That was sort of a compliment coming from a construction worker out of the oil fields, and I said: "I reckon those horses can do just about anything. It ain't the horses you are having trouble with, it's me. I don't want to do any dirt work."

He said: "I know where there are some fresnos, turnin' plows, and everything you'd need to do some dirt work—and you could do it in a week or ten days."

I said: "Yeah, that's about the length of time it would take me to get home."

I knew that if he was hurting, he would buy a team of these horses—or two teams—or he would get somebody to buy them and contract his dirt work. I knew that I wasn't a dirt work man and wouldn't know how to figure it and would get cheated anyhow. By this time I had finished my breakfast; so I paid the cashier and went out on the sidewalk and started toward my wagon.

He had gone out ahead of me, and when I looked up he was closer to the wagon than I was and just stepping right up and walking around my horses when I got there. I had the black horses hooked to the wagon, and they were the most stylish pair I had. They were good six- and seven-year-old horses, both geldings, and good true pulling horses with nice dispositions and good legs—the kind of horses that could go out and do a hard day's work at a fresno or any other kind of work.

I said: "I might sell you that pair."

He said he didn't have any business with one pair of horses. If he had to do any fresno work, he had to have from three to five.

I said: "Well, I might sell you more than two, but the more of them you take, the higher they are going to come because I don't want to get rid of these horses too bad."

He said: "What'll you take for five head and me pick 'em?"

I could tell by looking at him that he had been a mule-skinner in the oil fields. An old teamster would know what kind of horses he was going to pick. I knew that when he got through he'd get five as good horses as I had. Of course these were all good horses, and there wasn't a whole lot of difference in the ones I had left since I'd sold the gray pair—they were the oldest—and I'd sold that other pair that went into the chile business. So he couldn't hurt me much, whatever he picked out. I told him I would take $200 a round, and he could get five head.

He said that he wouldn't give it; that he would give

$100 a round. So I said: "Well, I've just found out you don't have much dirt work to do, and there ain't no use in me and you taking up each other's time. I just as well get on up the road."

He said: "I'll give $125 a head for five of 'em."

"Well," I told him, "you're still talking like a cheapskate. I guess I gotta go. Good-bye." And I clucked to my team and drove off.

Going east out of Albany you go up and cross the railroad track and pass the schoolhouse. I was topping out on the hill at the edge of town when he overtook me, driving some kind of a red automobile.

He stopped me and said: "I'm going to make one more pass at you. I'm going to give $150 a head for some of these horses if you've got harness to fit them."

He had decided that he could make do with four head instead of five; so after he walked around and walked through them and looked at their mouths and picked up their feet, and showed off and made you understand that he was sure enough a horse man—he picked out four good horses. He took the two black horses, and he took a pair of dark-gray young mares. Said he'd rather not have any mares, but he couldn't do much about it. The two blacks were the only geldings I had left. He gave me a check for $600 for four head of horses and the harness that fit them. His check was on the Albany bank, and I just thought that would be a good place to get the money —where the check was written—so I just pulled my wagon out by the side of the road, fastened my horses up along the fence, and got on a saddle horse and rode back to town. It was early and I had to wait a little while, but the bank opened soon, and sure enough the man's check was all right. I put the money in my pocket.

I went back up on the hill and had to figure out another team and another set of harness to hook up so I could get on the road. I was getting along pretty good. I had gotten rid of eight of my horses out of sixteen and had taken in two mules. I had my five saddle horses and that made fifteen head. I still didn't know just how that café deal was coming out, but I had half-interest in a café, two mules, $750 of my $1,200 back, and still had half of my big horses. I began to think that business wasn't too bad after all.

I got to Breckenridge in a couple of days. There was a trade lot on down close to town in the flat. I stayed there a couple of days and rested—visited around, ate some town grub, and went to the picture show. I didn't do anything smart and didn't have any horse business. I heard some more about tractors and how much big horses ate. It had got to where it didn't worry me much, I'd heard so much of it—and then, too, I was getting a lot of my money back. I just let those smart people advise me, but I didn't pay it much mind.

The day I left Breckenridge—it was up in the middle of the afternoon—there was a farmer that had plowed out to the end of a row and had seen me coming down the road. He stopped his team, did up his lines, and walked over to the fence and waited for me to get there. He had been breaking some sandy land that he raised peanuts on. He bragged on how big and how pretty my horses were and told me how they used to have such horses there in the days of the oil boom—which was before my time. He noticed the little bay mules, and he liked them real well and asked me if they were for sale. We had quite a visit while he walked around them, and he had a long hard time making up his mind about them.

He thought they would be awful nice. I offered to take $100 a piece for them. He said he guessed they were worth it, but he was a little short of cash. He didn't think he could give that, but he could give $150 for both of them if I wanted to sell them. I didn't think that was all the money he had, and I didn't show much interest. I told him I guessed I'd better take them on with me—that I believed they would be a little higher down the country and somebody would have more need for them than he did. He crawled back over the fence and said he guessed he'd better get back to plowing. I had started to drive off when he turned around and said he would give me $165 and that was all.

I told him: "I guess that will be all. That's enough. I'll just sell them to you."

I pulled on down the road a little piece where the gate turned into his place. He walked on down, opened the gate, came out and got the mules, and said: "I guess you're throwing the halters in."

He was being just a little stingy with me, so I said: "Well, no. At the price these mules are going, I guess I'll want my halters back."

He led them through the gate, took the halters off them, and threw the halters back to me. He went to the house and told his wife to write me a check for $165. I sat outside the house and listened, and it sounded like a young war. She told him about how many different things they needed worse than they needed a pair of mules. He would beg her and plead with her and say: "Now honey, you know we've got to have an extra team."

I listened to this domestic warfare about twenty minutes, but he finally came out of the house with a check for the mules. That cut my herd down a little more and added a little more to my pocket money. Now I had $915, still had eight head of big horses, and it looked to me like I was as good a trader as I thought I was before I heard about those tractors.

It was still fall weather but a little chilly, and it was threatening. A bank was in the north, and I was still four or five days from home. I thought I really ought to drive a little harder and get on in before bad weather set in; but still, I didn't need eight head of big stout horses to feed all winter. I was just wondering if maybe I ought to stop in Palo Pinto or Mineral Wells and spend several days and try to get rid of the rest of my work stock. I camped that night on a creek about eight or ten miles from Palo Pinto. It was a pretty cold kind of night and the wind blew hard. I had plenty of feed, and I was camped down in the creek bottom away from the wind, and had all my horses put away pretty good. But that wagon was a little lonesome. A few horses moved around in the middle of the night, and I began to decide I didn't want to stay on that road during the winter. I sort of made up my mind that the next morning I'd just start on in home and take my chances on trading on my horses through the winter.

A little before noon the next day I pulled up on the courthouse square in Palo Pinto. It was a nice, quiet, peaceful-looking place. There weren't many cars parked around and there weren't many people on the street. It was a bright, sunshiny day, and the wind had died down. This was kind of a pretty looking place, nestled down in a cove of the mountains. I saw that my horses would be all right—they were content to stand there tied to the wagon. The team was standing good; so I did up my lines and looked around for a place to eat some dinner.

I noticed a big store on the side of the square. I walked over to it and up and down the side of it. I didn't see any signs sticking out up or down the street about an eating place; so I thought: "Well, maybe I'll go in the store here and get me some cheese and crackers, or sardines or something"—the kind of stuff you could buy in a store those days to eat on.

As I stepped inside I noticed back over in the corner of the building toward the back that there was a meat market, and you could smell some meat cooking. I walked on back—there weren't any customers in the store —and the man that ran the outfit was behind the counter in the meat market. There were three or four stools at a side counter; he had a barbecue pit in there, and he was cooking up a batch of barbecue. It smelled good, and I could tell that I had found a pretty good place to feed that day.

I said: "That sure smells good. You must have got your training as a camp cook."

He kinda laughed and said: "Well, it'll do to fill up a hungry man."

I told him I'd like to have a batch of that stuff. Up to now he never had said: "What's it for you?" or "Can I help you?" or "Did you want to buy something?" You wouldn't have known it was a commercial place of business from the way he was acting. He got a tin plate out from under the counter, went over to this barbeque pit, raised the iron lid off it, and took out a big chunk of meat. He chopped it up, and it filled up the plate. He slid it over to me, reached in a bread wrapper and pulled out a loaf of bread, and started to cut me a chunk of bread. That was before bakeries had learned how to slice bread and then wrap it—bread all came in one chunk.

I said: "I like the tailgate."

He just cut off both ends of the loaf of bread and said: "There's you two tailgates."

I started in on this barbecue, and it sure was fittin'. I began to brag on it, and he said: "Reach over in that box behind you and get you an onion and peel it."

Well, I thought that would help, too; so I reached over and got an onion and sliced it and peeled it and started out eating again. That made everything better. I was mighty hungry.

We were talking, and he looked up and saw all these horses standing on the courthouse square and wondered who owned them. "They're mine," I told him. I said I had been up in Kansas and I was going to Weatherford to winter. I never let on but what I had been working these horses all summer. I didn't tell him I was trading on them. Then I added: "I'll swear, this is good barbecue."

He said: "Look around there in front of that glass counter and reach in that barrel and get you a pickle to go with it."

Well, that set it off some more, and I just kept eating and visiting and talking. Nobody came in for a while—but directly here came a fellow. He came up and said his wife was washing and he thought he'd better take some barbecue home for dinner. They had small talk while he got fixed up with some barbecue in a little cardboard box with some gravy in it, and he went out.

The storekeeper turned around to me and said:

"There'll be four or five of them kind of fellers by here. There's several different reasons besides washing, but that's just the one they tell you about."

"One reason is," I said right quick, "that their wives can't make barbecue like this."

Well, you could tell that didn't make him mad. He said: "Yeah, and another reason is, some of these fellows don't take no meat home for their wives to cook nohow."

While I was sitting there eating, I was looking around this store. Back behind me—it was a kind of L-shaped building—on the back part of it he had some feed and some seed, some farm tools and some chain harness and collars were hanging on the wall. Up around on one side of the meat market there were some cases of canned goods, and stuff that wasn't too common in just everybody's store. You could look up the other side, toward the front, and there were about three big aisles going up through there. You could plainly tell which aisles belonged to the women's kind of merchandise; the floor was swept, and there were bolts of goods up and down the counter and in the shelves. There were some fancy kinds of women's shoes, some of them laced and some of them had bows on them. And there were even two or three pairs of right fancy ones with bows on them—sitting right out on top of the boxes.

Then on the men's side there were good ducking britches, jackets, and work clothes—and Stetson hats. Any direction you looked there was something else that had to do with living in a ranch or farm country. You could just tell right off that this was a good general store. If anybody wanted something this store didn't have, he sure was looking for luxuries, because the necessities were all here. I mentioned this to the proprietor—about how much stock of stuff he had in his store.

"Yeah," he said, "I sure am proud. I try to keep everything that people need, but ever now and then I hear of somebody going off fifty or sixty miles to Fort Worth and buying something."

I told him there would always be people hunting things that came from Paris, or something that didn't have any practical use, but he had a right to be proud of a store like this—and this wasn't any country store, the way I saw it. It was an up-to-date store.

He began to appreciate me pretty good by then. He reached over and got my tin plate and said: "Heah, young fellow like you—been a-drivin' that bunch of horses a long way—can eat more beef that you've had." So he loaded up my plate again.

I didn't fight him any over it. I figured I could eat a bunch more of it, too. And besides that, I was going to have to make a camp supper somewhere down the road. It just might be I wouldn't want much supper, the way he was feeding me.

In a minute he spoke up and said: "Surely you don't need all those horses at home. You mighta needed 'em in the summer, but you ain't gonna be doin' anything this winter to take that many horses, are you?"

I said: "Well, I might be. I have the horses, and I pretty near have to do something if I keep them."

He said: "There was somebody in here a few days back a-talkin' about needin' some big horses—some teams to dig dirt tanks with. I didn't pay much mind to who it was. You don't reckon you'd want to sell 'em, do you? I might try to think of who that was."

I told him: "Oh, I'd keep my saddle horses and sell some of my work horses, if it would help a man out—but I'm not hankering too much."

He didn't know that was a piece of information I was waiting for—the name of somebody around there that might be needing work horses. I tried not to show much interest, and after all I was pretty much busy with that second plate of barbecue he had cut for me. About that time somebody else came in. I had finished eating, and he said: "Well, don't run off. Come back 'fore you leave and I'll try to think who that was that wanted some horses to work."

I walked out on the sidewalk and kinda stretched and yawned and started over toward my wagon and horses. I saw a fellow coming out of the courthouse astepping pretty nice. It looked like he was either after something or running from something, and about that time I noticed he had a big star on the side of his chest. I decided he was probably the high sheriff. He got to my teams about the time, or a little before, I did. He was looking around, and he said: "Nice bunch of horses you got, kid. Who do they belong to?"

I said: "They belong to that kid you're talking to."

He kinda laughed and said: "Well, I guess they could. I just figured there was a grown man around somewhere."

I kinda took that like it was an insult, but I thought since he was the high sheriff maybe I'd best not cuss him out—and he kinda laughed when he said it, anyhow. We got pretty well acquainted, and he was a good kind of a fellow. He was an old-time stocker, had been a cowboy and a teamster and a mule-skinner; then he got into politics. He was right likable, and his name was Abernathy if I remember right. And I thought it was a shame that a good fellow like that would take off to devious means of making a living—like being a sheriff—when he was a good stockman.

He brought up the matter of whether the horses were for sale. I told him that I guessed I'd sell some of them, but I wouldn't want to run myself short. Of course he didn't realize how many I could do without and still not be short. He said: "There's a fellow down here in the south part of our county that runs a big land company: the T and P Land Company. There's a lot of that old ranch country that they can't get windmill water on, and they're having to build some dirt pools in some of the pastures. It's been a dry fall, and the manager down there has been wanting to get some dirt work contracted. I imagine you could get a job building some dirt pools and tanks through the winter."

I let him on the fact that I didn't think that would be a pleasant way to spend the winter—camped off there digging a bunch of dirt tanks. And that I'd started home and wouldn't be interested in a job.

He said: "Well, in a case like that, would you sell some of these big, heavy, dirt-working kind of horses to my friend if he wanted to buy them?"

I could tell then I was sure about to have some more business. I said: "Well, I don't know. It depends on what your friend knows about what good horses are worth."

He said: "It's Mr. Cox, and he runs that T and P Land Company out there. He'll know more about horses than you or me either one."

It's always nice to do business with a fellow who knows, or thinks he knows, so I told this high sheriff that

I would be interested in talking about selling some of my horses if Mr. Cox was really interested in paying what horses like mine were worth.

He said: "Mr. Cox has a phone. I'll go over to the office and see if I can ring him. It's about dinnertime and he ought to be at the house. If he lets on like he could use these horses, I'll come back and tell you."

I said: "That would be just fine. I'll appreciate it. Maybe we'll have some business, and you'll be doing us both a favor. It doesn't hurt a man in politics to be doing people favors, even if they are strangers."

He kinda smiled and said: "That's a fact." And I learned later that's how he had been in office pretty near all of his life.

He came back out of the courthouse after a while and said sure enough that Mr. Cox would be here in a little while. If I could stay around, he just knew that we would have some business. I told him it was an awful nice time of day for me to be getting on down the road, but I appreciated his trying to help, and I would wait a while on Mr. Cox.

In about thirty or forty minutes, here came this man Cox, and he was another nice gentleman—well spoken, wasn't insulting, knew a lot about horses and a lot about people. He and this Sheriff Abernathy sure were big friends. We visited, and they talked about the size of the teams and how good they could work and what all they could do, and how it might be smarter to buy them and do the dirt work than to contract and have it done. I thought that was a lot of favorable conversation, and I just felt like I was going to have some business with this Mr. Cox.

He finally got around to asking what I would take for a team, but before I answered him he said: "No, I mean two teams."

I asked him $300 a pair for them. He said that was a little high, but that he would try to buy them if I would try to sell them. I thought that was a pretty good attitude, and I said: "Well, it seems like you know more about the horse business than I do. What do you reckon you'd give for them?"

He decided that he would give $250 a pair for two pairs, but I told him I couldn't quite take that. So he said: "Well, supposin' I bought them all?"

"Then I'd be out of teams!" I said it just like I'd be ruined, but he didn't have any idea how well that would have suited me. "I don't know. If you bought the eight head, I might take off a little."

"How much is a little?"

I said: "$25 a pair."

"You're trying to split the difference with me. I offered $250 and you wanted $300—but I just got to thinking, what am I going to hook these big horses up with? If you had some harness, I'd try to buy them."

I said: "That wagon is full of harness, but I can't put that in at no such price."

About that time the high sheriff raised the wagon sheet and saw that, sure enough, there was a lot of heavy harness in there. Then this Mr. Cox, he stuck his head in there. You could hear them talking low to each other about how good that harness was. Then Mr. Cox asked me what I was doing with my ponies along. He didn't know it, but these were my cow horses and I wouldn't have given them for all these big horses at any time.

I told him I needed them—that I had been up in Kansas handling a bunch of steers through the summer, and I would probably handle mules through the winter, and that I'd need my riding horses. None of them were for sale.

But when I said I would handle mules, you could see his eyes light up considerably. He asked: "What kind of mules?"

I said: "Just mules—any kind of mules."

"How would you like to trade these horses for some mules?"

I said: "Well, I wouldn't want to trade all my horses for mules. I need to get some money out of 'em if I'm going to let them go."

"We've got some mules. There's just a little small matter about catching them. They're in a big pasture on Pinto Creek, and if you'd trade for them range-delivery, we'd sure try to have some business."

"How many mules you got in this wild bunch?"

He said there were five three-year-olds that never had been broke, and one six-year-old mule that had got out and got so wild they couldn't catch her—which made six head in all. I asked him about the colors of the mules, and the sizes, and so on.

He was a pretty fair kind of a fellow, and this high sheriff was a-vouching that he was telling me the truth all the time. He said there were brown and bay mules, the six-year-old was a sorrel mule, and they were all fat. Some cowboys had run them a few times, but nobody had been able to catch them.

I asked him if there were any corrals anywhere that they could be put in, and he said: "Oh yeah, there's a

good set of pens out there in the pasture on Pinto Creek—
made out of rock—if I ever could get them in there. But
those mules—seems like they got a little something against
goin' in a corral."

Well, by now he sure had tapped my number. I was
getting interested fast. I asked him if I could keep the
wagon to camp in and maybe a span of the mares at the
wagon until I caught the mules—if we had some kind of
a mule trade. He said the wagon wasn't going to be much
good to him, that he was going to need scrapes and plows
and slips and fresnos. I could camp in the wagon to catch
the mules, provided I caught them before they got too
smooth-mouthed; that he didn't want the wagon sitting
out there seven or eight years. Of course he and Sheriff
Abernathy, they had a great big laugh about that.

I laughed, too. I said: "Yeah, well, you got something
there. It might take a long time to catch those mules. Tell
you what I'll do—I'll take $250 a pair for these four pairs
of mares—and your mules—and I'll put in a set of harness
for every mare. You get the wagon, but I'll want my pack
out of the wagon." I meant by that my cooking gear, bedroll and stuff like that of my personal belongings.

This would amount to selling the mares for $250 a
pair and trading the wagon and harness for six mules, the
way I figured it right fast in my head. So I told him if
he would show me the pasture and the pens and a place to
water, when I got through I'd leave the pair of mares and
the wagon right there. He could take the other teams and
their harness and go on getting his dirt work done.

By now we had all got well acquainted, and we were
liking the deal. He was anxious to get rid of those wild
mules he couldn't get caught, and the sheriff was feeling

like he had done everybody a big favor; so the sheriff said: "Let's go over here and all have something to drink."

We went back in this good old mercantile to the meat market part, where the proprietor poured up coffee for everybody but me—and I was a coke-head. He got me a coke and we sat there and visited. Mr. Cox was quite a business man along with being a nice fellow, and he brought up the matter of were the horses and wagon mortgaged to anybody.

I told him: "No sir."

And the high sheriff had to put in a little humor, so he asked: "And they ain't stole?"

And I said: "No sir, they ain't stole."

Mr. Cox said to Mr. High Sheriff: "I believe I'll just have a trade with this boy."

I said: "Well, that will be fine. I'll try to catch the mules. If I don't catch 'em, they ain't mine—but when I catch 'em, they are mine."

"Yes," he said, "that's the trade. We'll show you how to get out to the camp, and I'll bring some men in the morning to get my horses and my harness. I'll go by the office and write you a check and bring it with me."

So since they had contested me about my mortgages and whether I stole the horses or not, I couldn't help asking the sheriff did he think it would be all right to take Mr. Cox's check. That created a little more good humor, and by now we were all big friends.

They drew me a map about how to go out of town and twist around south to the pasture gate. They said it was a good ways, and I would have to get up and drive pretty hard to get down on Pinto Creek, where those rock pens were, by dark. So we all shook hands, and I went back to get a package of barbecue to eat that night.

I said to the store man: "I believe I'll pull around here to this back door and get a few sacks of feed."

He had some good red oats, some shelled corn, and a few bales of hay. We stacked the stuff in my wagon—got all in that my wagon would hold—and I pulled out of town. I held a tight line on these old mares, clucked to them pretty good, and drove them on down the road. It had begun to get a little dusky when I came to this gate they told me about. Mr. Cox was there waiting. He had been back to his office at Gordon or Mingus or Thurber or maybe Strawn, wherever this big land company had its office. He showed me the way to go down there on the creek and said he would be back early in the morning.

I got to the creek in time to gather me some firewood. I put my horses in this big rock corral. This corral fence was built out of native Palo Pinto red stone—placed by hand to a height of about five feet, which is about shoulder high to an average man. The fence was full two feet thick. (A horse or a mule will not jump anything that high that is solid, where it can't see what the ground is like on the other side.) On the inside of this corral was a partition fence, cutting the corral into two pens. There was one big gate in the north side of the rock fence— a gate made of heavy, rough-sawed timber and swung on large bolt hinges. And I thought to myself that this mule-gathering deal wasn't going to be too serious.

I built a fire and sat around a while, warmed up my barbecue and ate another batch of it. I shook out my bed-roll and made my bed down in the wagon. When the fire died down low, I went to bed.

Early next morning I crawled out of the wagon and

stretched myself and looked around. The stock was all in good shape, I'd fed them the night before. It was late in the year, and the grass had been frosted on. It was dead and dry. There wasn't any green in the pasture, but there was a lot of good cured grass. You'd know that anything that you caught in that pasture was going to be fat.

Mr. Cox showed up pretty soon after I had fixed my breakfast and fed my stock. He had a couple of men with him. One of them was going to ride one of these mares and lead a team and the other fellow the same thing. Mr. Cox asked me what team I wanted to keep at the wagon. I had a pair of eight-year-old, dapple-gray mares that were real gentle, well mannered, and easy to catch; so I told him I wanted to keep them. He said he couldn't imagine what I wanted with them, but that was the trade, so for me to just keep them until I got through with them. When I got ready to leave—after I'd given up and hadn't been able to catch the mules (he laughed right big)—I could just take my saddle horses and pack up.

Mr. Cox and the men laughed some more about my catching the mules. I tried to laugh a little, too, but I had some pretty positive ideas about how I was going to catch these mules.

After they got their harness and horses—they took the six head—I had my five saddle horses plus the two mares, which left me seven. My saddle horses were all gentle and easy caught. I had old Beauty with me, and you never had to tie Beauty. You could turn her out in the pasture with whatever else was there and never have to worry about her. She would come when I called her. Beauty would come if I turned her out when I had just fed her or just curried her or just rode her hard; whatever

I had just done to Beauty, when I called her she would come, regardless of the hour of the day or night. A man is mighty lucky if he has one horse in a lifetime like Beauty.

So I fed Beauty and left her in the lot. I left the dun horse in the lot with her for company. I turned the gray mares and the other three horses out. They knew where the pens were by now, and the water was in the creek just below the pens. I knew that they would be back for feed that night or next morning.

Then I got on my dun horse and rode around the pasture. It was a great big pasture. It had about five thousand acres in it and no cross fences. Pinto Creek was running through it—real cow country with lots of curly mesquite grass and lots of mesquite beans that had cured lying on the ground. Stock would eat that through the winter.

It must have been about two o'clock in the evening when I got back to the corral where I had made my camp, let loose the dun, and turned out Beauty. I had a pretty good lay of the country about now and knew kinda how things were. I had got a glimpse of the mules, but they were running off into thick brush. I guess they thought I was after them and they would lead me off into a wild chase, but I didn't bother about them. I just rode away and left them and came on back to camp, where I got to thinking that I had camped in the way of the gate on the north side of the pens. I ought to be camped on the south side of the pens with my wagon if I ever aimed to get the mules to come in this rock corral.

Next morning I got out and squalled and hollered right loud, and my saddle horses came in. Beauty was in the lead, with the other saddle horses following. It was cool weather, and they didn't stop for water. They came on in the rock pens, and I put out some feed in an old trough in the first pen and some feed in the other pen on the ground around the edges inside of the rock fence. I hollered a few more times and, sure enough, here came the big gray mares. They just came trotting on into the pen, gentle and nice.

Something that most people don't know about wild mules—or any kind of mules—they will take up with a gray mare or a spotted mare. These horses had been out there all night, and I knew the mules had winded them and come to them; so I fed the gray mares in plain view, in the feed trough in the front pen. I looked around and, sure enough, it wasn't but just a little bit until those mules were sticking their heads out through the brush, looking to see where the gray mares went. I just whistled and sang and payed them no mind. I walked around my horses and rubbed them while they ate—and talked to them some more. The gate was open, but I crawled over the fence on the south side.

Later I caught the gray mares. And I moved my camp to the south side of the pens that day, so I wouldn't be in the way of the mules getting through the gate. When we got a north wind, I didn't want them to be able to wind me before I ever got a chance to shut that gate.

I spent the morning brushing and currying these gray mares—and kept the other horses up. You could see the mules grazing over there in a little glade across the creek. Ever now and then one of the mules would look up, and the oldest mule—that was the sorrel—brayed a time or two. I sure would have loved to see my mules up close and know what kind of stock I had, but I didn't want to take the chance of running them off. I got my camp moved and let my horses all out, except one saddle horse that I thought I might need in the night.

I didn't go to town or do anything that next day. I stayed out of view, but along late that afternoon Mr. Cox drove up to my camp. He got out and shook hands and said that he saw I was set up all right. Was I getting along all right, and had I had any luck catching my mules? I told him I had been resting, that I hadn't tried to catch them.

He asked: "Where are all your horses?"

I said: "Oh, I turned them out and just kept up a saddle horse."

"You'd better always keep up one," he said, "or you're not even gonna be able to get out of here. They'll all go wild with that bunch of wild mules, and then I'll have all your horses. You just better always keep one up so you can leave."

I thought this was kinda funny. I laughed about it, and he did too. I asked him how far it was over to the closest town. He explained to me that I was camped a little closer to Santo than I was to Gordon. He asked me if I needed anything from town, and I told him no. He asked me if I was going to town and try to hire some help to catch my mules—and I told him I didn't think I would need any help, I wasn't too much worried about my mules.

He kinda began to get his curiosity aroused, and he began to tell me the different men he had hired to catch these mules. He had caught the mares that raised the three-year-olds, but he never did catch the mule colts. He had moved everything out of that pasture one time, but they still never did have a chance to catch these mules. He said they had worked at it several times since the mules were two. He thought that I was going to get some experience in this mule-catching business that maybe I hadn't contracted for in the trade.

In the meantime he had given me my check, but I hadn't been in to town to cash it. He asked me where his gray mares were, and I told him that I had used them to move camp that morning and turned them back out—but they would be in his pasture. He said: "Well, there's just one more little thing. If they get loose with those mules and we can't catch them, I'm not going to want to pay you for those two mares."

I thought this was a little amusing, but I didn't bother too much to explain my business to him. I told him it could be I was going to winter here and stay longer than I thought; from the way he was talking, I might just as well saddle up my horse and go into town this evening late and kinda get acquainted with the people—if I was going to be a native there. He thought that was funny, but he told me I might be more settled there than I thought I was, if I was going to stay there until I caught those mules.

Finally he guessed he had something else to do besides talk to a man who didn't know when he couldn't catch mules, and he believed he would go on his way. We shook hands, and I told him to come back to see me—that I might be there for some time yet.

After he was gone, I saddled up a nice brown horse that was quite a road horse. He wasn't a very big horse, but he carried himself nice and had a fox trot that slipped over the ground. I just thought I'd ride him up to this

Santo and look around. Santo was kind of a pretty little town, had a few stores and a bank. I visited around and found a place to eat supper. Some of the natives were sitting around talking, and I got into conversation.

They finally found out what I was doing there—I wasn't too secretive about it. Didn't any of them want a job helping me, and they talked about how many and who-all had run at those mules. They said Mr. Cox was a fine man, but he was a good business man and a good trader and it could be I was cheated. I told them that wouldn't be a new experience, but that I was going to wait a while before I decided it was a fact.

I rode back to camp that night kinda late, fed my saddle horse, turned him loose, and went to bed. This was getting to be a pretty permanent camp. I had a nice way to build a fire, on a big flat rock just south of my wagon a little piece. It wasn't far to the creek where I was getting good fresh spring water. I was sure getting along all right, and I got to thinking it might not be too painful to spend the winter there in case I didn't catch these mules—like people thought might happen.

Next morning I got up, got out of the wagon, walked around and shook a feed bucket, stepped on the wagon tongue and shook the doubletree and the singletrees—made a few noises. Old Beauty nickered at me from across the creek and came trotting over. She ran up and stuck her nose in my face. I rubbed her and visited her and we talked. She was sure enjoying that good mesquite grass and mesquite beans. She shook her head and looked around in the wagon and acted like I was a little slow serving breakfast. Instead of feeding her at the wagon like I've done lots of times, I walked on out to the rock corral and went around to the north side where the gate was. I shook the bucket and went in and poured out some feed and hollered and squalled and talked around. She nickered a couple of times and threw her head up, and I knew the rest of them were coming in. This time the big work mares were in front, my saddle horses were behind, and the mules were all just kind of mixed up among them. I left the corral real fast—got out of the way.

The mares came running into the corral, ran up to the trough, and went to eating. Some of the other horses went on into the back corral, so I went and got some more feed, crawled over the fence on the south side, and fed them on the ground along the rock fence like I had done the morning before. I looked up and there this sorrel mule was—up there eating between the two gray mares. That fresh taste of oats was something this mule hadn't had in a year or so, and you could tell it was making quite a hit with her. She was a nice sorrel mule that would weigh about eleven hundred pounds. She had a good big ear and a nice head, and she had a good-size bone and her legs were clean. Her mane and tail, of course, had grown out to where they were shaggledy, and her forelock was hanging down between her ears. A mule's mane is never pretty, but when it has grown out awhile it is uglier than common. But I just said to myself I knew that if I wanted to, I could catch one mule—so I was sort of winner at that.

I peeped over the rock fence, and there were two of these young mules grazing out on the side of the creek next to the corral—but they were still a couple of hundred yards away and they weren't coming any closer. I didn't see any use in boogering them. I just crawled over the rock fence back the other direction and went to the wagon, where I peeped around and watched everything eat. My saddle horses and the gray mares ate good. My sorrel mule, she stayed at that trough until all the feed was gone. She threw her head up and blew a little wind through her nose and whistled a time or two, like a mule will do if she sees or smells something strange. The mares and my saddle horses didn't pay any attention to her.

As the horses kinda worked their way back out of the corral—they took their time and went toward the creek —I stepped from around the east corner of this rock fence and whistled to old Beauty right low. She turned around and followed me over to the wagon. I put a rope around her neck to keep her at the wagon because I was going to use her that day. And after the horses and the mules had all gotten down to the creek, had a drink, and gone out across the glade and disappeared into the mesquite on the other side, I saddled old Beauty up and rode around them and pretty close to them. I got a good look at them but never did offer to run them. These young mules would throw their heads up, throw their ears up, and snort right loud—which from a mule makes a noise more like a whistle. I just acted like they weren't there and rode away. You could tell that wasn't what they were used to, and I had begun to get them a little perplexed.

This kind of business went on for about four or five days. One of these young mules would sneak in to get a bite of feed, then break and run out of the corral. I wouldn't pay any attention to him, and the horses wouldn't either. The sorrel mule got to where she would be there every time the gray mares were up in the morning for feed. But I never ran at any of these mules one single time, nor made any motion like I wanted them.

By the sixth morning I had got to where I was putting out lots of feed. I wanted them to stay in there and eat—and let the ones outside come look inside that rock fence. On the sixth morning every mule from that pasture, and my saddle horses, and my gray mares were all in the corrals eating. It was a little bit of a temptation to try to get around that rock fence and get that gate shut on these wild mules—but the wind wasn't just right. If I had left the wagon and started around the pens, the mules could have winded me, and they would have broke and run out of that pen before I could have ever got to the gate. So I just tried to content myself that I was playing the game the right way, and that I'd better wait until I had a little more favorable weather to trap that bunch of wild young mules.

Mr. Cox had been by. He asked me if I was fishing or hunting or how did I plan on entertaining myself through the winter—if I wasn't going to try to pen those mules. I told him that I wasn't quite ready, that I hadn't gotten well enough acquainted with the pasture yet, and that I wanted my saddle horses to be rested and ready before they made the wild run. I told him I thought I still had plenty of time to catch the mules and get home before Christmas.

He said that was all right with him. He just wondered how a man could be so unconcerned about catching wild stock—seeing that I had five saddle horses and hadn't broke a sweat on them in the week's time I had been camped there.

I told him that I was sure he was a business executive and very capable of running a huge land company, but that he evidently wasn't in too close communion with a mule—that I didn't believe his advice would be worth too much to me, nor his ideas about catching mules. He had known these mules longer than I had, and he hadn't caught them either. I didn't say this hateful; I just said it and smiled. He laughed and said he guessed that was right, but if I got around to the point where I thought I needed any help, he would try to find somebody that I could hire to help me catch the mules.

I asked him if he thought he was running short of grass or short of time. He answered: "Oh no, take all the time you want. I was just concerned. I hate to cheat a boy, and the way you're doing your saddle horses are all going to the wild with the mules. Be sure, now, to keep a horse up, so you'll have a way to leave."

On the eighth morning there was a little norther blowing. I got up pretty early, and some of the horses were standing around in the pen. Beauty was nickering, the gray mares were nickering, and the sorrel mule had her head over the fence. By this time these young mules had all had a taste of feed, and they had gotten used to the idea that they were all going to get some feed every morning. They were all up there, but there wasn't any feed in the pens. I came along with two great big buckets full of feed and just went in at the gate and poured the feed in the trough. Then I went down through the back corral and poured the feed out on the ground along the rock fence like I had been doing.

When the last mule walked up—and he was a great big nice horse mule, brown with a white nose and a white belly, big ears, and looking around at the world—he stood there at the gate watching me pour out feed. Everything else was eating. He could hear them eating, so I didn't pay him any mind. I just crawled over the fence on the south side; but when I did, I stopped real still and stayed there, hunkered down low enough so that my head wouldn't show. Directly I heard the horses kinda scuffle—and I knew that another one was trying to get up to the trough.

I didn't want to make any noise. I started around the east side of that rock corral on my hands and knees. The wind was out of the northwest and blowing against me, and they couldn't smell me. They were all busy eating; I had been a little late with their feed and they were all a little greedy and anxious. So when I thought I knew that this last mule was over there at the trough, I came right easy around this corral and got near to where the gate was.

I knew when I hit that gate I'd better hit it fast if I was ever going to get it closed. I'd already found out that when the gate went to, you had to tie it with a chain. There was also a big pole lying there that you could prop the gate with and brace it and keep it from flying back. So when I raised up, I did it right easy and got ahold of that gate. About that time the hinges squeaked—all these wild mules threw their heads up—and this one big horse mule charged at that gate just as I slammed it to. I slammed the brace pole against it to hold it; I didn't have time to fasten the chain. I threw my hat over the fence right in that mule's face and squalled at him. He boogered and fell back through himself, and I got the gate chained hard and fast.

This was the eighth day, and I hadn't broke a sweat on a horse or throwed a shoe or rode myself down or got skinned up in the brush. I was running low on horse feed, but I had every mule and every mare and every saddle horse inside those big tall rock corrals with the gate shut.

I stood there and looked over the fence and bragged on myself awhile—and squalled at the stock and shook the gate and made them get back away from it. I made them understand it was fastened good and tight. I brought some feed sacks and tied around the planks on the gate. With those feed sacks flopping in the north wind, I knew they wouldn't try to come through that gate. The rock fence was high enough all the way around that they weren't going to try to jump it. I felt like if I left my saddle horses and the gray mares in there with these mules, they would quieten down better than if I got everything else out and just left them in there to get nervous and excite each other.

These mules had cost me nothing except twenty bushels of good red oats that I had bought from the man in Palo Pinto. It sure had been a nice, easy way to make money. Waiting hadn't been too hard on me, because I had been riding into these little towns and visiting around and drinking cokes, going to the picture shows and taking on a little rest. Just riding one saddle horse a little bit every day, they were all about to get soft. It was time I was doing something with them.

I was a little afraid to get in there and go to roping these mules and trying to put halters on them the first day. I knew that they were already nervous and mad about those sacks a-waving in the breeze; so I just walked around through the corrals a little bit and let them run away from me—run up in the corners and snort and blow their noses and throw their heads up and pop their ears. I would just walk away and climb over the fence. I never did open the gate or unchain it, for fear one would come by me. I just climbed over that rock fence, one way or another.

I spent the whole day going back and forth and around through them, but I didn't offer to take any horses out of there. I didn't offer to rope one; I didn't even carry a rope with me. I separated my horses from my mules that night, into two different pens. I fed my saddle horses good, fed the gray mares good, and just gave the mules a bite of feed—which didn't hurt them. They had been full all their lives, and they were so nervous they wouldn't eat much feed, anyhow.

Next morning when I got up it was awfully cold. Sure enough, that norther had finally gotten there. Mr. Cox drove up about the time I had my fire built up. He asked me if I was going to stay out there and freeze to death. I told him no, that I thought I'd leave that afternoon sometime.

"Without your mules?"

I said: "No, I don't think I will. I got 'em in the lot."

Well, you could have knocked him down with a feather duster. He wouldn't believe me; I said: "Well, Mr. Cox, just step out of your car and walk right light and speak right soft and behave yourself—don't scare my stock out of the corral, and I'll be glad for you to ease up there and look over the fence."

He was a well-dressed man, and he had an overcoat on, and it was flopping and a-popping and the wind was a-blowing. I said: "Now pull your hat down tight and take that overcoat off and lay it here on your car, because I don't want my mules to see any fresh, man-made boogers."

Sure enough he did what I told him, and he went there

and looked over the fence. We came back to the fire and stood and visited a while. He told me it had been a pleasure to do business with me. He only hoped I would be able to catch these mules and put something on them to get them out of the pasture—that he would be glad to get rid of them and he wanted them to make me a profit.

I told him I appreciated his attitude, and in view of the fact that it would be advantageous to him and me both, would he send a couple of men over to help me rope and tie these mules down and put halters on them?

He said he felt like he owed me that much—that he just hadn't realized what a good mule man I was. He would send two men over right after dinner, and they could help me all afternoon and the next day if I needed them. I told him I wouldn't need them more than two or three hours, and that next day I would drive out of there and leave all his belongings and his gray mares.

About two o'clock that afternoon a couple of big old boys came over. They weren't too bright, but they were stout. I roped the mules, then they would get on the rope with me. The mules would choke and bawl and carry on and try to get away—and then they would try to paw us, and then they would try to kick us. But there was a big snubbing post, that is, the gatepost between the two pens was a big heavy post. One by one we tied these mules to that post, and then I would get a rope around one hind foot. Riding a saddle horse, I would pull this foot out from under the mule. When he fell, one of these big old boys would jump on the mule's head and get a halter on him while he was down. By the time he came up, we'd have the lariat rope off of his neck and he would quit choking—and he'd have that halter on with a drag rope tied to it. He would run all around the corral two or three times and step on that drag rope and throw himself and jerk his head and jerk his nose.

We got them all haltered and went back to camp, and the boys ate a bite with me and drank some coffee. They said they had better get home to their families before dark. We all shook hands and I thanked them, and they asked me about coming over the next morning and helping me to get out of the pasture with my mules. It was about three miles from where I was camped to the gate, but I told them they needn't bother, I would make it all right. And they said: "We believe you will."

So they went on home and left me with my mules all haltered—and me well satisfied with the day's work.

These mules walked and tromped and stepped on those drag ropes all night. By morning the tops of their heads were kinda sore and their noses were sore—and when they would step on one of those ropes, they would give to it instead of running or pulling away from it.

That morning I saddled old Beauty—got the rigging on good and tight and tightened the breast harness. I would catch one of these mules and tie him to a post. Soon he would quit pulling on the post too much. Then I would catch another mule and pitch my rope over the mule that was tied to the post—draw them up pretty tight and tie them together at the necks with their own halter ropes. These halter ropes, or drag ropes, were plenty long, and I tied them up real close to where they couldn't go around a tree with each other or get loose anyhow. That left two rope-ends long enough to drag on the ground, so the mules were still stepping on each other's ropes and pulling on each other's heads. But I had three pairs of wild mules tied in pairs.

I took three gentle saddle horses and—with lots of stout, soft ropes that I had been using for stake ropes at night on this trip—rigged them each one with a loose rope collar around the neck, down close to the shoulders. Then I tied another rope fairly tight around the body to make a surcingle, and tied short ropes from the collar rope to the surcingle.

I would crowd a pair of mules up in a corner, lead or push one of the gentle horses up close, get ahold of a mule drag rope, and tie it to the collar rope on the horse. With this collar rope tied back like it was to the surcingle rope, lots of strain was being taken to the surcingle, which went around the horse's entire body. My saddle horses had everything done with them and knew how to pull from a saddle horn or a breast collar; with this rigging they could drag a pair of sore-headed mules easy.

Well, I had three spans of wild mules tied to three saddle horses and one saddle horse left to put my good heavy pack on. I had worked that night before to get my pack ready—my bedroll, cooking gear, extra ropes, and halters and stuff that I had to have—and I put it on this dun horse. He was a good big stout horse and used to carrying a pack, and I had my pack harness and my pack saddle on him good and tight. Old Beauty looked wise and ready when I got on her, opened the gate, and eased in and started the horses and mules all out in the open.

These mules tried to run, but these gentle saddle horses they were tied to would jerk them and pull them back. They couldn't very well get away. I herded them out there on the glade by the corrals about thirty or forty minutes, maybe an hour. I had a bullwhip in my hand, and I would ride in to these mules that were pulling back and hit them with that bullwhip and drive them back with the others. Finally I had them bunched up pretty good. I never did fight my saddle horses that the mules were tied to, but I got them headed out toward the road. They ran crossways a few mesquite saplings and had to get unwound and start over, but by the time I got these mules to the road they were pretty well beat and had begun to line up and walk pretty good. They realized they were caught. The saddle horses had been kind of careful. Hadn't any of them got hurt or pulled very bad, and they had been a controlling influence on the pairs of mules they were tied to.

I rode out in front and opened the gate and drove them all through the gate. I had my packing outfit that I had left Kansas with, before I bought any big teams. I had my saddle horses I started with. I had six head of good young mules worth $100 a head. I had my money in my pocket that I started with, and a profit besides.

I was only about two days from home, a week before Christmas. If it hadn't been the dead of winter, I might have gone back to Kansas for more big work horses.

Traveling Mare

When I was an aspiring young cowman,
still not quite twenty years old,
I had gone to the brush in the
fall to winter a large string
of steers. My partner

and I had several pastures leased, and we stocked them with steer yearlings and two-year-olds which we would winter on the range and sell fat off the grass in the late summer. This kind of operation took a lot of cowboyin' which could not be done without some good, stout, hard, usable horses. They didn't have to be pretty, but they had to savvy a lot of cow and be able to take a good deal of abuse from long, hard rides and bad weather.

This particular winter I had a black horse in my string that you wouldn't fall in love with because of his appearance, and after you rode him all day you would almost hate him. His back was long, his shoulders were straight, his hindquarters were powerful, and he was a little jug-headed but deep in the body, with heavy bone and lots of muscle. The hair up and down the backs of his legs would well denote that his grandma had more than likely pulled a plow. One of the pastures the steers were in joined the Brazos River, and when the river was out of banks, the fences would be washed away and we would have steers in the bog. You could tie this old black horse to a steer and pull him out with the saddle horn and lariat rope without too much strain on the horse. He was also useful for lots of other heavy jobs.

This explanation will cause you to understand why I had endured this old black horse; but now it was spring, and the grass had begun to come in the draw, and the cattle had begun to fill up and shed a little of their winter hair; so I had it on my mind to get me a road horse, and the black was the one I thought needed trading the worst.

I saddled up bright and early one morning and rode into Cleburne, Texas (about twenty-five miles), by noon. Sterling Capps ran an old-fashioned livery stable about a block from the public trading square, and he was always glad to put up a cowboy's horse, gather news about the country he came from, and inform him on the most important happenings since he was last in town.

I rode into Sterling's livery stable and got down off the black, about half churned to death from riding that short-trotting horse with all that power clear to town. As the man led him away to unsaddle and clean off, Sterling remarked about what a big, fine, stout horse I was riding. I wasn't about to explain to my friend Mr. Capps that the horse was jarring the pigtails on the Chinamen on the other side of the earth every time he hit the ground; nor did I explain that the main purpose of my trip was to trade him for something with an easier movement and a more appealing general conformation.

I walked to the main part of town—it was a short distance or I wouldn't have walked it—got a haircut and a shave, which after a long winter improved my appearance some, and went over to the hotel and ate a town-cooked dinner that was sure good after a winter's siege of batchin'. When I moseyed back down to the livery stable, Sterling's handyman had my horse brushed and curried—and to a man not too well versed on stride and ease of motion who was looking for a big stout horse, he would have made a striking picture.

As I had ridden into town, I had noticed a gypsy horse traders' camp on the creek; I also had noticed that the men and horses were gone from the cap wagon. I resaddled the black horse and tried to hold myself up nice in the saddle and let him walk real slow across the market square. There was a wagonload of pigs that a farmer was trying to sell, so I sat on my horse and looked over into this load of pigs—not that you could have given me a pig, but I needed some way to kill a little time until someone noticed my black horse.

After not too long a spell, I looked over to one side and there stood a gypsy horse trader. You could tell them from way off; that was before cowboys had heard about TV, and it was the gypsy horse traders that wore loud shirts. This old boy had on one of the loudest shirts and the baggiest britches; his feet were little bitty, and he had on soft-toed shoes. He looked at me a minute, took his shabby hat off, and that greasy black hair fell down over his ears. He said in a very humble and polite voice: "Meester, you have a very fine horse, and I need heem to work to my wagon. Vould you care to trade?"

In a very unconcerned manner and uncouth voice I said: "I don't know. What you got to trade?"

He motioned toward his trading wagon, which was just a few yards away. I rode up and looked at his horses without getting off mine. There was a beautiful chesnut-sorrel mare about fifteen hands, well kept, with a flowing flax mane and tail. She was tied to the endgate of the wagon, and his other horses were tied along the side and up toward the front. You could tell she was really something special, because he gave her lots of room where the other horses couldn't kick her or get their heads tangled in her halter rope. She had a beautiful short back, a long sloping shoulder; the arch of her neck and throat latch and the beautiful chiseled head were something to behold. Her flax mane and tail had been combed out with a fine toothcomb, and her tail almost drug the ground. I knew without untying her that she would be a dream walking, so I said to this gypsy: "You got no business with a mare like that. She won't match anything you got to work, and these clodhoppers around here don't know how to appreciate that filly, so I guess I'd let you trade her to me."

The gypsy put on a real good act and told me how precious she was to the family, and that they just never traded her off, and that I'd have to pick something else. I said: "That's your mistake. I don't have to pick anything else 'cause I don't want to trade for anything else." And I reined my horse to ride away.

The gypsy said: "Wait a meenute, Meester. Maybe you would geeve me a leetle deeference between thees mare and your horse."

I knew then that I was smarter than the gypsy, so I got down off my horse to look at the mare. She didn't have a pimple or a pin scratch on her and was about an honest six-year-old (by honest, I mean that her mouth had not been changed). He insisted that I ride the mare, and it wasn't hard to get me to try her out. I put my own saddle on her, and she stood very nicely. I stepped on her and rode on off across the trading square. I got out on a back street with her, and she was the nicest mannered mare that you ever could imagine. She had a long, sweeping fox trot and nodded her head just enough to rattle the bit—and didn't jar you the least bit out of the saddle. I told myself that I believed I'd cheat that gypsy out of that mare.

In the meantime, of course, he and his kinfolks had gathered around the black horse and gone over him with their beady black eyes and nervous little twisted fingers, and they knew all there was to know about him. After a batch of unnecessary conversation about the good and bad points of both horses—which no horse trade would be complete without—I offered him $50 difference, which was a pile of money in those days. I never did get off the mare, and the gypsy and his brothers never did quit talking—with all six or eight hands in the air—about how that would be stealing her and she was worth many times more than the black horse.

The reason I didn't offer to give him any more was because that was all the money I had in my pocket, outside of a little change I had to pay Sterling at the livery stable and eatin'-money to leave town on. They had a meetin' between where I sat on the chesnut mare and the black horse; when they came back out of the huddle and went to putting their hands in their pockets, the first gypsy said: "Me take $50."

I paid him and rode off back down to the livery stable so Sterling and the rest of the town boys could congratulate me on a good day's work as a shrewd horse trader. As I rode in, I had the mare reined up just a little so she was hitting her best stride, and people up and down the street had to stop and watch her pass. Sterling said: "She moves like a thief in the night."

I stepped down and said: "Ride her off a little ways, just to realize she's real."

As he came back and got off her he said: "She's real nice."

We put her in a stall, and I visited a little while longer. Late that afternoon I started out of town. Just as I rode out of the gate my old friend Sterling, with a whimsical smile on his face, said: "Ben, does that tail belong to that mare?"

There was a little question mark in the tone of his

voice, and to this least of my worries I answered: "I reckon so. It's following her." And it didn't cross my mind but that all was well.

I rode back to the ranch in solid comfort, fed my new traded-for mare off the porch of my batchin' shack, and left her in the yard instead of putting her out with the other horses.

Along about this stage of my life, all I knew a currycomb and brush were for was to scratch the sweat off horses' backs and knock the dry foam and sweat off their sides where the cinch rubbed. And sometimes I did this with a short broken piece of wood, or I found a corncob was just about as good as a currycomb. I fed, watered, and rode the mare, and her mane and tail soon were hanging in ropy-like strings and lacked the beautiful fluff they once had displayed. But that didn't bother me much, until one morning I walked down to the pen where I had left her the night before, picked up my bridle, and started into the pen to catch her.

The mare was standing with her hindquarters to the gate, and as I walked through the gate I thought she had sprouted an elephant tail in place of a horse tail. That long, beautiful flax tail was hanging by a snag on the fence on the other side of the corral. And the stump of that mare's tail didn't have a hair on it.

The gypsies had fashioned a tail for the mare which they had fastened on with elastic bands—and she was a sickening sight to behold with her "falsy" off.

The Parson's
Mare, Bessie

When I was ranching in the Brazos River country
of West Texas, I had a lot of horses of various
and sundry kinds—might even have been
a few sorry ones among them.
All my horses were on the
light-boned side, and I
was in need of a work
horse or two to use
to a wagon.

It was in the late summer, which was about the time of year that people in the country used to have "Brush Arbor Meetin's." They generally imported some good old preacher from across a few counties to hold these summer meetin's. It wasn't uncommon for preachers to trade churches and hold a meetin' away from home. These saintly old gentlemen generally drove buggies or two-wheel gigs, and some few of them rode saddle horses with huge saddlebags on the backs of their saddles to carry a Bible and their other shirt in.

It so happened that one of these fine old gentlemen came to the farming community down below my ranch to hold a summer meetin'. He drove a nice big fat bay mare named Bessie to a little bitty light two-wheel gig. Bessie's size and proportions suited her much better for a work mare, I thought, than pulling the preacher's gig at a slow walk. The Reverend brushed and curried Bessie, combed her mane and tail, and fed her the good brethren's corn wherever he might be; so her condition was nothing but the best. Wherever he might drive during the day to have dinner, he drove Bessie in a slow walk. And that irritated me a lot to see a great big fat mare pulling a little bitty gig and a small preacher in a slow walk. I just thought the preacher should have a faster and lighter horse, and if I had Bessie she would have a better load to move at a faster step.

Being young and a little on the rough side, and it being the season of the year that I usually loved to run wolves at night with a pack of hounds and good horses, I hadn't been too regular an attendant at the good preacher's meetin's; but I really got to thinking that I might ought to hear the good Reverend preach and—purely as an afterthought—mention the possibility of a little horse trading some night when the meetin' was over.

I rode down to the brush arbor tabernacle one night, and I was being real gentlemanly: I had taken a bath and shaved, and when I got off my horse, I took my spurs off and fastened them on to the saddle instead of wearing them under the brush arbor. Any good close observer would be able to tell by this action that I was properly impressed with the solemness of the occasion. Quite a few of the more devout members of the community took notice and made some mention of my presence, but the kind old preacher acted as though I had been coming all the time and made no mention of any of my past sins, such as wolf hunting, horse and mule trading on Sunday, and the like. I found this attending church rather painless, and as I walked out to where my horse was tied to leave that night, it just occurred to me that everybody had been real nice to me.

I noticed that the preacher's mare was standing tied close to my horse, and even in the dark I could tell that she didn't have any bad wire cuts, big knees, or similar blemishes; but I didn't feel like I ought to mouth her and see how old she was the first time I went to the meetin'.

The weather was hot and dry, and it wasn't a good time for wolf dogs to be able to follow a trail at night; so I attended the meetin' a few more times right straight along, but I still didn't get a chance to mouth that preacher's mare to see how old she was. There was a country store in the community just a few miles from the ranch. One day right after dinner, when most people were taking their naps, I was on my way over to another ranch and rode by the country store to get a cold coke—which was quite a treat in a country where there was no ice—and get posted on the local gossip. The country store-keeper was my good friend and he generally had something interesting to tell, either about the cow market and whatever trades had been made in the country, or maybe he would drift off on the political trend or gossip of the neighborhood. But to say the least, you could always get more than your nickel's worth of conversation along with your bottle of coke.

He had hardly started into conversation when up drives the country preacher with his big mare, Bessie, hooked to that little bitty gig. He shook hands with us and remarked about the heat of the day, and consented to accept my hospitality in the form of a cold drink. I didn't waste any time bringing up this horse trade that had been troubling me the times I had been listening to him preach. I said: "Reverend, that sure is a big fine mare that you've got there, and it seems to me a shame to waste her ability as a work horse pulling a little bitty gig like that. And, too, as valuable a man as you are to the community, you ought to be able to get around faster and do more good tending to your flock."

He pondered my statement a few minutes, and with very carefully chosen words he told me that he had had the desire for a speedier animal, but that he was so fond of Bessie it hurt him to think of parting with her. However, he guessed if the right trade came along, he would be tempted to get a better driving horse that would be more suitable for his needs. I invited him over to the ranch to look over what I had and pick out something that would suit him, and we made a date for him to be at my place the next morning while it was still cool and see if we could have a trade. He further told me that another reason he would consent to look at my horses was that he knew Bessie would have a good home and wouldn't be mistreated.

The next morning the preacher showed up driving Bessie in that usual slow walk, and he had gotten up early enough to give her that nice brushing and combing and grooming that causes any horse to be attractive. By this time in life I was a little better than half smart; so the afternoon before, I had rounded up my trading stock and cut out a few of the very best ones and driven them over to the back of the ranch. I put them in a pasture so the preacher wouldn't have them to pick from. Several of the other horses were broke to work and ride, and I had one red roan mare that was a little Roman-nosed, a little pig-eyed, and just a shade prick-eared; but she was a good driving mare and had plenty of go and plenty of endurance, and I felt like she would be the ideal horse to jerk that little two-wheel gig across the country. I showed the preacher eighteen or twenty head of horses, but I did emphasize the driving qualities of the Roman-nosed, red roan mare.

I began to get aware of the fact that the preacher hadn't told me anything about Bessie. I looked in her mouth, and she was about an eight-year-old. She had a good set of legs and a heavy body and probably would have weighed fourteen hundreds pounds. I asked: "Reverend, does she work hitched double?"

He replied: "I would have no fear of hitching Bessie double or single."

I said: "Is she a good puller in a tight?"

He stated: "Why, I would have no fear of hooking

Bessie to a green load of wood or a wagon loaded with a bale of cotton in a sandy field."

I thought this was sufficient comment and didn't press the old gentleman for any more proof as to Bessie's working qualities. The good preacher made me quite a talk about the scarcity of money with a member of the clergy, and how much better horse Bessie was than the Roman-nosed, red roan mare, and it was so impressive that I paid him $20 boot between Bessie and the red roan mare.

We took Bessie out from the gig and had to punch holes in the harness to take it up enough to fit the red roan mare. We got her hooked up, and the preacher sped along on his way because the red roan mare was for sure a road-eater hooked to a cart.

When the preacher was out of sight, I had to sit down on a stump in the shade of a tree and have a real big laugh and brag on myself about cheating the preacher out of that big fine work mare. I felt then that my only problem was to find another one good enough to work with her, and in the meantime I would just have to hitch that big fat mare up beside a common mule.

I lost my interest in the meetin's, seems like, and it was three or four days before I had an occasion to work Bessie. I was cleaning out a corn crib to make room for some fresh corn, and I backed the wagon up to the crib by hand and loaded it with corn, then proceeded to harness Bessie up. I had to let out my harness and take the pad out from under the collar in order to get the harness big enough to fit Bessie. Then I harnessed a good common mule that I knew would pull, and hooked the two up to the wagon that was loaded with corn. Bessie was very nice and easy to hook up and was gentle to walk around. I put my hand on her hip as I stepped on the doubletree to get up into the wagon, and thought how lucky I was to have such a big, fine mare. I tightened my line and spoke to the team.

The mule started to go—but the tone of my voice didn't seem to impress Bessie, and she didn't move a foot. I looked around to see if I had hitched her wrong or if something was bothering her—if the lines were too tight or something. Her lines seemed to be in order; so I shook the bits and spoke to them pretty plain to "Get up." The little mule lunged at the load, but Bessie stood real still.

It was almost about to dawn on me that Bessie might not work too good to a wagon. I reached out with the end of my line and tapped Bessie a firm, stinging lick on her nice fat rump. The only thing it did was cause her to chew her bit a little faster, but Bessie didn't move. I finally proceeded to use a strong brand of language that Bessie may not have heard before, and I even resorted to a good heavy bullwhip to try to impress upon her the responsibilities of her new position in life. Well, I damn near wore out the whip. And I ran out of any fresh profanity, without repeating myself. And I decided that Bessie wasn't going to pull that load of corn. I took Bessie out of the harness and got another mule, and moved the load of corn with the team of mules.

It was late in the afternoon by now, so I saddled up a horse and rode off down to the country store to confide in my old friend about the preacher's mare, Bessie. I was sitting on a sack of salt drinking my second coke, and my old storekeeper friend was having a belly laugh that he was thoroughly enjoying at my expense. He told me that he thought I should have paid the $20 on the expense of the meetin', anyway. The good preacher had been by the store and told him how well pleased he was with the road performance of the red roan mare.

As I was about to leave the store, up drives the preacher. He had been brushing and currying the red roan mare and feeding her the brethren's corn, one of the brethren had shod her, and she already looked a lot better. There was no one else in the store but the storekeeper and preacher, so I contested the preacher about that statement of his concerning hooking Bessie to that load of wood or that bale of cotton; then I said maybe she knew the difference between these and a load of corn, and maybe she just doesn't like to pull corn.

The preacher smiled and asked me just exactly what he had said. By this time I had had time to ponder it, and I remembered well what he had said. He had said he would have no "fear" in hooking Bessie to a load of green wood or a wagon loaded with a bale of cotton in a sandy field. He smiled, and in a very satisfied tone of voice quoted me Webster's definition of the word "fear" which is, "apprehension of evil or danger, dread or anxiety." And he told me that he had no apprehension of danger of Bessie trying to pull that load, and he had no dread of hooking her to that wagon as she would not kick or hurt herself, and he had no anxiety that she might break her harness or tear up the wagon trying to pull the load.

As he turned to walk away he said: "Young man, you were also truthful about the red roan mare. She is everything that you said she was—and more, too."

The Gray Mules

One winter I was feeding a bunch of steers on the Brazos River on a big old rough ranch—rough pasture and lots of canyons and draws. The river was winding, and it was a hard kind of country to get your feed out into the pasture to feed cattle. Of course, in those days we used wagons and teams for everything.

I had a young team of horses that were thrown in on the deal when I leased the ranch, and that were supposed to be unbroke. Well, that was putting it mildly. Generally when you say a team is unbroke, you are talking about young horses three or four or five years old that just never have been worked. When I got this team up, they were a pair of well-matched bay, bald-faced horses that weighed about fourteen hundred, and instead of being four or five years old and unbroke—they were eight or nine years old and had been broke *at*. But there was sure nobody had ever done much of a job of breaking them.

They were the rankest, big draft-type horses that I had ever had any experience with. When you roped them, they choked and pawed and fought. Then when you got them up and got your hands on them, you would have to tie a foot up on each one to harness them—if you didn't, they would kick you from behind and paw you in front and bite you anytime you weren't looking. Generally, big horses are gentle, but these weren't.

Every morning after I'd load my feed wagon, I'd start to hitch up this team. That meant I'd have to rope them and tie them to a tree and try to get harness on them. And after I'd get them harnessed—each one separately—I'd have to get them up by the side of each other and hook them together and then run them over the wagon tongue —two or three times—before I ever got them to stop where I could draw them back in position to hook them to the wagon. After they were hooked to the wagon, they would either try to run away or try to balk and fly back two or three times when you tried to start them with a load.

I had been carrying on this kind of a battle every

morning for about three weeks. It was taking me twice as long to tend to my steers as it should have, and I decided I had to have another work team. One Saturday morning I hooked them up to the wagon loaded with feed and started through the pasture gate; just as I got the gate open, they came through it and tried to run away. They hung the back wheel on the gatepost, broke the coupling-pin, and ran off with the four wheels. It just happened they ran astraddle a tree—got it between them—and didn't get very far. But this was the final performance that made it easy for me to get rid of them.

The ranch was about thirty-five miles west of Fort Worth; so Sunday morning I saddled up a good saddle horse, led this pair of great big horses over to Fort Worth, took them to Ross Brothers Horse and Mule Barn, and checked them in to be sold the next day at the auction. I got a stall for my saddle horse and cleaned him off and fed him good before I went up to Mrs. Brown's boardinghouse to spend the night.

This was a big old boardinghouse on top of the hill overlooking the horse and mule barns, on the west end of Exchange Avenue. It was kind of horse traders' headquarters, and it was about the only place along about then that I knew to spend the night in Fort Worth—unless I went away over across town to the big hotels.

Next morning I was out at the horse and mule barns early, looking around to pick me out a good team that I knew would be safe and a sure-pull and wouldn't cause me any more grief through the winter while I was trying to tend to those steers. Since I had gotten in with my horses Sunday, they were in the early part of the sale Monday morning.

When they came in the ring, Jim Shelton was doing the auctioneering. He looked down and saw my name on the ticket and said: "Ben, tell me about these horses."

I said: "Well, they're a big stout pair of green-broke horses." My name was Green and I had put the breakin' on them—what little they'd had—so I guessed I could say they were green-broke, although that usually just meant a pair of horses that hadn't been worked much. Anyway, they sold for more money than I had hoped to get for them.

I had been up and down the alleys and back of the barns and looked at some horses and some mules. I had watched them hook-in some various teams of mules to the try-wagon out in front, to see how they would work. I had decided that a good pair of steady mules would be better for me to try to finish feeding cattle through the winter than horses would be. Mules are always more dependable to a wagon in a hard pull, and they usually are quieter than horses are; so I had made up my mind that I'd buy me a nice pair of mules.

I sat there and watched horses and mules sell for three or four hours and got pretty well posted on what I thought mules like I wanted ought to bring when they'd come in the auction ring. About two-thirty in the afternoon I had already decided that I couldn't ride home and lead a team of mules that day—that I'd have to stay over; so I wasn't in too big a hurry to spend my money.

Late that afternoon a great big nice pair of dapple-gray mare mules came into the ring. They were well made and fat, they had good dispositions, and when the man led them around the ring he touched their ears to show they weren't shy about their ears when they were being bridled. Parker Jamison looked in their mouths—he was the ring man—and he hollered out loud: "The prettiest mouths you ever saw. Mark 'em about eight-year-olds."

Wad Ross started them at $200. A few people bid on them—people you could see were commenting on them. I couldn't hear what they were saying, but there was something unusual. The bidding went up to $240, and I bid $250. Didn't anybody else raise my bid. Two or three fellows turned around and looked where I was standing to see who it was bid the $250. I just thought to myself that they were looking at me because I knew a good team when I saw it.

Well, directly Jim Shelton—he was the auctioneer—knocked the mules off to me and hollered: "Sold!"

I watched them go out at the gate and run down the plank alley. They were so near alike, you would have thought they were twins. I saw the pen they turned into, and I had got the numbers off their hips while they were in the ring. When you bid on horses or mules and bought them, then a ticket boy would bring you a ticket. So when I got the ticket, I tore off down the barn alley to look at the mules I'd bought.

I walked in the pen and drove them out on the plank alley to themselves and stood there and looked at them and rubbed them a little bit with my hands. Oh, they were nice, well-made, beautifully dappled mules. I got ahold of the barn foreman and asked if he couldn't put them off in a separate pen where wouldn't anything happen to them—they wouldn't get skinned up or maybe kicked in the night.

He was real nice, said he knew I was proud of that pair

of mules and he didn't blame me—he would be proud of them, too—and that he would put them over to one side in a pen to themselves. Of course he knew me, knew I was horseback. He said he would sure help me with them and I could go on and forget them.

Well, I had seen a lot of horse and mule selling that day and I was kind of tired of the barn; so I got on the streetcar and rode over to the big main part of Fort Worth to eat a big steak at the Siebold Hotel. I went up to the picture show—the Majestic Theater—and saw Richard Dix in *Cimarron*. Then I went back to Mrs. Brown's boardinghouse and went to bed about nine-thirty. I had a long ride ahead of me the next morning.

I got to the horse and mule barn by daylight. After two nights and one day's rest, my saddle horse was in good shape and ready to go. I got him saddled and rigged out and got my mules out. They had nice woven grass halters on them like used to come on horses and mules that were bought at auctions, and I tied a long lead rope to these halters. Somebody held my lead rope while I got on my saddle horse, handed me the lead rope, and I started out of the horse and mule market and up Exchange Avenue. I was going to hit the White Settlement Road and head out west. It was pretty chilly, but not real cold, and the sun not near in sight.

I was way out in the edge of town before it got good sun-up, and my horse settled down to a nice long sweeping walk. This was a good pair of mules, and they traveled nice and walked right up by my horse. I crossed plank bridges with them and they didn't shy or pull back—or get scared from meeting anybody—and the farther I went toward home with them, the better I liked them and the prouder I was of them. It was a little after dark when I rode into the ranch, and I put my new mules in a small pasture next to the barn and gave them plenty of feed. I turned my saddle horse loose and fed him and went to bed thinking how much nicer it was going to be to tend my cattle through the rest of the winter with the right kind of a work team.

This was about the nicest colored pair of dapple-gray mare mules anybody ever saw. The dappling was real smooth and beautiful and uniform over their hindquarters and up and down their sides and around their shoulders. Their heads and necks were just a little lighter color, just as they should be. Then their feet and legs from their knees and their hock joints to the ground were real dark, just the way they should be. They had a beautiful color for a pair of eight-year-old mare mules, just about as nice as anybody could ever have wished for. I don't believe a real good artist could have painted them any more perfect than they were.

In the meantime, I had left instructions to get my wagon brought in and fixed, and I had the wheels and the coupling-poles all ready to hook up to it that morning and start back to feeding my cattle. I got these mules out, and I had to let the harness out some to where it would fit them. They were a nice, big pair, and it took big harness to fit them. I had several collars, and I had to change around until I got the collars that would fit on them good —to where they could pull good and not hurt their shoulders. I just could hardly take my eyes off of them, they had such a beautiful dapple-gray color.

I hooked up to the wagon and drove them around the lot two or three times to the empty wagon. They didn't do a thing wrong. They didn't make a bobble or take a wrong step. And I backed them up to the crib of the barn where I loaded my feed, dropped my lines, and said: "Woah." They just stood there. As I threw feed into the wagon I made noise throwing the sacks around; they never moved. I finally had a team that were just broke to perfection.

I put on a big load of feed and started out through the pasture. It was a big old long rough pasture, some hills and bad places to pull over, and one place I went down into the valley and across the creek. It was the common way you forded a creek—no bridge or nothing—and coming out of the bank on the other side it was a little slick. The load was heavy, and these mules got down just as smooth and even and pulled with each other as steady as you every saw a team pull. It was quite a relief from the work team I'd had in that pair of horses.

I had my saddle horse leading behind, tied to the back of the wagon. I drove up to the feed grounds where generally I'd feed my cattle, and they weren't all there. I called and hollered a few times, and you could hear a few cattle bawl. Some were coming; some were up on the side of the mountain and weren't trying to get down there to the feed grounds. I left my new team standing with the lines done up, but not tied to any kind of a tree or post or hitched in any way. I thought: "This pair of mules is so perfect, they won't run off with the wagonload of feed."

I got on my saddle horse and loped up in the hills and started the cattle moving toward the feed ground. I circled around, and after I knew everything was coming in good, I rode back down to the wagon. There that pair of dapple-gray mules stood, just perfect. They hadn't offered to get scared or run off or twist around or try to graze or do anything that a good mule oughtn't to do.

I fed my cattle at this pasture and tied my horse to the back of the wagon again. I stepped in and took the lines down from the stick I had them wrapped around. Since I had unloaded some of my feed, I trotted my mules off in a pretty good trot and started over into another pasture about a mile away. This good pair of mules didn't mind trotting to the load. They stayed in step good, and it was a pleasure to stand up in the wagon and look over them and watch how nice they worked. It was just hard to believe an eight-year-old pair of mules would be so near perfect.

By the time I got to the next feed ground, they had begun to break a sweat a little around the collars and up and down the backbands and around where the breeching worked on their hindquarters. I didn't think a little sweat hurt a mule, so I just trotted them on to the next feed ground. I had to round the cattle up in this pasture, and I left my mules standing out in the feed ground, close to a feed trough. They were just perfect. They stood there until I got back. I rode up and put out the feed and tied my horse back to the wagon. I had one more pasture to feed.

I drove across the creek again and up the bank on the other side—pulled them pretty hard. I thought there was a little dirt working out of their hides and their hair maybe. I noticed some black lines coming along the backbands and around the collars where the sweat worked out. I didn't think much about it, only I just thought they sure were a nice pair of mules to be that dirty. I hadn't noticed too much dirt in their hides when I was harnessing them, but that didn't bother me much. I stopped them at the next feed ground to wind up my morning's work. It was kinda clouding up and misting a little bit, and these cattle came to feed better than the others had.

I did the reins up on my saddle horn. My saddle horse knew the way back to headquarters—he didn't have to follow the wagon—so he trotted on out the road in front of us, and I stepped the mules up to a good brisk trot. When they moved out, I noticed the backbands were working the sweat back and forth—and that every time they did, the hair got a little whiter around the backbands and a little bit more dirt piled up and down that ridge. There was a little sweat coming on their hind legs, and I noticed some black lines running down their legs. I didn't think much about that. I just thought these mules must have been wallowing somewhere in the blackland and just had a lot of dirt down next to the hide—and I hadn't noticed it.

When I went through the last pasture gate and started up to the house, a little shower came and sort of washed everything off. It was a quick little hard shower, and I pulled my jacket up over my head and rode along. The mules were trotting along good; my saddle horse was on ahead, probably to the barn by now; I wasn't looking too close—just letting the mules go, following the road at a good brisk trot. When we pulled up at the barn another pretty hard shower hit, and I ran in the barn. I thought I would stay until it let up, and then I would unhook my team.

Well, my team was pretty warm—of course, it wouldn't hurt a good mule to get rained on—so I stood in the feed room a few minutes until it slowed raining, and then I went out. I was keeping my head kinda ducked—to keep the rain from hitting me in the face—as I unhooked the traces and unhooked the coupling-pole and drove the mules up to the edge of the barn where the water wouldn't hit quite so much. I went to taking off the collars and the harness, and after I stripped it off and hung it up in the barn—I turned around and looked.

My mules had sure bleached out a batch—between getting sweaty and getting rained on! And I had a lot of stain all over my hands—and all over my sleeve where I had run my hand through the harness to carry it in and hang it up in the barn!

By this time I had forgot that it was misting rain, and I rubbed my hand down one mule's neck and across where the collar had worked—and I just rubbed off great, big, wide streaks of those beautiful dapples. And the farther I rubbed, the more dapples I rubbed. And the more I rubbed, the sicker I got. When it got through raining, and I got through rubbing, I had a pair of mules as white as gray mules can get in a lifetime. Now, they were just as white as white mules ever get to be! This was sure the first time I ever lost $100 on a pair of mules in two days—without one of them dying.

Well, I had that color all over me, and I hadn't decided yet what kind it was. Anyway, I kinda washed my hands in a little puddle on the ground by the side of the barn where it dripped, and I opened one of these mule's mouths. She had a cup in the corner tooth like an eight-year-old ought to have; but her tooth was too long for an eight-year-old, it was too wide across the top, and it was too ridged up and down the side. My mules were a good thirteen or fourteen years old. Somebody had worked their mouths and made them an eight-year-old corner, and evidently somebody had given them a dye job. I didn't know what they were dyed with or how anybody did it. The dapples were so natural and so purple and so well shaped—nobody in the world could ever have guessed that they didn't belong to these mules.

Then it kinda began to dawn on me about that whispering and looking that those people did when I was bidding on this pair of mules. And I got to thinking how that barn foreman smiled when he said he would help me take care of them—that he knew I wouldn't want anything to happen to them. I don't know whether women had beauty parlors by then or not—but there was bound to have been a mule beauty parlor somewhere, because that pair had as nice a hair job done as could be done on any kind of animal.

They were a real nice work pair, and I was busy wintering a bunch of cattle, and the weather was bad. I kinda hibernated and stayed at home and fed steers and worked my mules. There was just no fault in their working qualities or their dispositions. They stayed fat, and they were easy to shoe—never offered to kick or do anything wrong. There was just nothing wrong with them except that dye job. The color had made it pretty deceiving about how old they were. The dapple-gray color went with an eight-year-old tooth, but the white color they had now went with a mouth that looked about fourteen years old when you got to looking at it close. When Parker Jamison called the age on them, I don't know whether he knew the difference or not. I imagine he did, but he was trying to match the mouth up with the color.

I got to hunting through my vest pocket, and I found

the ticket that showed who owned the mules when they were consigned to the sale. Of course, I never bothered about who bought that green-broke pair of horses—that was their trouble. What I was bothered about was that dye job on this pair of mules. I saw that the name on the ticket was that of a very prominent horse and mule man who lived off down about Hillsboro somewhere.

I went to two or three First-Monday trades around over the country, and I'd get into conversation with a bunch of road traders or old-time horse and mule men. I would just sort of bring up casual-like about: "Wouldn't it be nice if a dapple-gray mule could just keep its color like that all its life."

It generally didn't start much conversation, except that everybody would say: "Yeah, but the older they git the whiter they git." Which wasn't news to me.

I would just say: "Uh-huh," and walk off.

Hardly anybody knew about my mules because I had kept them at home and worked them, and I had got them home without anybody seeing them. Oh, maybe some of the neighbors had noticed they had whitened out on me, but it didn't ever dawn on them how come it. One man did say something about them turning awful white. I said: "Yeah, the hair has got out on them long, and I guess they'll blue back up when they shed in the spring."

I knew an Irish horse trader that was about a half-breed gypsy—been raised in a road camp. I kept laying for him, but it didn't seem like he was ever going to come through the country again. I figured he would know how you manage to do a blue job on a mule.

I took some saddle horses to Decatur one trades day, to trade maybe for something different. These horses weren't good and they weren't bad, it was just that once in a while you would want to change colors on your stock —or sizes, or ages, or something. Anyway, you needed to have a little variety among your livestock, some new experiences about what could be the matter or what could be good about some of them. So in Decatur, about the middle of the morning, I spied my old Irish horse trader friend.

He and I had traded a few times in years past. It never had been anything big. We always hurrahed and tried to cheat each other if we could—but for a horse trader he was sort of on the honest side, and I was just a great big wild rough young boy and he kinda liked me. A time or two he had told me things I needed to know, so I propositioned him to let's go up town and eat some dinner. He lived in a road camp and ate his own cooking, or camp cooking, so he said he believed he'd like a little change and he believed he'd just take me up on my proposition.

We got some chile or some stew or something—I don't know. We ate a pretty good little batch of dinner and visited and talked about how the country looked and where he had been since I saw him last. By this time we were about to order pie and wind up the dinner; so I decided I'd better ease up on these gray mules. I said: "It's a pity that a nice dapple-gray mule or horse can't stay that color all its life."

"Yeah," he said, "but we all get gray when we get old."

"I know," I said, "You are getting a little gray, but I ain't worried about you—and it's a long way off for me— but I got some mules that got gray pretty soon."

He had a sharp black eye, and he glanced up at me

real quick. A little twist came in the corner of his lip, and he said: "How do you mean?"

Well, I hadn't told anybody else, but I didn't think he would tell on me; so I explained to him what had happened about my mules. He thought it was real funny, and we had a good laugh. Then he said: "Where did the mules come from?"

I told him about this high-class horse and mule man from down around Hillsboro who had sent them to Fort Worth—that his name was on the ticket when I bought them.

"Oh, you mean him! I remember when he was a road trader—till he married that rich woman that had a good farm. Then," he said, "he got respectable. He's not supposed to remember any old tricks like that—much less play 'em on people that are buyin' work stock."

"What do you mean—old trick?"

So he described how the dapples looked on the mules, and sure enough, he knew. He knew that they were darker and bigger around on the sides and down on the lower part of the belly. And he knew that they were smaller and lighter up around their necks and shoulders. He just knew exactly how these mules were colored— and he never had seen them.

I said: "Damn, did this man from Hillsboro learn how to color them mules from you, or did you learn from him? Evidently you all are using the same color pattern."

He kinda laughed and said: "I'll tell you—I'll go down and look at your horses and see if there is anything I want to trade you out of that would be worth a little boot between mine and yours. Then, I'll tell you how to recolor your mules—and call it boot."

We laughed, and I told him that would be sort of like blackmail, I reckoned, but it might not be anything new in the horse and mule business. We visited on—and I asked him where he was going from there. He said it didn't make much difference, that he could drift down south. He would kinda like to be in Waco in about a month, so he believed he would come by and see my mules in a few days.

I told him that sure would be fine, that I had a good little pasture he could camp in, and he wouldn't have to stake out his stock. He could let them run loose for a few days and fill up before he went on down the road. He said he thought that was a good proposition—for me not to worry too much about the color on my mules because they just might gain it back.

I said: "Well, I've heard of mules gaining weight back, growing out their manes and tails and things like that—but I've never heard of one gaining its color back."

"You boys," he said, "that stay at home and feed cattle —there's things you haven't heard about. Let's go on back down to the trade ground. If I don't see you no more there, I'll come by your place in two or three days."

He knew where I was ranching and how to get there. It wasn't too much out of his way if he was going to go on down into central Texas.

I traded a saddle horse or two that day—didn't do anything too smart or too dumb, which was a fair average for me along about then. I started home along about the middle of the afternoon, rode by his wagon and waved at him, and told him I would be looking for him.

He said: "That's fine. Kill a yearling and get some fresh groceries and I'll stay a few days."

That was a common remark, and we both waved and laughed and I rode off thinking that maybe I was going to be able to lead my mules back through the fountain of youth after all. It was getting to be up in the spring of the year, and it was nice to travel horseback and have my bunch of trading stock on the road. They could graze along the way, and there was water in the road ditches.

Sure enough, in four or five days my Irish horse-trading friend pulled up to my ranch gate in the late afternoon. I saw him coming—I was out at the barn doing something—and I went and opened the gate and let his stock in and let him drive his wagon in. I waved to him to turn down toward the creek and some great big pecan trees to set up his camp. I walked alongside his wagon until he pulled up between two big trees where he would be in the shade all morning and afternoon both. I helped him unhitch and shuck the rigging off his team—untied the ones that were tied to his wagon and just turned them loose there in the small pasture.

We got through and sat down on the wagon tongue and talked a few minutes. "I want to see your changeable mules," he said.

"I don't know whether they are so changeable or not," I said. "They just changed once since I've had them —and it wasn't for the better."

We walked up to the barn where the mules were in the corral on the other side of the barn. Regardless of their color, they were still nice mules, and I had kept them fat and their feet were in good shape and their shoes weren't too worn. They were just good mules. I had let their manes grow out—I hadn't roached their manes or sheared their tails—and they looked a little ragged. But you couldn't make mules like them look too bad regardless of what you neglected about them.

This old Irish horse trader was, I guess, about sixty years old. He said: "Kid, you've sure got a pretty pair of mules, and it is a shame that they seem to have lost that youthful bloom so all of a sudden."

I started up again and I said: "Well, if there's any way to color a mule—and there's bound to be—then they had been colored. But I can't understand how you could get the dapples so smooth and even—and small where they needed to be and large where they needed to be. It's a mystery to me—it was just a work of art. I guess you might brush it on. But how would you get the mule to stand long enough?"

He just died laughing. "It's easy," he said.

We sat there a few minutes on the feed trough out in the lot—just looking at our stock. His horses and mules that he had brought in with his wagon—they had been to the creek and drunk and wallowed and had begun to graze. He said: "It's going to help my tradin' stock to get two or three days rest in here—in that good pasture."

I said: "Yeah, you needn't be in any hurry gettin' on down the road. Let 'em fill up."

"That might give me time to help the looks of your mules some, too."

I said: "Well, you know, the main reason I'd want the looks of these mules helped is—our friend down at Hillsboro must like this dapple-gray color of mules we are talking about, or else he wouldn't have colored this pair. And I just felt like maybe he'd like to have another pair back—if they were the right color."

He laughed and he said: "I don't believe that'll work.

He's too sharp for that." We sat in silence a few minutes and then he said: "But I'll tell you what would work," and his face brightened up like he had just seen the light.

"What's that?"

He said, "He's got a son-in-law that's a-buyin' mules at Cleburne and a-usin' the old man's checkbook. The son-in-law, he's not too sharp a mule man, but his daddy-in-law has got to keep him up someway—so he lets him buy horses and mules for him and use his checkbook. He's a-stakin' him on the halves, hopin' he'll make half as much as it's costin' to keep him up."

I said: "Well, maybe we can make it be half-color and half-mules and have a little deal with the son-in-law—if you know how to put the blush back on them that they had when I got 'em."

"Kid, it's easy—if you know how."

"Yeah, you said that before, but you cut me out ever time you add that if-you-know-how to it. Besides that, if you was to put that cloudy color on 'em here, I don't know how I'd get 'em to Cleburne without it running on 'em."

He stayed around and we visited two or three days. His trading stock filled up, and he enjoyed resting under the big trees. He slept in his wagon and I slept at the house, but he ate with me and visited, and he told me a lot of things about trading that I never knew. He rode around the pasture with me, and he told me that when he was a young man he thought he would be a cow man. But, he said, he never could figure out how you would make any money just waiting for a cow to have a calf. He said if you went to trading in cattle you couldn't cheat any-body—because about the time you thought you knew all

273

there was to know about a steer or a cow, all they had to do was weigh her and make a fool out of you. So far as he was concerned, he had rather have swapping stock than beef stock.

Along about now, that all made sense to me, too.

The afternoon he was ready to go, he never yet had told me how he was going to color that pair of mules—or how for me to color them. It seemed like a deep, dark-gray secret. All he would ever tell me when I would bring it up was: "It's easy, Kid. It's easy."

Well, that "Kid" with me and "it's easy" was about to drive me beyond the kid stage. I was aging fast from wondering how we would do it. He got all harnessed and hooked up one morning and pulled out in the road in front of the house and started to leave. I said: "You never have . . ."

"Yeah, I know, I never have," he said. "In about three nights from now I'll camp down close to Godley. That won't be far out of Cleburne. You bring your mules and spend the night at the wagon with me, and I'll get 'em in shape that you can take 'em to Cleburne the next morning and show 'em to this promisin' young mule buyer. The trip will be so short that I don't think the dye job will run on 'em."

Well, I'd finished the winter, and I'd fed my cattle, and I was through with the mules, and they were a year older by the calendar but six years whiter. So on the appointed day I saddled up, tied my mules to the saddle horn, and started off to find my Irish gypsy friend's wagon.

I went through Granbury and on down through Cresson and on over to Godley. My old Irish friend was camped down below Godley two or three miles—out by the side of the road where there was a little pond of water and some fresh grass, a nice place to camp and not too far from Cleburne. The next morning was Monday, and it would be a Trading Monday, which would be an ideal day to be in Cleburne.

I rode into camp and we had our "howdys" out, and I staked my mules over to one side where they wouldn't mix up with his. He had a fire going, and it was sort of late. He was frying up some meat and stuff and had a Dutch oven full of sour dough biscuits; so we sat down and ate a big supper. It was the spring of the year and it got a little chilly, so we sat around the fire a little while before we unrolled the bedrolls and went to sleep. I still didn't know about coloring these mules—but he knew I was there, so I wasn't going to bring it up.

The next morning was a bright, sunshiny morning and he said: "Well, this is a nice clear day for our little chore."

I said: "It don't seem to me like it's such a little chore."

"Oh," he said, "it won't take but just a little while. I got the fixin's the last town I came through."

I said: "Well, I'd still like to know about these fixin's."

"Oh," he said, "Don't let it bother you. It's easy. These mules are gentle?"

"Sure, they're gentle!"

Well, in the meantime I had roached their manes and sheared their tails up neat to their bodies, and they were looking good. I had trimmed a little of the long hair off around their fetlocks and under their chins. The mules

275

were in good shape so far as dressing and brushing and currying were concerned. They just lacked that little tinting job.

We finished breakfast, and my Irish horse-trading friend set the black kettle off the fire, over to one side, and said he was going to have to let that cool. "I still don't know what you're doing," I said.

"Kid, don't worry. I know what I'm doing."

"I believe you," I said. "I'm just waiting for the demonstration."

He reached back in the wagon into a little box and brought out some black Easter egg dye. I told him, "Now this ain't Easter—and anybody knows that the bunny didn't bring these mules—and I don't see how that is gonna work."

He said: "Kid, don't let it bother you."

Well, he made up that black Easter egg dye in that pot with me asking: "How in the world are you gonna get it on 'em?"

"Oh," he said, "that's the simplest part about it."

He reached back in the cooking part of his old wagon and got three great big brown hen eggs. He didn't cook them, and he didn't crack them. He took those hen eggs and dipped them in that Easter egg dye. Where he wanted a little dapple, he would mash the small point of the egg into the hair and turn it around. That dye would come off the egg in a nice little round circle. Then where he wanted a big dapple, he would change ends and dip that egg in the dye and turn it around on the hair. The dye would come off the egg to where the hair would stay white in the middle. Then if he wanted a long, oblong kind of dapple along the bottom of the belly, he would use the egg the long way. I stood and watched him, and he worked just as nimble and fast as anybody can ever imagine. In about an hour's time he had a nice pair of dapple-gray mules with the little dapples where they belonged, the big dapples where they belonged, the dark dapples where they belonged—and of course the lower parts of the legs were already black and didn't need any touching up.

When the sun got up higher and brighter and the dye dried on these mules, they were just simply beautiful. They were just as nice a pair of mules as I had bought before, and I thought about taking them back home with me. But I knew we might have another shower, or I might get them wet with sweat again. And too, the teeth hadn't changed any. They were still too long, and too rough, and too wide. That corner that had been put there changed their ages in part of their mouths only.

When he got them dappled out pretty he said: "Now, Kid, you'd better go back to the ranch and feed your cattle and see how much you can get 'em to weigh. This is a professional job, and I'd better wind it up for you."

I told him that I'd let him wind it up for me, but that I was going to go along to watch the show.

We pulled in on the trades square in Cleburne, and it was the middle of the morning and lots of other traders were there. A good many mules were standing around, but it was still early enough in the spring that there was a good demand for mules, especially good stout heavy well-fed mules that could go to work. I sat around on my horse and watched. Didn't anybody know me much. I'd mosey around horseback from one wagon to the next. I didn't have any other trading stock with me.

Sure enough, after a while here comes this overly

dressed son-in-law with a big diamond horseshoe stickpin and a great big diamond ring and a great big white hat—and a bigger mouth. He came to buy some mules for his father-in-law, and he was carrying that long checkbook. He walked around the wagon and talked to my Irish friend a few minutes. He picked out a brown mare and he picked out a bay horse. Then he said: "I think I'll have to have that pair of dapple-gray mules." He looked in their mouths and asked: "How much for them?"

My friend said: "$300."

"Aw—they're a nice pair of mules and they're ready, but they're not worth quite $300."

My old horse-trading friend said: "I don't get many mules with that quality, and I'm really not capable of knowin' what they're worth. What do you think you can give for 'em?"

"Well, I could give you $250."

My friend said: "I couldn't take that, but I'd take $275."

"Aw—that would be too much. I'll give you $265."

I was holding my breath, and my Irish friend was a-pawing around on the ground like a horse that was tied to something he didn't like, but directly he said: "I guess that'll be all right. You can just pay me."

The son-in-law whipped his big long checkbook out and made out a check for the bay horse and the brown mare and the gray mules. He hollered across the yard at a Negro to come and get them and lead them off for him. He wouldn't have wanted to get his gloves off or get them dirty leading that stock around. After all, he wasn't spending his own money.

So I waited until he got away with them, and I got

down off my horse and leaned up against the wagon wheel and stood there and laughed a while.

My old Irish friend said: "You don't want this check. I've got the money on me, so I'll just pay you."

He gave me my $265. I told him that I had $250 in those mules, but I had worked them all winter, so I would take $225. I gave him back $40 for his trouble.

He said that was getting a pretty good price for Easter egg dye that early in the season, and he thanked me. I told him to come by and camp any time he was in my part of the country.

He told me that I'd better go back to making cattle get fat—then when I got cheated, it would be by weight and not by color.

The Schoolmarm and Ol' Nothin'

Along in the early thirties, I had passed
all winter in a two-room shack out
on a ranch and wintered a string
of big steers with intentions
of sending them to

northern feeders the following summer or fall. It had been a mild winter. The cattle had not been too much trouble to tend to, and I'd had lots of good horses to ride, with plenty of time on my hands to socialize.

There was a schoolmarm in the nearby village that I had been giving the rush act through the winter, and we had been having lots of fun. There was a bunch more young folks in and around the little ranch town, and we had parties, moonlight picnics, and wolf hunts for social entertainment through the winter, as well as eating hamburgers and going to the picture show on Saturday night.

I guess I had gotten farther away from the cow business, with this schoolmarm, than I realized. I had been keeping a special ordered blue serge suit in the pressing parlor in town, and I would ride in horseback, put my horse in a corral next to the feed mill, then go to the pressing parlor and the barbershop and get smoothed off and dressed up.

This schoolmarm had a new Model A Ford convertible coupé—the first Ford I ever saw with a standard shift and two pedals in it—and we would get in it and take on whatever social activities were going on.

So the winter had passed and had been very enjoyable. It was spring of the year and grass had put out. The mesquites were leafing out. Cows were licking themselves and having baby calves. Horses had all slicked off, would swell up when you cinched them and hump up when you tried to ride them. It was hard to get the big boys and girls to go to school, and it was still harder to keep the little ones in the schoolhouse after they got there. So it was the natural time of the year for a school-closing.

One Friday afternoon my schoolmarm picked me up

to take me down about twenty-five miles to another town where her daddy was superintendent of the schools. She said that there was going to be a big weekend—a party Friday night and Saturday night and some kind of goings-on Sunday—and she wanted me to go home with her and stay at the house with her folks, and we could come back Sunday night or Monday morning.

Well, I wasn't too well house-broke for such affairs, but it sounded like a lot of fun, so I went along.

Sure enough, the old folks were expecting me to come home with her, and they were all set. The old man was a fine old Southern gentleman, very light-complexioned and probably of Irish descent. His wife was a good-looking, black-headed woman, and this schoolmarm had gotten her features and his coloring—which sure did turn out to be a good cross. But on second glance at her mother, you could readily determine that the professor had kept school close to the Reservation when he was a young man; and my schoolmarm's grandmother was probably the daintiest little creature that ever dusted out a wigwam with a wild-turkey-wing duster.

Sure enough, we went to parties, dinners, and feeds, and had a big time over the weekend. Sunday, after church, the old man and I were a-settin' on the front porch waiting for the schoolmarm and her mother to get dinner ready. There was another little girl about nine years old, almost a tomboy, and cute as she could be. She came out and took me by the finger, wanting to lead me off to show me her pets. She had a black and white pet rabbit and a banty hen with some baby chicks. Well, I had raised lots of rabbits and banty chicks, so she and I had a big visit. She was a real sharp, likable little kid.

We had started back to the front porch with her leading me by the finger when she said: "It sure will be fun having you for my big brother. We can just do all kinds of things together."

I tried not to booger from a little girl—but that double harness rattled in my face and spooked me just as bad as shaking a chain harness at a saddle horse.

We had a real good Sunday dinner. I minded my table manners and didn't eat with both hands all the time. I bragged on the old woman's cooking and laughed at the professor's jokes.

We started back in the middle of the afternoon. This cute little schoolmarm was full of talk and plans, so I hardly opened my mouth—which was quite unusual for me. When she finally did slow up, she told me that her mother thought I was real nice and her father said I was just like an "own son." There was that double harness shaking at me again.

We got into town about dark, drove around to the corral where my horse was, and she told me the coming Friday night was school-closing. There was going to be a big country play and an ice cream and cake supper after the play was over. She said she was going to be awfully busy with the details and arrangements, but that I could come over to the school horseback. I told her that suited me just fine.

There was an old camp house next to the corral where I had thrown my saddle and work clothes when I left my horse. I changed clothes in the moonlight and went over to the pressing parlor and stuffed my good suit in the back screen door. Of course the pressing parlor man would know what to do with it when he found it the next day.

My old horse was full and seemed to have enjoyed my being gone. I saddled him up and rode out of town. It normally was my habit after dark, riding home from town, to drop off to sleep and let my horse take me home. He would paw on the gate when we got there and wake me up. But tonight I wasn't sleepy. I had left home when I was thirteen years old and wrangled horses on a chuck wagon. I had batched and ranched most of the time ever since and had ridden back and forth from the ranch to the school during my high school years. I was twenty-odd years old now, a lone wolf, and sure a-scared of that double harness!

I spent the rest of the week up and down the Brazos River, riding over my ranch and my neighbor's, kinda dreading that school-closing Friday night. By Friday night I had lost my taste for such sweet stuff as ice cream, cake, and schoolmarms, and didn't feel like the play would be too interesting. I rode up the creek into the back of the pasture, which was about three miles, carried a little grub sack with me, built a fire, cooked some meat on the end of a forked stick, unsaddled my horse, lay down on my saddle blanket, and took a nap. I knew that there wouldn't anybody find me up there unless they came horseback, and I didn't think that schoolmarm would come up the creek horseback hunting for me. When I woke up the moon was hanging over toward the west, and I thought it was late enough to go back to the shack.

I had some steers to change pastures with and left the shack early the next morning. I rode back in just a little before dinner time, and that Model A was parked out in front of my batching shack. As I rode up, that cute little schoolmarm came bouncing out of that shack, walking mad all over. She must have just had a visit with Emily Post. She told me all the un-nice things that I had done by not coming to the school-closing, and that she was fixin' to straighten up and change a lot of my ways. She said she would be by late the next afternoon to take me home with her, as Mamma and Daddy were planning a party for us Sunday night—and for me to be dressed up and ready. Then, with this set of orders and instructions, she turned and got into that Model A and went over the hill in a cloud of dust. I just stood there holding my horse, and never had a chance to answer back a word.

I went into my shack, and it had an uncomfortable look to it. She had done made up the beds and straightened stuff up to where I couldn't find my frying pan to fix dinner—and I *knew* that wasn't going to suit me.

I didn't leave the ranch the rest of the day, and that night I ate a big supper of bachelor's grub—beans, beef, and potatoes. About this stage in my life, I could eat just about anything I got to that didn't eat me first and sleep anywhere I got still.

The next morning I woke up a little before daylight. Ol' Nothin' had walked up out of the pasture and stuck his head over the back fence. I hadn't ridden Ol' Nothin' much all winter, and he was feeling fit and looked like he needed to go on a long trip.

Ol' Nothin' probably had the best legs, the deepest chest, and the most powerful hind-end that was ever put on a horse. He was fifteen-one hands high and covered all the ground he stood on. But there was one bad thing about Ol' Nothin', his neck was poorly shaped and was away too long. There was about a foot, right behind his ears, that you wondered why it had been put there. This caused him to be limber-necked and high-headed, and he didn't have much mouth. I hesitated to ride him in the brush or rough country because he ran with his head up and seldom saw where he was going. He was sound, gentle, a real good pack horse, and a brush race horse that wouldn't quit.

I had just shod Beauty the day before. She was always my standby and favorite, and she hadn't been ridden too hard lately. And when I got to thinking about that party the old woman and the professor had planned for me and the schoolmarm, and I looked at Ol' Nothin' and Beauty, I thought about what a good time it was to take a long pack trip and maybe buy up a few good bronc horses to break and sell that fall.

I let Ol' Nothin' in the yard gate and fed him some feed out on the front porch. I always kept a sack of feed in the house, in case a horse came up and wanted a bite to eat. I whistled at Beauty and let her in, then fed her off the other end of the porch.

While my horses were eating, I gathered up my personal belongings and riggin' and fixed up a pack to put on Ol' Nothin'. I saddled Beauty, put my bedroll and clothes, my frying pan, and a few other belongings in my pack, cinched and tied it down on Ol' Nothin', and put a halter on him. He led the best of any horse I ever took with me. He would lead right up beside the horse you were riding and never tighten the halter rope.

By late in the evening, I rode up to an old friend's place and told him I was going on a little horse-buying trip, and I wished he would see that my steers had salt and would look about my batching outfit until I came back.

He was an old bachelor and a sure-nuff cowboy. He busted out laughing and said: "Ben, is that schoolmarm crowding you?"

I didn't admit it, but I told him I thought I would do better in some other country for a while.

In five or six days I rode into Abilene, Texas. I hadn't hurried much; I had visited along the way, and my horses didn't show much sign of the trip. Jenks McGee was an old-time horse and mule dealer in Abilene and had a barn not far from the main part of town. I rode into the barn in the late afternoon. There was nobody around. I found an empty corral and put my horses in it. I threw my pack saddle and my saddle in the harness room and fed my horses out of his grainery (graineries and barns and saddle rooms didn't come equipped in those days with locks. Locks were something brought on later by the machine age).

After I had my horses well looked after, I thought I would mosey off up into the main part of Abilene, eat supper, and go to the picture show. I walked into the lobby of the hotel, next to the post office, and there was one of the gals that had taught school with my schoolmarm. She had already made it home after the school-closing. She was real glad to see me and was full of conversation. She didn't try to pry into why I was in town or where I was going. While we were drinking a coke, some more gals came in. There were three or four of them gathering there to go to the picture show. She asked me to go along, but I flinched and got out of it. It had just begun to dawn on me that this country was overstocked with young female wimmin. I had supper and made my way back down to the mule barn. I undid my bedroll, spread it out on the saddle room floor, and went to sleep.

The next morning, about daylight, Jenks McGee kicked me to see who he had for a night guest. I got up, and we had a little visit while we were feeding my horses. He asked me what my business was, and I told him that I was going to buy some young horses to take home and break. He said I might not have any more sense than to give what a good horse was worth, and that might mess up his business; so he would rather I would move on farther west than to be buying horses in his territory. He had a truck going to Carlsbad, New Mexico, to pick up some polo horses, and he would send me to Carlsbad for nothing. He thought I could probably buy some broncs a little cheaper out there than I could around Abilene. It sounded like a good proposition, so I took him up.

I didn't tarry around Carlsbad long. I saddled up and rode off into northwestern New Mexico, high up in the mountains, where I knew there were lots of good horses and mighty few buyers.

I drifted into Cloudcroft, then back into the Apache Reservation, and was camped one night near an Indian trading post about fifty miles up in the mountains, south of where the Ruidoso race track is now. There were lots of good horses in this country, and I had begun to put out the word among the natives and the Indians that I wanted to buy a few young horses. I stayed camped high up in the mountains, between Almogordo and Ruidoso, close to this Indian trading post.

About the third afternoon I was there, some Indian bucks rode over to the trading post—four or five of them, I don't remember which. After they ate some cheese and crackers and drank red soda pop a while, they began to get rather friendly. They said they didn't have any horses to sell, but they had a race horse they would like to match a race with. The man running the trading post was named Watson, and the Indians called him "Wat." They said they would sure like to match a race against one of my horses for $10, and that Wat could hold the stakes.

These Indians had some store-bought duckin', pale-face britches on them, but their shirts were Apache colored and Apache made. They all wore hats but one. The oldest Indian among them had his head tied up with a headband, and instead of having on store-bought boots, he was wearing moccasins. He was much smaller than the rest, and real bowlegged.

After a little talk and discussion, we put up $10 apiece with Wat and went down to a mountain meadow, just below the trading post, where we marked off what the Indians said was about three hundred yards. I thought it was closer to a quarter of a mile, but it didn't make any difference because Ol' Nothin' could outrun them anyway; and the farther he went, the better he got.

They stripped the saddle off a little brown Indian horse that they were riding, and this old Indian turned out to be the jockey. Ol' Nothin' was staked out to graze a little piece from my camp. I walked out and got him, took the halter off, slipped a limber-bit bridle on his head, and thought I would just ride him bareback. I probably weighed 160 pounds and was as hard as white men get, I guess.

The Indians got Wat to quit the trading post, and he walked off and left it open. He came down into the flat and was going to be the starter. We had marked off the place where the race was going to be over, and we broke down a bush to one side so there could be no argument about the end of the race.

The Indian and I got on our horses. We had scraped a line on the ground, and Wat was standing on the end of the line holding his hat in his hand. The Indian's horse was a little fidgety, and Ol' Nothin' had savvied what was going to happen and had pertened-up some, too. We were standing on the line, and Wat dropped his hat and hollered: "Go!"

Ol' Nothin' jumped past that Indian horse the first lick and outran him so far to the other end of the race that I had him turned around and looking at the Indian when he got to the end of the race. There was no argument about who won.

We went back to the store and got real well acquainted. The Indians told me they had another race horse that they wanted to bring the next day and run against Ol' Nothin'. Wat asked them how much money they wanted to put up. They grunted and had a little meeting among themselves, then decided they would have to bet $20 to get even—if they won. I told them that would be fine and that I would be at the store waiting for them the next morning.

They rode off, and Wat and I got a little better acquainted. He had paid me my $20 and said tomorrow there would be a good many Indians come down to see the race; that if I wanted to bet a little money on the side, he would be glad to help me with it. I didn't want to brag too much. I told him money might be a little short with me, but I would talk to him about it tomorrow.

It is plenty cold up in the mountains early in the

morning, and it was about ten o'clock before the Indians
showed up with their other race horse. This time there
were about forty Indian bucks, all ages and all sizes. They
were all mounted on good Indian ponies. These ponies
were a little better than average Western horse size, even
though some of them were paints. For the most part, they
showed quite a lot more breeding than was commonly
found in those days among Indian horses. The horse they
had brought with them to race was a bigger than average
Indian horse, a dark chestnut color, and was shod with
light cowhorse shoes. I'd say this horse had been picked
out of the bunch and was the best horse this particular
band of Indians owned, more than likely.

We visited around the porch of the trading post and
put up our $20 apiece with Wat. Then I slipped him $25
more to bet on the side. He didn't seem to have any trouble getting it covered by the Indians. I began to think
maybe Wat was on their side—that I was the only paleface there, and that I might be fixin' to lose my money.

We went back down into this flat below the trading
post, and this time they wanted to run the race for a little
bit more than a quarter of a mile; so we marked off a little
longer track, which was sure a long quarter of a mile.
But, like I said, the farther Ol' Nothin' went, the better
he got.

Wat did the starting, the Indians did the hollering, Ol'
Nothin' did the running—and me and Ol' Nothin' won
the money.

This upset the Indians a right smart, and they said I
ought to stay around a day or two until they could get
another race horse that was farther back up in the Res-

ervation. I told them I wasn't in much hurry as long as I was winning horse races, and I would camp at the trading post 'til they showed up with a better race horse.

What I didn't know then was that they had already sent up the smoke signal for this other horse—in case they lost the race.

In about three days they came in to match the big race. They brought a palomino mare that belonged to Chief Treeheart and was called something which meant the Daughter of the Sun. She was truly a beautiful mare, well kept, with every hair in place. She had a beautiful light mane and tail that had been plaited and unplaited by the squaws, giving the hair a wavy appearance.

The Chief wanted to bet a great big turquoise bracelet against $50. This turquoise stone was as big around as a tin drinking cup and about as thick as your thumb—mounted in a huge silver band. I didn't know whether it was worth $3 or $300, but we almost had to match the race to get any side bets; so I put up the $50 with Wat at the trading post, and the old Chief gave him the bracelet. Then Wat went to taking side bets, and he had about $150 to bet when he asked me if I wanted to take part of it. I told him I would take it all, and he looked pleased. I know now that he was working for the Indians and hadn't bet anything himself.

We led our horses back down into this meadow below the trading post. It was a nice, brisk, spring day, and we got our horses at the end of this line to start the race—which was to be the same distance that we had run the last race. The meadow where we were running our horses had been watered in the early spring by melted snow, and the grass was up tall and waving in the breeze. Green pines covered the side of the mountain. The peak of the mountain was covered with snow that it was holding up above the heat of the earth as a marker for the snows that would come that fall.

I heard a peculiar noise, and when I looked up along the side of the mountain, the whole tribe of women and children was seating itself on the ground and perching on boulders to watch the horse race. These Indian women and children had blankets and dresses whose colors must have been rubbed off the rainbow.

The old Chief wanted to stand on one side of the line, and Wat on the other, to be sure the horses got an even start. The Chief stood on the same side that my horse was on, and when Wat hollered "Start," he whooped real loud and threw his hat under my horse. But this didn't booger Ol' Nothin'.

The Daughter of the Sun was a good race mare, and at the end of the designated race we were nose-and-nose. Neither of us had won. A little argument started, and I thought there was no one at the end of the line who really knew; so I wasn't trying to claim that I had won the race. But among the squaws on the side of the mountain was a white woman who lived with the Indians, and she had been standing even with the end of the line. I didn't know this until a little black Indian kid ran down and whispered in the old Chief's ear; then he raised up and said it was a tie. This worried me a little, because I knew he was on the starting line and wouldn't have been able to tell if it was a tie. That was when Wat decided that it was appropriate for him to explain to me about this white woman on the finish line. What he neglected to tell me, and I learned later, was that this was a frame-up in order to get more money for a race to be run that afternoon.

After a little grunting among the Indians, the Chief and I agreed to run the race over that same afternoon about two o'clock. This is not in keeping with present-day racing practice—to run a horse two races the same day—but it looked to me like it would be fair because they were going to run the same mare, just as I was going to run Ol' Nothin'.

The Indians lay around the trading post all day and made business real good for Wat. Their horses grazing in the meadow below the trading post made it look like they had gathered for a summer powwow. Nobody drew down his bet, but Wat had begun to act uneasy about the $150. He eased up to me and asked if I wanted to draw my money down—he might get the Indians to call off the race. I felt a little lonesome among that bunch of redskins; and Wat, the only other white man, I had decided was on their side. But I told him that I would leave my money up. As an afterthought, I added that I sure was glad that race wasn't any longer because I didn't think Ol' Nothin' could run more than that distance twice in one day.

It was about eleven o'clock in the morning. I took Ol' Nothin' and eased back over to my camp, threw some more wood on my fire, and heated some water in a bucket to rub his legs down. Ol' Nothin' was ten years old. His legs were hard and sound, and I guess I was just trying to pamper him a little bit. He wasn't used to having his legs rubbed down after a brush race. I fed him some oats out of a morral (nosebag) and while he was eating, I got to thinking he might enjoy a drink of strong coffee. It was an old trick in brush races to drench an old, seasoned race horse with about a quart of black coffee thirty or forty minutes before a race. It seemed like the dope in the coffee sure would perten one up, especially when he hadn't been used to it.

I walked back up to Wat's trading post and told Wat I was fresh out of coffee, so for him to give me a pound. He handed me a yellow package of Arbuckle's, which was too strong for most white people although most Indians liked it. I boiled me up a bucketful of that coffee and poured it in a whiskey bottle, then raised Ol' Nothin's head and drenched him with it. I was far enough off from the trading post and in a little draw, so I knew nobody would know that I gave Ol' Nothin' that coffee.

This was about an hour before the time we had decided we would run the race. You could see Indians all up and down the meadow, standing and sitting down in the grass, and they were taking turns about keeping the Daughter of the Sun limbered up. They rubbed her with beautiful Indian blankets that today would be worth a fortune. Some little Indian boys would run up ever now and then and give her a bite of feed out of their hands. I never knew what kind of feed they were giving her.

As the time drew near for the race, you could see the squaws and little children gathering on the side of the mountain and getting their grandstand seats. I put the bridle on Ol' Nothin'. I had brushed him and cleaned him off good and fed and walked him a little bit. So I began to walk him around, and I led him up by the trading post.

Old Wat came out and had a very confidential talk with me. He told me that the Indians wanted to put up another $50 and increase the length of the race about a

hundred yards. He pointed to a red boulder in the side of
the mountain that they wanted to use for a marker, letting
the race run out to a line even with the boulder. I hemmed
and hawed, rubbed Ol' Nothin' on the shoulder and
slapped around on him, looked over his back and kinda
kicked my boot-toe in the dirt a few minutes. Then I told
Wat that I was running awful short of money, but that I
believed I would put up that $50.

He motioned back at some of them, and an old Indian
walked up bringing the other $50. We gave our money to
Wat, after agreeing that the boulder would be the line to
end the race. I had to turn and lead my horse off in order
to keep from showing that I was well pleased. They had
took the bait that I had planted when I told old Wat that
I was glad the race wasn't any longer, that I didn't think
Ol' Nothin' could run more than that distance twice in
one day! I knew Ol' Nothin' could run from then 'til sun-
down if he had to.

We all got set for the race, and I told Wat that I
wanted the Chief to sit on the other side and not throw his
hat under my horse. All the Indians thought that was
funny, and they had a great big laugh. The truth of the
matter was, I didn't care if he sat in front of me; when the
race started, Ol' Nothin' could have jumped clear of him
—but I wanted to complain a little bit about something to
make it seem like I was a real paleface.

Old Wat dropped his hat and hollored: "Go!"

The Daughter of the Sun was a beautiful mare, and
the old Indian rode her like some more of her own hide.
It was a nice race for a little piece, and then I decided I
had better quit taking a chance. So I leaned way over and
squalled into Ol' Nothin's ear. He must have gotten the

message, because when we went past the line where the boulder was sticking out of the montain, the Daughter of the Sun was about even with the point where we ran the first race. I would say Ol' Nothin' daylighted her 150 feet.

You never saw Indians disappear back into the woods like that bunch of squaws and kids as they went up the mountain. By the time I got back to the trading post, which was just across the valley, you couldn't even see them. Half of the younger men walked off with their horses and with the Daughter of the Sun, and eight or ten real old, dried-up looking Indians were sitting on the porch of the trading post when I got there.

I walked into the trading post, and Wat acted like he was awful busy wrapping up something and talking to an Indian squaw. He didn't even notice me. I opened the lid of an old, homemake ice box and got a coke which I stood around and drank. And that was an awful quiet bunch of Indians sitting on that front porch with their backs toward me. I don't know how Custer felt at his last stand, but I was beginning to think I knew. So far as I knew, there hadn't been any Indians on the warpath in a good many years, but the way these were acting, it seemed like we were about to have an uprising over Ol' Nothin's outrunning the Daughter of the Sun.

The Indian squaw finally walked off, and Wat couldn't help but turn around and see me, so there was nothing he could do but start conversation. He reached down under the counter (he didn't have a cash register) and pulled out my $250 and another $200 in various bills and silver and counted it out on the counter. He wasn't saying anything; and the Indians, lined up with their backs to us on the front porch, weren't saying anything either.

Then I said: "Wat, where's the Indian bracelet?"

He began to change feet and look off. And I saw the Chief's back straighten up some, on the front porch. Then Wat went to painfully trying to explain to me how the bracelet was a piece of tribal jewelry and that the Chief couldn't give it up; that he and the rest of the Indians out there on the porch wanted to have a powwow about trading me a blanket for it.

Well, I thought about it a few minutes, and I didn't think that bracelet would fit me anyhow, though I might use a blanket. And the trade might make a difference in how long I got to stay, and what shape and how many horses I got out of the mountains with. So I cleared my throat and in a loud voice told Wat that I wouldn't think of taking any of the Chief's precious stones—that I would be more than glad to have the blanket instead and would cherish their friendship every time I put it on a horse.

When I looked up that time, all the Indians had stood up, turned around, and started walking into the store. Indian fashion, they didn't display very much surprise or gratitude. However, the old Chief said that for a paleface I was a good rider and a good horseman, and since I took the blanket I must be part Indian. The little Indian jockey was carrying a beautiful black and white handwoven Indian blanket—that has been on a horse or in a car for lo, these many years, and is folded and lying across the head of my bed in place of a pillow to this good day.

I took my money and my blanket and Ol' Nothin' and went off down to my camp. Strange to say, none of the Indians had ever come close to where I was camped or paid any attention to Beauty, who was by far the best-looking horse of my two. I cooled Ol' Nothin' off a little and then stretched out on the ground, leaned back against a tree, and thought about what a nice trip I was having and how different this was from that double harness.

In the late afternoon, the old Indian jockey and two young bucks walked up to about fifty yards from my camp. One of the young bucks made some kind of noise that made me notice them, so I asked them to come on down to the fire. I had a little of that black coffee left from what I had given Ol' Nothin', and I took the chance of letting the Indians drink some of it because I figured the races were all over. We sat and looked at each other a while. Then finally the young buck who did the talking said that old Indian jockey had many ponies and he wanted to own my race horse. We talked about the ponies, and they explained to me that they were over east of the mountain in a valley, that they were all young and most of them had been ridden "some." It sounded like a good proposition, and I told them that when I broke camp the next day I would ride back that direction and look at the ponies—then we would talk trade.

The valley they described was on a little narrow road that led out across the mountain range and down to a small town called White Tail, then over the mountains toward Hondo. However, I didn't intend to go to Hondo after I got the ponies. I thought that I would bear back on an old ranch road that went by the Flying H and in toward Artesia.

I broke camp the next morning about sunup, went back to the trading post, and got another supply of grub which I put on Ol' Nothin's pack saddle. As I came out of the trading post, there was one of the few white men that I had seen crossing the country. He was stopped to get some gasoline. Wat had one of those hand-grinding gasoline pumps. His gas business was of minor importance, though he did have a little for white people who rode in automobiles. When the fellow got out of the car, I recognized him as being a friend of mine from Lubbock, Texas. Wat filled his gasoline tank, and we had a great visit.

We walked off from the car a little piece, and I whispered to him what I had in mind. Then we went back to within earshot of Wat, and I said: "That sure will be nice. I'll get a paper sack here from the trading post and wrap it up for you."

When he started to pay Wat for his gas, I asked Wat to get me a paper sack that would hold about $400 worth of money. I had the money stuffed in my shirt pockets with the flaps buttoned down; so I took it out and put it in this paper sack, then folded the sack down to a small wad, tied a string around it, and handed it to my friend. I told him I sure would appreciate his mailing it back to my bank. Of course, that was for Wat's information. My friend was going to keep the money until he heard from me. I wasn't going to accuse Wat and those Indians of anything. I was just making arrangements to disappoint them, in case they had anything in mind.

The old Indian jockey, who had many ponies, lived in a valley that was about a two-day ride. On the morning of the third day I topped out on a ridge and looked down in a narrow, rough kind of a little wooded canyon, with a trail leading down to something a little more than an Indian hogan. It was sort of a 'dobe, houselike affair with a porch on the front of it, built out of cottonwood poles with Spanish dagger tied in little bunches and laid over the top to form a roof. As I came into view of the porch,

I saw the old jockey sit up on a little cot against the wall. As it turned out, the white squaw who was at the race belonged to the jockey, which was the reason that dwelling looked more like a house than a hogan.

We visited a little while, and he said that he was ready to show me the ponies. I didn't tie Ol' Nothin', or unpack him, or leave him—I just led him along with me. About four miles down the canyon, against a little stream, was a well-hidden little valley.

The ponies were fat, good-sized for Indian horses, good solid colors, and showed more than a little breeding. The old Indian jockey started out by telling me that he would give me five ponies for the horse that outran Daughter of the Sun. I didn't show much interest. I had counted them, and there were twenty-three in that valley. We got down off our horses and walked around among the ponies. They seemed to be real gentle. There were only two that had saddle marks to show that they had actually been used. But the others didn't shy from us— didn't booger or try to run off—and acted like they had been raised in a lot by a farmer, instead of on an Indian Reservation. I had already decided that the old jockey was the top horse-Indian of the tribe, and I was giving him credit for these ponies all being so gentle.

We spent about three hours, and he kept inching up a few more ponies until he finally got pretty mad and said he wouldn't give more than fifteen ponies for any horse he ever saw, and that he didn't like making talk with a paleface horse trader all day. I told him fifteen would be enough if I got the two that had the saddle marks. He agreed, and I unshucked the riggin' off Ol' Nothin'— using a bay horse with saddle marks for a pack horse. He stood still until I got the pack on him, and he led off pretty good when we started out. However, I decided to turn him loose and drive him with the rest of the ponies.

I started out of the mountains, driving the ponies in front of me up the trail that I had come in on. They were the gentlest, slowest moving, young fat horses that I ever saw. You could ride up and tap one on the rump with a lariat rope, and he would hardly flinch.

I made camp that night at a little set of corrals by a spring. They evidently belonged to some rancher who used them occasionally to pen livestock. I had about run out of oats for Beauty, but I had enough for that night.

The next morning I saddled Beauty and went into the corral to catch the bay horse that I had used for a pack horse the day before. He was a little bit snorty and didn't want me to walk up to him, so I had to hem him up in the corner to catch him finally. I thought this was just because I wasn't an Indian and that he would get used to me in a few days. But when I started to put my packsaddle on him, he threw a walleyed fit, and the rest of the ponies crowded up in the back side of that corral snorting and acting like wild broncs. I had to tie this pack horse's foot to his shoulder and put a twitch on his nose before I ever got my packsaddle on him. I sure did cinch that pack-saddle tight, and then I wrapped him and that whole pack up with a big rope, which I tied with a diamond hitch. I had an idea that he might be going to buck with the pack, and I intended when he got through bucking for him to still have it on. Sure enough, when I let his foot to the ground he threw a fit, but it didn't last long. There was no gate on this corral, just some long pole bars. I pulled them down and rode around the back side of the corral, easing my ponies out onto the trail and heading them east. I was getting back down into the lower country, and the road was getting plainer and easier to follow; I could see that I would come onto a fenced road in another two or three hours.

These horses were snorty and rearing a little bit when I turned them out. They were afraid of the horse with the pack on him, and they tried several times to break across the opening and get away. But Beauty and I had different plans. I had gotten them onto a fenced road when a car came along, so all of them tried to break over the fence. By this time I *knew* there was something wrong with these horses. I had begun to get real suspicious of my Indian jockey friend.

I penned these horses that night at a little town called Hope. They had gotten wilder all day, and by that night they were so spooky that when I threw them a little alfalfa hay, they tried to run over the fence.

The next night I camped at Artesia. I was sitting up at the Cattleman's Café in Artesia, after supper, when I got into conversation with an old-time cowboy. After we visited awhile, I told him about my horses. He said he hated to laugh at a stranger—but he damn near got down on the floor of that café. There were a couple more fellows came in, and he told them about it—then they broke out laughing, too.

I finally said it didn't seem so damn funny to me, and if some of them could get their breath long enough, I would like for them to tell me what they were laughing about—then maybe I could laugh, too. After all, I was furnishing the horses for the laughing.

This old pock-marked, half-breed, new-found friend

of mine wiped his eyes and told me that the Indians had
herded those ponies down into the valley and had held
them there on *sleepy grass*. I know now, though I didn't
then, that the seeds of sleepy grass contain a dopey substance that acts on a horse much like today's modern tran-
quilizers. And that good trade that I thought I had made
turned out to be a bunch of wild, unbroke horses.

I went to the hardware store the next morning and
bought me a bunch of three-quarter inch rope, then cut
and tied myself some fifteen hackamores. I drove the
horses over to the railroad stock pens and got them into the
chute. Then I put these hackamores on them, with each of
them dragging about ten feet of rope. This was new treat-
ment for the sleepy-grass horses; and every time they
jumped, one stepped on the other's halter rope and pulled
his head around. The pack horse wasn't much trouble to
put the pack on that morning, and the young horses
couldn't run away because of the rope they were dragging
that they stepped on all the time.

I got back home in the late summer. All my Indian
horses had their heads sore from the hackamores, were
easy to catch, and had begun to get civilized. But if I
hadn't had a three-weeks' drive for them when they came
out from under that sleepy-grass dope, I would have never
broke 'em to ride.

I regretted that I lost Ol' Nothin', but he wasn't as bad
off with the Indians as I would have been in that double
harness!

A Note about the Author

*Ben K. Green, a native of Cumby, Texas, was the
kind of a Westerner who almost crawled out of the
cradle and into a saddle. He spent his childhood,
adolescence, and young manhood on horseback.
He studied veterinary medicine at Cornell
University and did postgraduate work at the Royal
College of Veterinary Medicine in England. Dr.
Green did subsequent research on toxic plant life
involving more than three hundred different plants
that are deadly to domestic livestock. After he gave
up his practice and research, he returned to Cumby
where he lived, raising good horses and cattle, until
his death in 1974. His other books are* Wild Cow
Tales; The Village Horse Doctor, West of the Pecos;
and Some More Horse Tradin'.

A Note on the Type

*The text of this book was set on the Linotype
in Janson, a recutting made direct from type
cast from matrices long thought to have been made
by the Dutchman Anton Janson, who was a
practicing type founder in Leipzig during the
years 1668–87. However, it has been conclusively
demonstrated that these types are actually the
work of Nicholas Kis (1650–1702), a Hungarian,
who most probably learned his trade from
the master Dutch type founder Kirk Voskens.
The type is an excellent example of the influential
and sturdy Dutch types that prevailed in England
up to the time William Caslon developed his own
incomparable designs from these Dutch faces.*

*This book was composed by
Brown Bros. Linotypers, Inc.,
New York, printed by Halliday
Lithograph Corp., West
Hanover, Mass., and bound by
The Haddon Craftsmen, Inc.,
Scranton, Penn.*